GEORGE WOODS
AND THE
WORLD BANK

"Little people only think in rates of return."
—George Woods

GEORGE WOODS
AND THE
WORLD BANK

by
Robert W. Oliver

LYNNE
RIENNER
PUBLISHERS

BOULDER
LONDON

332.153092
W890

Photo credits: Courtesy of "George D. Woods Papers," Rare Book and Manuscript Library, Columbia University: pp. 2, 18, 62, 218; Courtesy of the World Bank, by Fabian Bachrach: jacket, frontispiece, p. 94 left; Courtesy of the George Woods family: p. 88 top; Courtesy of the World Bank, by Edwin G. Huffman: all others.

Published in the United States of America in 1995 by
Lynne Rienner Publishers, Inc.
1800 30th Street, Boulder, Colorado 80301

and in the United Kingdom by
Lynne Rienner Publishers, Inc.
3 Henrietta Street, Covent Garden, London WC2E 8LU

Library of Congress Cataloging-in-Publication Data
Oliver, Robert W.
  George Woods and the World Bank / Robert W. Oliver
  Includes bibliographical references and index.
  ISBN 1-55587-503-3 (alk. paper)
  1. Woods, George D. 2. World Bank—Presidents—Biography.
  3. World Bank—History—20th century. I. Title.
HG3881.5.W57043 1994
332.1'532'092—dc20   94-8738
[B]   CIP

British Cataloguing in Publication Data
A Cataloguing in Publication record for this book
is available from the British Library.

Printed and bound in the United States of America

     The paper used in this publication meets the requirements
  ⊗ of the American National Standard for Permanence of
     Paper for Printed Library Materials Z39.48-1984.

With Love

To Darlene and Jean,
Lesley, Jim, and Stewart

CONTENTS

FOREWORD

George Woods was a banker with a heart. He was a man of genuine affection, who at all times was ready to cast aside his own problems to share in yours. His friendship ran both wide and deep.

George came into my parents' life in their adult years, but it wasn't very long before it seemed that he and his wife, Louise (whom we all called, as he did, Louie), had been family friends forever.

George cared deeply about both the New York Times and the Sulzberger family role in that institution. Today's continuity of ownership and the underlying strength of the institution are a direct result of George Woods's creative approach to problem solving.

Over the years, first my folks and then my sisters and I came to rely evermore on George's advice. His agile mind absorbed an extraordinary understanding of the press and the Times's role. He was convinced that the Times needed to remain fiscally sound if it were to maintain its independence, and that its independence was important to our country.

George was, of course, more conservative than the Sulzbergers. There were those days when, after reading the editorial page, he could no longer contain himself. The phone would ring, and it was George berating me for some "damned fool liberal solution" recommended by an editorial writer. But his venting was personal to me: I never heard him criticize the paper in public.

As a director of the New York Times Company and later, upon the death of my father, as a successor trustee of the Ochs Trust that controlled the Times, George in his quiet way preached fiscal responsibility and editorial independence. He played a giant role in setting out the markers for the trail we still follow, and we all are fortunate for his having passed this way.

Arthur Ochs Sulzberger

FOREWORD

U
nder George Woods, the World Bank came closest to living up to the ideal of an international institution. George Woods's Bank was unique: it was entirely objective; nonpolitical; and had a highly competent international staff of unquestionable integrity, single-mindedly devoted to assisting the economic development of the poorer of its member nations. Although under his predecessor, Eugene Black, the Bank evolved to be more than merely an international investment bank, under George Woods it was firmly established as a development institution; and so it has since thought of itself. Woods's term was also the last in which the Bank gave priority to achieving better economic management for its borrowers as opposed to generating ever larger volumes of lending.

The process of economic development is too complex to be managed by a single policy prescription. But (bearing in mind this reservation) there is a fundamental difference between those who emphasize the dependence of development in the poor countries on the volume of the transfer of resources from rich to poor and those who, instead, emphasize that development depends, first and foremost, on improvement in the allocation and management of the resources (in the widest sense) at the command of the poor country. In simple terms, the difference is between those who emphasize giving a starving man enough fish for a meal and those who believe it is better to equip him with a fishing pole and teach him to fish. Partisans of both views ("transfers" and "economic management") recognize the importance of the other's policy, but the different emphases result in very different methods of operation—and results.

It was George Woods's firm belief that the main objective of the Bank was to help countries to achieve development through improved economic management. Loans, credits, economic studies, and technical assistance were all means to this end, rather than ends in themselves. When Robert S. McNamara, succeeding Woods, announced as his first major policy objective the doubling of the total of Bank loans in five years, the contrast was stark. And since then the Bank has highlighted the volume of the resources it disburses annually. The result has been a reversal of roles: under Woods, the focus was on what the member country could do for itself with the help of the Bank; under McNamara and his successors

xi

the volume of loans became the objective—member countries sat in judgment on the success of the Bank in attaining a given target of lending.

Professor Oliver documents George Woods's approach. For example,
in India Woods's Bell mission succeeded through working with a cooperative minister of agriculture in changing Indian agricultural policy. As a result, within a few years India moved from being a food importer, threatened by famine whenever the monsoon failed, to being self-sufficient in
food. Woods's attempt to persuade India to dismantle its maze of licensing
restrictions and trade controls (restrictions that still largely choke its industries) failed, but this was in large part because donors were unwilling to
help the Bank to come up with the required package of inducements.

With his emphasis on the need for better economic management,
Woods expanded the economic work of the Bank and strengthened the
role of economic analysis in its operations. Through a Bank program of
economic publications, he encouraged Bank staff to make widely available
their knowledge and experience, including for the first time an economic
section in the Bank's annual report. This evolved into the current series
of valuable World Bank Development Reports. But publication was secondary; the purpose of economic work was, first, the betterment of country economic management and of Bank policies and operations. Woods
gave Bank economists, for the first time, equal weight in the lending
process with the loan officers and project analysts.

George Woods fostered a unique process of promoting economic development. There was close collaboration between Bank staff and the key
personnel of a borrower in technical assistance, fact finding, analysis, and
problem solving. In the course of loan, economic, and project missions,
and in the day-to-day work of Bank resident staff in the country, Bank
professionals worked with the personnel of the member government in
planning projects and sectorwide investments, institution building, and
the training of management, policy, and administrative staff. In most
cases, policy reforms and better administration and management flowed
naturally out of this process without the need to try to hold a government's feet to the fire or to exact public commitments to drastic, and sud-
den, structural change. In the few cases where agreements were not lived
up to, loan disbursements were quietly suspended until the problem was
resolved without public confrontation or loss of face.

Woods himself was bigger than life. Everyone who worked for him
knew that he was someone special, ranking with the other great statesmen
of the post–World War II era. I acquired a great liking and admiration for
him, even though early in my work for him he gave me the worst calling-
down in my whole career—justified, I should add. One of the staff stories
during his administration explained his outstanding originality by the fact
that he had never gone to college and so never had his mind molded into

conformity. Professor Oliver has accurately captured his personality—warts and all.

Robert W. Oliver is singularly qualified to write about George Woods and what he made of the Bank. Professor Oliver, an economist, knows the Bank's history as does no one else. His book *International Economic Cooperation and the World Bank* describes how nations were persuaded to consider organizing an institution like the Bank and how the negotiations at Bretton Woods produced the Bank charter. Oliver recorded oral interviews with most of the key personnel of the Bank as it evolved. On sabbatical, he worked as an economist for a year in the Bank, participating in Bank missions and operations. In brief, Professor Oliver has unequaled credentials and ability to write this account, and the book shows it.

With the majority of the people of the world poor and increasingly conscious of being poor, the high-income countries are realizing that the economic development of the poor countries is essential. The World Bank can be an effective organization for this purpose. While the Bank does much good now, it could be much more effective if it learned again the lessons of the George Woods era as narrated by Professor Oliver in this book.

Andrew M. Kamarck
Director, Economics Department, World Bank, 1965–1970

PREFACE

This is a book about the World Bank. It is a book about the transformation of the World Bank from a relatively passive investment organization, owned by many governments, to a development-assistance institution that actively sought more and better ways to assist the less-developed nations of the world.

This transformation did not occur overnight. In a sense, it began with the first Bank loan to a less-developed country (Chile) as the Bank used its leverage to influence the terms and conditions of lending. By 1955, with the establishment of the Economic Development Institute (EDI) under the noted British economist Alec Cairncross, the Bank began to teach government officials from less-developed countries about the economics of growth. In 1956, the World Bank spawned the International Finance Corporation (IFC) and, in 1960, the International Development Association (IDA). Collectively, they become known as the World Bank Group. Today that group has as members virtually all the nations of the world, including China and the nations that once were parts of the Soviet empire.[1]

The World Bank Group was in place when George David Woods became president of the World Bank on January 1, 1963, and Woods was largely responsible for transforming the Bank Group into a development-assistance institution.

I was first employed by the World Bank in 1961 when I was invited by Bob Asher of the Brookings Institution to conduct tape-recorded interviews about the Bank.[2] I worked happily with Harold Graves in the Bank's Information Department, which provided me with a splendid, state-of-the-art Ampex, reel-to-reel, tape recorder. With Ed Mason, Bob Asher was contemplating a massive volume, *The World Bank Since Bretton Woods*.

I had finished my dissertation in 1958 under the direction of Professor Jacob Viner at Princeton University. Published with modifications as *International Economic Cooperation and the World Bank*,[3] it dealt mainly with the attempts of international economists during the years between the two world wars to induce leaders of the important nation-states to cooperate in decisions concerning exchange rates, international trade, international investment, fiscal and monetary policy, and related issues. The mistakes of the pre–World War II era, particularly the depression years, were apparent to most observers in 1944 at the Bretton Woods Conference, where the articles of agreement of the World Bank and the International Monetary Fund (IMF) were negotiated.

During the summer of 1961, on leave from the California Institute of Technology where I was an assistant professor of economics, I interviewed Eugene Black, Robert Garner, Crena de Iongh, Burke Knapp, Richard Demuth, Leonard Rist, Paul Rosenstein-Rodan, Martin Rosen, William Diamond, Andrew Kamarck, and many others.[4] Eugene Black graciously invited me to his home for dinner before our tape-recorded conversation. It was an experience I shall always remember.

In 1965, I was elected to the Pasadena City Council. While I was an economist with the Stanford Research Institute, I had published *An Economic Survey of Pasadena*, which contained suggestions of how the second-oldest city in Los Angeles County might overcome symptoms of aging. I had hardly embarked upon my career as a part-time politician, however, when Andrew Kamarck, who was at UCLA as a regents professor, on leave from the World Bank, invited me to spend a full year at the Bank in the Economics Department. Kamarck had had an exciting and meritorious career in the Bank as an economist, most recently as an economic adviser to the Africa Department. He was on leave partly in order to finish a book, *The Economics of African Development*.[5] While he was at UCLA, Kamarck was asked by Irving Friedman, the newly appointed economic adviser to the president of the World Bank (George Woods), to return to Washington to establish a revitalized and expanded Economics Department. For my part, as my four-year term on the Pasadena City Council neared its conclusion in 1969, the siren song of Washington grew louder, and I decided to forgo seeking a second term on the council. My wife and I accepted Kamarck's invitation in the autumn of 1970.

We sought a house that we could lease for a year. Kamarck suggested that we call on the Irving Friedmans, who were about to spend a year at Yale and Oxford on sabbatical leave from the World Bank.[6] We asked if we might lease the Friedmans' beautiful home in Bethesda, Maryland. The Friedmans stipulated that they would like to return to their home occasionally while they were in residence at New Haven. It was agreed, and the Friedmans and the Olivers soon became close friends.

The year spanning parts of 1970 and 1971 was a happy time for the Olivers. I was employed in the Economics of Urbanization Division, where I wrote the working papers "Djakarta, the Capital City of Indonesia" and "The Major Cities of Taiwan." I also visited the places named in the titles. But I had bypassed George Woods. I had met Eugene Black when he was president of the World Bank in 1961; but by 1970, when I was in Washington, Robert McNamara was president.

Irving Friedman knew about my earlier interviews in the World Bank and about my dissertation, which was slowly becoming a book. Partly for fun, in March 1974, when I was visiting the Friedmans, I proposed that Irving allow himself to be interviewed by me. I used a tape recorder, as I had done in 1961. Friedman's long 1974 interview was typed by my secretary, but it lay largely unused for another decade.

George Woods died in 1982. I had not met him. But in his interview, Irving Friedman spoke so glowingly, so personally, of George Woods that I almost felt that I had known him: had observed Woods with his senior staff—his leadership, his wit, his sayings, his occasional anger, his resentment at being slighted, his basic wisdom even in the face of adversity. I had ended my book about the Bank with a quotation from Woods's Gabriel Silver Lecture on April 13, 1967, at Columbia University: "The founders gave the Bank a priceless gift in the form of an extraordinary charter called the Articles of Agreement." I had also referred to Woods's fitting analogy to an airplane as recounted in the Friedman interview: "I don't think you can have a development agency unless it has as its fuselage the loans which are being made, but one wing has to be project work and the other wing has to be economics."[7]

After George Woods died, Louise Woods, his wife of almost fifty years, wanted to have a biography written about her Woodsie. She hired John Mason, husband of the head of the Oral History Program at the Columbia University Library, to do oral-history interviews of people who, she knew, would speak favorably of her husband: Arthur Ochs Sulzberger, Sr., Martin Rosen, Ed Townsend, George Wishart, and Greg Votaw, for example. Mason interviewed Louise Woods herself on six occasions. He also interviewed, as did I, George Woods's sister, Grace Woods Johnson.[8] Mason felt, however, that he lacked the time to complete a book about George Woods. Knowing of Mrs. Woods's desires, Irving Friedman arranged for me to meet her. I showed her my book about the Bank and spoke about my work, including my 1961 interviews. She agreed to sponsor me in my efforts to write about the Woods years at the World Bank.

That was in February 1985. I was teaching full-time; I could work on my exciting new project, for the most part, only during the summer. I perused the George Woods collection at Columbia University in June 1985 and began to interview people in the World Bank in July 1985. I returned for additional interviews in July 1986 and subsequently. I was particularly interested through these interviews to seek an understanding of Woods the man—his motivation, his character, his personality.

Over the course of five years, I had long, rewarding, tape-recorded conversations about George Woods with Simon Aldewereld, Gerald Alter, Warren Baum, Bernard Bell, Munir Benjenk, William Bennett, Ken Bohr,

Aron Broches, Roger Chaufournier, Richard Demuth, Barend deVries, William Diamond, Irving Friedman, William Gilmartin, David Gordon, Harold Graves, Julian Grenfell, Ravi Gulhati, Ralph Hershtritt, Grace Johnson, Andrew Kamarck, Ben King, Burke Knapp, Michael Lejeune, Peter Lieftinck, Marie Linahan, Nat McKitterick, Robert McNamara, Bernadette Schmitt, Davidson Sommers, William Stanton, Rainer Steckhan, Alexander Stevenson, Richard Van Wagenen, Ladislaus von Hoffman, Willi Wapenhans, Mervyn Weiner, and Richard Westebbe. I conversed with Irving Friedman with my tape recorder in hand on six different occasions, with Andrew Kamarck three times, and with Simon Aldewereld, William Diamond, Harold Graves, and Michael Lejeune twice. To all of these fine people, I am grateful. To my secretary, Gail Peterson, who typed and retyped these conversations, comprising some two thousand pages, as well as my manuscript, which changed many times, I am more than grateful.

I retired from Caltech in the autumn of 1988, spent a term in England at Cambridge University as a visiting scholar the following autumn, and worked on my manuscript in November and December 1991 in Bellagio, Italy, at the Villa Serbelloni, the Rockefeller Research and Study Center.

I wish I had met George Woods face to face. Based on some two thousand pages of transcribed conversations about him and the World Bank, however, I have become acquainted with this man in a way no one else could have been. No two people I interviewed perceived George Woods in exactly the same way. No two objective events involving George Woods were interpreted by two or more observers in precisely the same way. I have been fortunate to see George Woods as others saw him, and I have had ample time, particularly in England and Italy, to reflect on the George Woods I was getting to know. Of course, I relied on the minutes of the senior staff meetings, the annual reports of the World Bank, Woods's speeches and letters, and books and articles about the World Bank and George Woods. But I relied most heavily on the interviews, the *Conversations About George Woods and the World Bank* on deposit in the archives of the California Institute of Technology and the World Bank.

Bernadette Schmitt, Woods's secretary, who served him from his days in the army until his death and who helped Louise Woods until Louise's death four years later, allowed me to go through many boxes of Woods's letters, articles, and speeches. In the end, she sent them to me at Caltech, where I perused them at leisure. Schmitty meticulously read every word of my manuscript and helped me to correct at least some of my errors.

My friends in the World Bank, Barend deVries, William Diamond, James Feather, Andrew Kamarck, and Charles Ziegler, read every word I wrote and commented on many of those words. William Diamond in particular sent me many pages of helpful suggestions. Bill and I have talked for hours, over the phone and across the luncheon table, about the Woods years at the World Bank. For Diamond, the Bank was an all-absorbing interest. He had great respect for Woods, "who is too easily forgotten despite his enormous contribution." "In my case," said Diamond, "it was a combination of respect and liking the man and wanting to see justice done." Andrew Kamarck, with whom I spent several wonderful days in Brewster, Massachusetts, and who wrote a foreword to this book, said much the same thing.

George Wishart read every word and sent from Switzerland many pages of constructive comments. Irving Friedman, before he died on November 20, 1989, had read my first four chapters. Edna Friedman has read them all. Bernard Bell, Ben King, and William Gilmartin read my chapter on India. My colleagues at Caltech, Kent Clark, David Elliot, and Thayer Scudder, read every word and helped me with my expressions. The archives of the World Bank, where I worked for several months over the course of several years, were made accessible to me through the generous assistance of Bogomir Chokel and Charles Ziegler. Chairman of the Board of the *New York Times*, Arthur Ochs Sulzberger, contributed generously toward seeing the book published, as did the president of Caltech, Dr. Thomas Everhart. I am also grateful to the Division of the Humanities and Social Sciences at Caltech for their support.

To all of these good friends, I am grateful. Of course, I alone am responsible for errors of both omission and commission.

Notes

1. At the end of December 1992, the World Bank had 172 member governments; the IFC had 148; and the IDA, 146.
2. See Author's Acknowledgements in Edward S. Mason and Robert E. Asher, *The World Bank Since Bretton Woods* (Washington, D.C.: Brookings Institution, 1973).
3. Robert W. Oliver, *International Economic Cooperation and the World Bank* (London: Macmillan, 1975).
4. These twenty-five to thirty interviews are available in the oral history section of the Butler Library at Columbia University and in the archives of the World Bank. They are cited collectively by Mason and Asher as "Oral History."
5. Andrew Kamarck, *The Economics of African Development* (New York: Frederick A. Praeger, 1967).
6. Irving Friedman had been the Bank's chief economist since 1964. See Chapter 5.
7. The Mason and Asher book (note 2 above) skipped rather hastily over the presidency of George Woods. It did not mention the role of the economists at all. I vowed that, should the occasion arise, I would correct this oversight.
8. Mason's interviews are on deposit in the oral history collection at Columbia University and in the archives of the World Bank.

INTRODUCTION

GEORGE
AND
LOUISE

George and Louise Woods in their early years

George Woods was not born to wealth but to a life of long hours and hard work. Business was his life. He had no real outside interests, unless they were the theater and dining well. He was a registered Republican, but took no great interest in politics. The *New York Times* wrote about him in 1964, "Sometimes they call him 'the radical from Wall Street,' but George Woods is no radical. He is an innovator."[1] He was an innovative banker.

George was born in Boston on July 27, 1901, to John and Laura (Rhodes) Woods. John Woods was a worker in the Boston navy yard when Laura and he married, but they soon moved to Brooklyn, in part to be closer to Laura's parents. In Brooklyn, George's only sibling, a younger sister, Grace, was born in 1904. That same year, the short and unhappy marriage ended in John's death from heart disease and cirrhosis of the liver, conditions probably caused by his excessive drinking.[2]

The Woodses were desperately poor after John died. George was three, and Grace not yet one. George's mother had not inherited anything. She worked at sewing, making things for people, repairing things. When Grace was old enough, she earned money by baby-sitting. George worked after school. As Grace—Grace Woods Johnson—later observed, "Our whole life was just the three of us. We were a nucleus."

> We were never affluent, but my mother was a very happy woman. She adored her children and that kept us from being underprivileged. We were certainly underprivileged with our contemporaries, our peers. We weren't wholly accepted. But at home we could do no wrong. . . . Mother loved George unbelievably. I always felt she favored him. Maybe she did, maybe she didn't. She just thought George was perfect, and I sort of went along with that too.[3]

When George was a little boy in Brooklyn, he swept the sidewalks and cleaned brass for a Doctor Treadwell, who lived in the neighborhood. Once Treadwell commented to George's mother, "That little fellow is going to grow up to be president of the United States." It must have been something in his attitude in performing those menial duties before he went to school. Everything George did, he did thoroughly.

3

George was sober even as a child. He had large, black eyes and very dark eyebrows that almost grew together. He was small when he was in high school and kept signs on his desk such as "Never cross a small man." Though younger, Grace was taller than George, and more athletic. It was she who taught George to roller-skate and ride a bicycle. When George did grow, however, he became almost six feet tall.

George was mentally alert but physically lazy. He joined the Boy Scouts but gave them up when he discovered that camping was required. If he could ride, he wouldn't walk; if he could sit, he wouldn't stand. After a long article about him appeared in *Fortune Magazine* in 1959, a friend wrote to him playfully, "What's that bunk about your being opposed to physical exercise of any kind? Hell, I remember once you walked up a whole flight of stairs to a speakeasy on 56th Street."

He participated in YMCA activities. True, he learned to swim at the Y; but he preferred to float. He would stand beside the piano at high school sorority and fraternity dances, fascinated by the music, though he was a lazy dancer. He was not agile. He loved the theater, but he refused, well into his twenties, to wear a tuxedo—even when the other men in his party wore tuxedos and his date was in an evening gown. If George could not do something well, he didn't attempt it. He was not good at languages, so he didn't bother to learn. He seemed to know his own capabilities. He was not competitive—except in banking, and he was very good at that.

George, though not a churchgoer, followed his mother's teachings. Laura Woods—herself a church regular—taught the children that they had to do certain things; that there was a right way and a wrong way. She explained very simply her philosophy of life, and the children listened. She continued to attend the Lafayette Avenue Presbyterian Church until, in 1950, she suffered a stroke. All those years, Grace regularly accompanied her. But George, when he was grown—though continuing to heed his mother's teachings—dropped out of church.

It was his mother's idea that George should go to Boys' Commercial High School in Brooklyn rather than, say, Brooklyn Prep or Erasmus Hall High School. Neither George nor Grace could afford to go to college. Grace entered high school at age thirteen, having skipped two grades in elementary school. George, too, was a good student, but he did not pass a required secretarial course (he was not interested) so had to stay an additional term. That was when he started to work in the school's bank, where he attracted the attention of Gilbert J. Raynor, the assistant principal. Raynor recommended George for a position as an office boy at Harris, Forbes & Co. It would not be his first job. He had been employed after school for five months by a local apron manufacturer, at $6 a week, and he was seeking "to improve his position."

On June 17, 1918, George began his career with Harris, Forbes & Co. in Manhattan. George kept a small photograph of the headlines in the *New York Times* that first day. The Austrian army had penetrated across the Piave River in northeastern Italy, while the U.S. troops had fired seven thousand gas shells during the preceding forty-eight hours and had inflicted heavy casualties upon the Kaiser's favorite divisions. The armistice was still five months away, war was increasingly fierce, and office boys of the dependable caliber of George Woods, not yet seventeen, were in short supply.

When Harry Addinsell, who had been with Harris, Forbes since 1904, returned to his job after World War I, he found a new office boy looking up at him with large, black eyes from behind the reception desk. George Woods reported to Addinsell and to Charles W. Beall, the executive vice-president of Harris, Forbes, "who knew practically everything there was to know about corporate financing—debentures and unsecured loans."[4] Phillip Krauthoff, another vice-president, induced Woods to enroll in night classes at the American Institute for Banking and at New York University. Krauthoff would confront Woods in the mornings and question him about what he had learned the night before. Woods frequently claimed that Addinsell and Krauthoff had brought him up. "He brought himself up," Addinsell would reply.[5]

In the 1920s, George traveled, largely for pleasure, to Germany, France, Italy, Argentina, and Brazil, polishing his social skills. When he was in New York, he stayed in a hotel in Manhattan, though he would usually go home to be with his mother and sister on Friday evenings. Grace would often drive George back to his hotel in time for his Saturday night date. George bought his first car, a Model T Ford, in 1920. Later, he bought a Chrysler convertible and then a Cadillac. He almost never drove in Manhattan, however. He kept his car in Brooklyn or, later, in Scarsdale.

One day George went home joyfully to announce that he had been offered the opportunity to go to Canada as a bond salesman, but his mother exclaimed, "George, you can't go to Canada and leave Grace and me. What would we do?" George didn't go. A year later he went to Japan for Harris, Forbes, but that was not a permanent separation from his family.

After George went to work at Harris, Forbes the family's fortunes began to improve. They improved further when Grace, then seventeen, became employed by the Prudential Insurance Company in Brooklyn. In 1929, the family moved to Scarsdale in fashionable Westchester County. Later they moved to a house at 277 Park Avenue in Manhattan, where the Chemical Bank Building now stands.

Grace stopped work when they moved to Scarsdale. She resumed her employment as manager of the Prudential office in Columbus Circle when

the family moved to Manhattan; but, when their mother had a heart attack in 1934, George asked Grace to stop work and care for their mother.
In 1935, George married. The following year, Grace also married.

In 1950, when Laura Woods suffered her debilitating stroke, she was
moved to a nursing home, where she spent three years. She recognized no
one, not even Grace. She would say to her daughter, "I haven't seen
Grace for a long time. Have you seen her?" At one point Grace called
George to say their mother recognized a picture of him and said she would
like to see him. George flew from Washington on the next plane, only to
realize that his mother did not recognize him after all. She said to George,
"I'd like you to meet my son. This is his picture." He did not go to see her
again.

When George's mother died in 1954, George had a heart attack and
was unable to attend his mother's funeral. His wife, Louise, was apprehen-
sive about George's recuperation. She wanted to whisk him away to
Florida, but Grace said, "You can take George anywhere you want, but unless I see him and talk to him and we get this straightened out in his
mind, he is not going to get well."[6] George and Grace had a long talk.
George seemed to feel he had neglected his mother. He was traveling a
great deal: he was in India; he was here, there, and everywhere. Grace assured him that their mother was extremely proud of him and loved him
very dearly. George put his arm around Grace and said, "Thanks, Pieface."
(He hadn't called her that since she was a little girl.) He smiled and began
immediately to recover.

Louise and the doctor attributed his heart attack to excessive smoking
and to drinking coffee, in addition to the turmoil he must have felt when
his mother died. "If you smoke and drink coffee, I won't be responsible for
you beyond five years. If you stop both, you'll live your normal life," the
doctor said. George never drank coffee nor smoked again, giving up a
habit of two or three packs of cigarettes a day. He just quit cold. But one
cannot help but suppose it was more than coincidence that George had a
heart attack the day after his mother died.

George liked to be with people who were interesting, but he was not
naturally gregarious. As a child, he never participated in group play, nor
did he relish debate or confrontation. He would listen to various points
of view, and then choose among them. He would delve into all aspects of
a problem before he made a decision, and he had little patience with
those who did otherwise. But once George made up his mind, the issue
was settled: he did not choose to argue. On one occasion, when Grace's
husband was baiting George by criticizing President Franklin Roosevelt,
George simply said, "He is a very difficult man to understand," and that
was the end of that.

George was a listener rather than a talker. He would pick other people's
brains. And when he did speak, he was usually careful about what he said.

He was sensitive, particularly if he felt he was being slighted. He was defensive about the fact that he had not gone to college. He spoke with a bit of a nasal twang, rather than with cultivated accents. What someone else might take as a joke, he might take seriously—he did not have an obvious sense of humor. Most notably, George was an honorable and generous person as is evidenced by his relationships with his many good friends (some of whom he helped for years after the stock market crash).

Woods was a great advocate of free education. After he had retired from the World Bank, he would talk with Irving Friedman (who had directed the World Bank's economic work) about education in New York City, making the point that the strength of New York lay in its education of one generation after another of immigrants—the English, the Irish, the Germans, the Jews, the Italians, and the Puerto Ricans. Through education, these immigrants had made their way into U.S. society. He loved to illustrate his point with people he met. "See that guy? He came over from Italy. He went to N.Y.U. (or City College, or wherever) and you can see where he is. He is the head of Manufacturers Hanover, or something like that."[7]

Speaking about banking, Woods said, according to Friedman, "It's a shame; it used to be such fun. I would never hire someone from another firm without calling the head of the firm and saying, 'I'd like to hire your Mr. So-and-So'. If he'd say 'no,' I'd forget it. Nowadays the poor guy who hired Mr. So-and-So in the first place finds out about it later." Woods's integrity as a banker was unquestioned.

George was always fond of the ladies. In high school, he was fond of Helen Jersey and Ruth Haidrich. He went with Ruth a long time. In 1929, he squired Agnes Ayres, Rudolph Valentino's leading lady. In the early 1930s, he was much in love with Louise Achilles, but that was before he met Louise Taraldson, whom he called Louie to distinguish her from the other Louise. He asked Louie to marry him.

Louise Taraldson met George Woods at a dinner party early in 1934. She had recently returned from three years in London and the Continent and was on the way back, more or less, to Long Beach, California, where she had grown up. She had set out for New York and London shortly after her mother had died and her younger sister had married. "You go and have fun," her sister advised, and Louie set out to do just that.[8] Louie had been able to afford a life in New York and London for the five years before she married George—Woodsie, as Louie affectionately called him. "I always had an adventurous spirit," Louie acknowledged. "I always wanted to know what was around the corner."[9]

Louie was living at the Waldorf when she met George. He asked if he could take her home from a dinner party. She hadn't wanted to leave so early, but she thought, "He can take me home if he'd like." He was a young thirty-three, attractive, a well-known banker. On the way home,

George whispered to the friend with whom he was riding, "You mightn't realize it, but I'm going to marry that girl."[10]

Before they were married, George frequently worked on Saturdays and Sundays. They dined in splendor two or three evenings a week, until George said, "I can't go out every night. I have business in the morning. I can't stay out at all these nightclubs, I have to be at my desk."[11] Louise liked him because he was quick and she couldn't push him around.

After a few months of going out in the evenings, Woodsie proposed and Louie accepted, but he set out almost immediately for California where he was involved in financing for the Southern California Edison Company. Louie stayed behind in New York. After several weeks, she wrote to him to complain that he wasn't writing, to which he replied by mail, "Dear Louise, mine is a silent love."[12]

Louie was patient. When George invited her to set a wedding date, she suggested that they be married on April 29, 1935, in Long Beach, at the Virginia Country Club, by the Episcopal minister who had baptized her. When George asked Louie what she would like to do for a honeymoon, she suggested sailing home through the Panama Canal. They found an apartment at 60th and Park Avenue in Manhattan before George returned briefly to Southern California to finish his work. This was their home for two years before they moved to 54th and Park. After sixteen years, they moved permanently to 825 Fifth Avenue.

At one point, when they began to entertain, George asked, "Don't you think it would be a good idea to get a chair or two?"[13] "Yes," Louie replied, and they began their collection of lovely things—largely antiques. George did none of the buying, however: he shopped for nothing other than men's apparel.

When George and Louise were first married, they went from time to time to Framington, Massachusetts, to visit John Macomber, chairman of the board of First Boston Corporation, who had a magnificent house and stables. Once Macomber put Louie on a horse without asking if she could ride. The horse started to go and Louie couldn't stop him. The horse wandered all over Macomber's golf course, with Macomber shouting, "Louie, get off the greens with that horse." Louie kept shouting back, "He won't stop. He won't stop. He won't stop." Later, after dinner, Macomber whispered to Louie, "Your husband is going to be chairman of this company some day. He will make it the top investment banking company in the world."[14]

Early in their married life, they frequently went to the country for weekends, returning home exhausted. They would have cocktail parties before lunch and cocktail parties before dinner, and people would say, "Come to us next weekend." Finally, George put his foot down. "This is the last time we are going any place for a weekend. Maybe people will be annoyed, but they'll get over it."[15] From that time on, they never went to anyone for a weekend. Instead, on Sundays they stayed in New York and enjoyed the *New York Times* and the *London Economist*, which George said was the best news magazine ever published, and went for a walk at about eleven in the morning. George would tell Louise about the different buildings, when they were built, and why business was moving slowly uptown.

Early in their marriage, Louie teased him, "If you don't tell me anything about your business, I won't advise you," to which George replied, "I am not about to tell you anything about my business."[16] Once, only once, Louie went to George's office. When she walked in, George looked up startled and asked, "What do you want *here?*" Louie backed out in a hurry and never returned. After that, she did not seek to "advise" him about his business. His business and hers were as separate as though there were a wall between them. As Louie expressed it, "I made the friends; he did the business."

In the 1920s and early 1930s, George had good luck in backing the stage plays *Sailor Beware, Dead End,* and *Outward Bound.* He said that plays were a great relaxation for him. He supported the Metropolitan Opera but did not care for opera performances and Louie was always looking around at the last minute for someone to go with her. George could make little sense of opera plots, and he could not understand the words. The theater diverted him, however, and the play always needed financial help. Woods would sit in a theater before the play opened and watch rehearsals. His friends would say "Oh yes, the Woodses backed that show,"[17] when, perhaps, they had invested only 1 percent of the total.

George also enjoyed the circus. Louie had known John Ringling North before she married George, and George became treasurer of the circus for several years after the historic Hartford, Connecticut, fire of 1944, during which a stampede in the main tent killed 168 people and injured 487. Woods worked out a plan for compensating the families of the victims and later reorganized the circus to keep it from collapsing. He enjoyed having the run of the circus: he enjoyed going backstage and being with the owner, who came with a long cigarette-holder, a fedora hat, and a cane; and he enjoyed the animals. The circus provided excitement similar to that which George felt in the theater.

He read books by leafing through them. If it was a book that Louie particularly wanted George to read, he would sit for an hour or so leafing through it. Louie would say, "You can't read a book that fast." He'd say, "Ask me a question," and Louie was unable to ask a question he couldn't answer.[18] If Louie expressed herself too violently about what she was reading in the newspaper at breakfast, George would say, "Calm down, calm down. Don't read the paper if you're going to get yourself in an uproar."[19]

In many respects, Louie was the antithesis of George. She was as outgoing, gregarious, and enthusiastic as he was sober and reserved. "My whole life has been an interest in people," Louie once declared.[20] In her youth, she had been a surfer. She loved to swim; and to dance. She had a penchant for foreign languages.

Louie acknowledged that she had never learned to cook. "I can't boil water without burning it," she would say.[21] They almost always went out for dinner. George and Louie had no children. When a close woman friend would announce that she was pregnant, Louie would be green with envy. Before World War II, she worked in the New York State adoption bureau.

Their lifestyle changed abruptly in 1942 when George entered the army as a major. They moved to Washington, D.C., where they lived for a time in one ancient room in Stoneleigh Court on Farragut Square. George slept on a cot in the hallway, and Louie slept on another cot in the bedroom with her toy dachshund. George would go off to work at 7 A.M. and return after General Somervell dismissed the staff at 7 P.M. George and Louie usually ate at Sholl's Cafeteria on Connecticut Avenue. When two rooms became available at the Shoreham Hotel, they lived there for the duration of the war in relative luxury. Louie was bored to tears on Saturdays. She worked in the blood bank five days a week; George worked six days. Their social life consisted of having dinner at someone's house. They would arrive at 8 P.M. and leave by 9:30.

During the war, Louie worked in hospitals so long and hard that she lost fifteen pounds and was ordered by her doctor to stop. After the war, but before George became president of the World Bank, Louie devoted herself to the young people from abroad who were sponsored by the Institute for International Education. She hired entertainers for them—such as Chubby Checkers, who performed a new dance called the Twist, and Teddy Wilson, who played piano for the Benny Goodman band. Sometimes she entertained the students at the institute, sometimes in her apartment. Sometimes she arranged picnics at the Stanford estate of her close friend Iphigene Ochs Sulzberger, whose husband controlled the *New York Times*. Louie took the students shopping; she took them to medical and dental appointments. If they were homesick, she would take them to her apartment and feed them or introduce them to the daughters of her friends. Later, when George was Bank president and she traveled a lot, she frequently came across young people she had known at the institute. She saw them worldwide—in France, London, Tokyo, Morocco, Ethiopia, Uganda, India. . . .

Louie was possessive about her husband. She traveled most everywhere with George and tended to shield him even from his family. Early in their marriage, George actually advised Louie not to have lunch with his mother. "You will become tired of it, and then, if you stop, you'll hurt her feelings."[22] But every other Sunday when they were in New York and before her stroke in 1950, George's mother came to dinner and spent the night. Relations with George's sister, Grace, and her husband were cordial, but they were all together only once or twice a year. Louie would talk to Grace frequently on the telephone, and George would have long restaurant lunches with Grace from time to time. The two would remain talking after all the other patrons had left. George loved Grace very much, and she loved him. George also loved Grace's daughter, Barbara Louise. When Barbara graduated from Mt. Holyoke in 1962, George chartered a plane so that he could be present at the ceremony. She was the daughter he never had.

George did not involve himself in politics. He felt that if he did, he might express opinions to which others might pay no attention, and that would be a waste. The closest he came to a political opinion was when he said, "If the time ever comes when forty-eight percent of the people are working to support the other fifty-two percent, there's liable to be trouble."[23]

He had little patience with small talk or cocktail parties. At the World Bank, he limited his nights out to three, seldom went to receptions, and went home early because he wanted to be at his desk in the morning. According to Louise, "He was not a social man."[24] When they traveled abroad and were met by a nation's president, finance minister, and/or governor of the central bank, each would want to put on a banquet for the Woodses, but George would say, "My wife isn't very strong and we can't have all these dinners. Can't you get together and have one dinner?"[25]

For her part, however, Louie loved sitting at the head table at the annual meeting reception of the World Bank in Vienna in 1961, shortly before George became president. She fancied Eugene Black was observing her to see if she could adapt to the social whirl of Washington life. She loved being at receptions with the Kennedys (and later with the Johnsons). Jack was handsome, and Jackie was beautiful. There was an air of elegance that Louie liked, even though she was a Republican. She felt proud of the president. Moreover, Kennedy liked George Woods very much: he had a wholesome regard for his opinion and wanted to talk with him, consult with him.

Once George was in his Bank post, Louie drew on her earlier experience with the foreign students she had mothered. She brought people together, particularly the wives. She loved to entertain. She was naturally gregarious. She was good at remembering names. If she missed a name, Marjorie Billings, the Bank's social secretary, was at her side to prompt her.

Perhaps the most important thing Louie did for George was to find a home in Portugal where he could relax in intimate surroundings. Louie said to George one day, "We have always liked to travel. Why don't we buy a little house in Europe so that when we semi-retire, we can travel all over and still have this to come back to within an hour or two?"

"Okay" Woodsie replied, "It's not a bad idea."[26]

With the help of Carlo Bombieri, second-in-command at the Banca
Commerciale Italiano, Louie started looking in Pisa: George and Louie
had always loved Italy. She wanted to be on the water, and searched down
the coast as far as San Felice, but she found nothing.

She tried Spain next. She moved into the Soto Grande for a week.
Joe McMicking said, "You and George ought to have a house here."
"Why," Louie replied. "We don't play golf, and the swimming is horrible.
What would we do? It's a long way from Madrid. It's a long way from
Seville." "I'll show you a location," Joe said, and he took Louie up to the
top of a hill where she could see the ocean on two sides. He said, "I'll
build you a house here. You can buy it if you want to." But Louie replied,
"Don't do it, I'm giving up the idea."

After looking in Pisa and in Spain, she went to see George Anderson,
the U.S. ambassador in Portugal. "I was in Italy looking for a house to buy.
I looked in Spain, and I thought I'd see you on my way out."

"What about Portugal?" he asked.

"I don't know anything about Portugal. I've never been here." But
Louie thought, "I'll be nice, I'll explore." So she telephoned Henry
Abecassis, who offered to show Louie around, but he only took her to
friends who recommended mansions large enough for ten kids. "I haven't
any kids," Louie said. "I want something nice and smart and available."

Finally he suggested a house that had been built by a Spaniard for his
wife. It was rented temporarily to a U.S. couple. Louie fell in love with it
immediately. "Henry," Louie said, "It's my house. This house I'm going to
own. Find out."

The owner was a man named Moreno, who lived in Portugal. They
made a date for the following day, but Moreno didn't want to sell. Henry
and Moreno conversed in Portuguese back and forth for at least twenty
minutes. Louie became impatient. "How much?" she asked. "He is asking
too much money. I'm embarrassed to tell you," said Henry.

"Henry, please tell me what he wants."

Henry relented, and Louie said, "I'll take it. I'll pay that."

That night she called Woods at midnight in Washington to say, "I
found a house." George said, "You'd better give them a deposit before they
change their minds," to which Louie replied, "I already have."

The house consisted of a double guest room and bath; a single guest
room and bath; master quarters—two rooms and a double bath and
shower; a dining room with pink marble; a living room with a slate floor;
an open kitchen and pantry; a basement with a shower; a maid's room
with bath; a powder room; and a double garage with a shower and toilet.
Louie immediately raised the wall around the acre lot so as to have complete privacy, and she put heavy iron gates at the entrance. She furnished

it with antiques and paintings. Later, they added a swimming pool.

Over the next three years, before retiring from the World Bank, George and Louie spent many happy weeks there, including two weeks in the summer. When George left the Bank, they went there for two or three months every summer. Sometimes they would go to Paris for two or three days, sometimes to London for four or five; but increasingly they just stayed in their home in Portugal. People would visit them.

* * * * *

The Woodses' life together saw several transitions. When Louie knew she had to leave New York for Washington (they kept their Fifth Avenue apartment and returned on weekends when they could), she wept. In Washington, they leased Suite G–400 in the famous Sheraton Park Hotel, formerly the Wardman-Park where Lyndon Johnson had lived. And when Louie left Washington to return to New York, she wept again.

Instead of—as earlier—there being a wall between George's business life and his life with Louie, they were partners in Washington. Louie was in her element. She was with people who were on the "team"; she was, in her own words, "fantastic."[27] The Bank years were years of "absolute joy" for Louie.[28]

Within reason, George tried to give Louie everything she wanted. For her part, she worshiped him and tried to do everything he wanted. As she observed in her memoirs:

> My whole life with him was built around the fact that I wanted to keep him happy. . . . I was married with this in mind. . . . As a result, he took me every place we went. I said, "I'll make the friends; you do the business." And this is the way of our life. I *did* make the friends and he *did* do the business. And we had fun, and were happy. He would be in business all day. He never saw those countries as I did. . . . I'd be up at 6:00 in the morning and going all day for fear I might miss something.[29]

Woodsie and Louie complemented each other to perfection.

Notes

1. *New York Times*, September 6, 1964, Part III, p. 1.
2. Little is known about John Woods except that he was probably born in Scotland. A fair amount is known about Laura and her family, however. Her parents, William and Elizabeth (Paige) Rhodes, were born in England, as were two of their three children (Laura, the third child, was born in Newark, New Jersey, soon after her parents emigrated).

William, a diamond cutter by trade, in due course made a small fortune in the United States and decided to retire in England. Laura was twelve years old by then: her education was interrupted and she found it difficult to pick up the threads in England. When William decided that he was too young to retire, he started a jewelry business but lost a lot of money when a salesman he had hired absconded with his samples. William decided to go back to the United States to try to recoup his fortune. Leaving Elizabeth and Laura with relatives (Ada, the second child, had died of diptheria in childhood), William set out with his young son, Will, promising to send for his wife and daughter when he could afford first-class passage. When he did send for them, Laura was glad to be back in America; but shortly thereafter Will, who had joined the U.S. Navy, started to drink too much. William complained that Will was a disgrace to the family, and Will decided he wasn't going home anymore. For a while, Will sent his mother Christmas cards and presents, but when these stopped the family assumed that Will was dead—a sad event for Laura, who loved her brother dearly. Laura, the surviving child and pride and joy of her parents, disappointed them by marrying John Woods, another person who drank too much.

William had a brother, George, and it was for him that George Woods was named.

3. Robert W. Oliver, "A Conversation with Grace Woods Johnson," *Conversations About George Woods and the World Bank*, New York, March 16, 1986, p. 6.

4. Arthur H. Dean, interview by John T. Mason, Jr., January 25, 1983, transcript, Oral History Research Office, Columbia University, p. 1.

5. Robert Sheahan, "First Man at First Boston," *Fortune*, June 1959, p. 146.

6. "The Reminiscences of Grace Johnson," *George David Woods Oral History Project*, Oral History Research Office, Columbia University, 1983, p. 24.

7. Robert W. Oliver, "A Conversation With Irving Friedman, V," *Conversations About George Woods and the World Bank*, July 23, 1985, p. 39.

8. Louie had graduated from Long Beach Polytechnic High School and had attended Long Beach City College for a year. She was born October 11, 1907, in Grafton, North Dakota. Her father was born in Lime Springs, Iowa; her mother, in Edmonton, Canada. They were of Scotch-Irish and Norwegian lineage. Louie's father was in the insurance business. The family had just moved to Minneapolis when he developed multiple sclerosis and died. This was in 1913, when Louie was six. After the father's death, mother and children moved to Long Beach, where Mrs. Taraldson (the family name is unclear; Louise called herself Taralton until 1931) occupied herself by buying and selling apartment houses. She must have done rather well, for she was able to leave Louie a fair nest-egg.

9. Mrs. George David Woods, interview by John T. Mason, Jr., January 14, 1983, interview 1, transcript, Oral History Research Office, Columbia University, p. 12. In this interview, Louise also reported, "A friend of mine who had lived here in New York talked me into going to Paris and London." According to Louise's passport, she arrived in London on September 23, 1930. While there, she was married (on January 24, 1931) to Montford Swan Steele. The marriage was brief.

10. Ibid., p. 2.
11. Ibid., p. 4.
12. Ibid., p. 4.
13. Ibid, p. 7.

14. Robert W. Oliver, "A Conversation with Louise Woods," *Conversations About George Woods and the World Bank*, New York, November 8, 1985, p. 1.

15. Mrs. Woods—Mason interview 4, March 4, 1983, p. 153. In subsequent notes, interviews that have previously been referenced are referred to only by number.

16. Mrs. Woods, 1, p. 8.
17. Mrs. Woods—Interview 2, January 20, 1983, p. 70.
18. Ibid., p. 95.
19. Mrs. Woods, 4, p. 174.
20. Mrs. Woods, 2, p. 64.
21. Mrs. Woods, 1, p. 34.
22. Mrs. Woods, 4, p. 167.
23. Ibid., p. 176.
24. Mrs. Woods—Interview 3, February 17, 1983, p. 111.
25. Mrs. Woods—Interview 5, April 21, 1983, p. 25.
26. Mrs. Woods, 2, p. 76.
27. Mrs. Woods, 1, p. 41.
28. Mrs. Woods, 3, p. 109.
29. Mrs. Woods, 4, p. 152.

CHAPTER 1

FROM
OFFICE BOY
TO
CHAIRMAN
OF THE
BOARD

Major George Woods, in the early 1940s

The firm George Woods joined as an office boy in August 1918, Harris, Forbes & Co., was a leading underwriter of municipal and utility bonds. Woods was given a desk in the buying, or underwriting, department. Moving on from his duties as office boy, he quickly assumed responsibility for helping clients put together a bond package that could be marketed. He helped with long-range corporate planning so that, if and when firms needed to raise capital, they could do so with expedition and on favorable terms. He was associated primarily with the buying or underwriting side, on advising clients, that is to say, on how to plan for their long-run future.[1]

The firm had an almost forty-year history when Woods joined.[2] N. W. (Norman Wait) Harris and Company opened its doors for business in Chicago on May 1, 1882. Born in Massachusetts in 1846, Harris had earlier been employed as treasurer of the Union Central Life Insurance Company of Cincinnati, Ohio, where he got to know real estate mortgages and railroad bonds. With the encouragement of S. M. Nickerson, president of the First National Bank of Chicago, Harris determined to start his own business. After conducting a thorough economic and legal investigation of a municipality, he would buy municipal bonds directly. He sought customers to whom he might sell his bonds, rather than waiting for bond buyers to knock on his door. Municipals led to utilities and, by 1916, utility bonds formed the biggest part of his investments. Harris established an office in Boston in 1886, and in New York in 1890. In 1896, his son, Albert W. Harris, became a partner. Albert operated out of Chicago and journeyed as far as Los Angeles to investigate bonds.

Five years earlier, in 1891, Allen Boyd Forbes, a twenty-five-year-old lawyer, had been induced to leave the legal department of Swift and Company for the Harris firm in Chicago. In 1901, he moved to New York and became a partner. In 1911, the New York office was incorporated as Harris, Forbes & Company, and in 1916 the Boston office also changed its name to Harris, Forbes after Norman Harris sold his majority interest to the New York and Boston partners.[3]

John R. Macomber, who was hired by Harris in 1894 after Macomber had finished one year at the Massachusetts Institute of Technology (MIT), was employed in the Boston office. Eventually, he became chairman of the board of Harris, Forbes and of First Boston. Harry M. Addinsell, a high school graduate who had worked for two years for the *New York Times* selling financial advertising, was employed initially as a buying department assistant in the New York office. He would become chairman of the executive committee of Harris, Forbes and later president of First Boston. Forbes, Macomber, and Addinsell were crucial to the success of Harris, Forbes. So was George Woods.

In 1927, at the age of twenty-six, George Woods became a vice-president. In 1928, he was entrusted with the task of opening Japan by marketing $9,000,000 of 6 1/2 percent first mortgage bonds for the Nippon Electric Company. He secured the assistance of a twenty-nine-year-old attorney, Arthur H. Dean, from the law firm of Sullivan and Cromwell. Earlier, George had suggested to Dean, whom George had recently met, "I have acquired a fair knowledge about stocks and bonds. You have a fair knowledge about the law. Why don't we just exchange information?"

In 1929, the total of all new financing of stocks, bonds, and notes in the United States was over $6 billion. Harris, Forbes & Co. headed a syndicate selling over $370 million. During the first six months of 1930, Harris, Forbes managed a total of over $238 million, principally public utilities issues, but, after that, syndications declined precipitously as the economy slid rapidly downhill.

The financial community was startled on July 1, 1930, by the announcement that the Chase National Bank of New York, the largest commercial banking institution in the world, would acquire Harris, Forbes, the largest securities distributing organization in the country. Woods conjectured that the Harris, Forbes senior management, advancing beyond middle-age, was buying financial security in a deteriorating economic environment. The stock of the Chase Bank, a Rockefeller bank, represented that security. John Macomber and Harry Addinsell survived the merger, as did George Woods and seventeen other vice-presidents.

The merger was short-lived, however. In 1933, with the passage of the Glass-Steagall Act banks belonging to the Federal Reserve System were required to separate themselves from their securities affiliates, so another reorganization was needed. Enter another player in this history of mergers. In 1903, a former bank examiner, Daniel Wing, had acquired, through a series of mergers, the name and assets of the First National Bank of Boston, formerly the Massachusetts Bank. The securities affiliate of this bank was the First National Corporation of Boston. In 1921, a branch of First National Corporation was established in New York under the direction of Colonel Allan Melville Pope, who had recently resigned from the U.S. Army after a seventeen-year tour-of-duty. A graduate of West Point, by 1928 Pope had become president and chief executive officer. James

Coggeshall, Jr., in charge of all sales, was second-in-command. On June 27, 1932, the name of the First National Corporation of Boston was simplified to the First of Boston.

On April 18, 1934, it was announced that stockholders of the Chase National Bank and the First National Bank of Boston would receive rights to purchase at $18 a share the stock of a new First Boston Corporation. Through a series of mergers and because of the Glass-Steagall Act, First Boston thereby became the largest publicly owned investment banking firm in its day. Macomber became chairman of the board; Pope became president; and Addinsell, chairman of the executive committee. George Woods and James Coggeshall, Jr., became members of the eleven-man board of directors.

On July 2, 1934, First Boston undertook its first public offering following its separation from the Chase Bank and the First National Bank of Boston. In October, the firm managed offerings of Edison Electric and Northern States Power. But the biggest and most successful offering was to occur in 1935. It would heavily involve George Woods. As long ago as 1910, Albert Harris had visited the forerunner of the Los Angeles Department of Water and Power and had made a hit with a startling prediction that in five or six years the Edison Company would have to relinquish some of its properties to the City of Los Angeles. He had subsequently been elected to the board of directors of Southern California Edison. Harris, Forbes had arranged most of the financing for Edison after that. Nevertheless, it was by no means a foregone conclusion that the team of John Macomber, George Ramsey, a vice-president, and George Woods, with Arthur Dean as legal counsel, would win the competition for Edison financing.[4]

Harry Bauer, the new president of Southern California Edison, was a tough bargainer. He sought terms for refinancing 5 percent bonds no worse than those enjoyed by Pacific Gas and Electric in northern California. (At that time, the world of banking and insurance had a higher opinion of San Francisco than of Los Angeles.) But George Woods prevailed. He broke the 4 percent barrier in April 1935, obtaining an interest rate of 3 3/4 percent for a total issue of $73,000,000, thus saving Edison $450,000 in annual interest charges and earning Harry Bauer's admiration as a lifetime friend.

This was much the largest securities offering since the Glass-Steagall Act. First Boston itself guaranteed the sale of $18,250,000 worth of bonds, roughly twice the size of its own capital. Significantly, the original First of Boston under Allan Pope had built an unrivaled reputation in U.S. government securities, and Harry Bauer had insisted that the firm financing Edison "be ace high in administration circles in Washington." The component parts of First Boston were fitting together nicely. George Woods—

taking time out only for his honeymoon—remained in southern California until September 1935 to negotiate three additional bond offerings totaling $91,500,000. Then he returned to New York in triumph.

In 1935, the first full calendar year of operations, First Boston earned a net income of $3,308,370; in 1936, $3,172,351. In 1937, however, First Boston suffered a loss of $2,484,004, the only loss in the firm's history. Industrial offerings to Bethlehem Steel and Puroil were disasters as the price of Puroil declined from $100 to $70 a share. First Boston had undertaken to market 40,000 shares. One of the results was the expansion of the executive committee from three to eight: Addinsell was chairman; with Pope, Coggeshall, Cowell, Ford, Linsley, Potter, and Woods as members. Macomber, located in Boston and reluctant to make frequent trips to New York, resigned. The new executive committee would hold regular biweekly meetings to approve all underwriting commitments and trading limits, with all action taken by the committee to be presented to the board of directors for approval.

In 1938, net operating profit amounted to $1,242,148, though a "write down" of $665,821 in connection with the unsold Puroil stock was subtracted, resulting in a net income of only $576,327. Utility bond offerings (Southern California Edison again led the list) were by far the most important. Net income for 1939 was a respectable $1,166,658. Income climbed in 1940 to $1,360,701, but declined in 1941 to only $491,256, as government securities became relatively more important than commercial offerings. In 1940, a new issue of 115,270 shares of the common stock of Standard Accident Insurance Company was accepted. The decision to undertake the financing of the common stock of an insurance company was attributed largely to George Woods. It foreshadowed the merger of Mellon Securities and First Boston. But that would not be until after World War II. Other duties first claimed Woods.

On November 18, 1942, George Woods was commissioned a major in the army's ordnance department. He was to work as executive officer for Colonel Frank Denton, who was on leave from the Mellon Securities Corporation in Pittsburgh. It was a relationship which, through yet another merger, would later modify the public utility and government bond orientation of First Boston and significantly increase its capital.

In 1931, the Mellon Securities Corporation had been organized to oversee the bond portfolios of Richard K. Mellon and Sarah Mellon Scaife, son and daughter of Richard B. Mellon.[5] Shortly thereafter, Frank Denton, a former bank examiner, was taken in to run the firm, and, in 1935, Mellon Securities entered the investment banking business. Its holdings included an awesome list of industrial concerns reflecting the Mellon family interests: Aluminum Company of America, Gulf Oil, Koppers Corporation, Westinghouse Air Brake, Jones and Laughlin Steel,

FROM OFFICE BOY TO CHAIRMAN OF THE BOARD   23

Crucible Steel, and others. Meanwhile, Richard Mellon decided to com-
bine Pittsburgh's two largest banks, Mellon National Bank and the Union
Trust Company, and to install Frank Denton as his chief executive officer
in the merged bank. Denton, anxious to move to his new post, suggested
George Woods as his successor at Mellon Securities.

Woods and Denton had known each other since Denton's days as a
bank examiner in the early 1930s. Now Mellon Securities had a branch
office in the building next door to First Boston at 100 Broadway in New
York.[6] First Boston on occasion loaned Mellon Securities its specialists.
Harry Addinsell had even proposed a merger of the firms, but in 1936 that
was premature.

Denton entered the army as a lieutenant colonel early in 1942.
Woods followed in November. Denton had urged Woods to go to Washington. "Let's get this war over with," pleaded Denton. So Woods enlisted.
Denton and Woods had adjoining rooms in the Pentagon and, with their
wives, adjacent rooms at the Shoreham Hotel. Denton and Woods served
on the requirements committee and the subcommittee for critical components. They reported, ultimately, to the chairman of the war production
board, Donald Nelson; but their immediate superiors were Generals
Somervell, Clay, and Minton, and Howard Bruce, a civilian. Woods, with
others, allocated scarce resources. Among other things, he was a trouble-
shooter: he visited plants having labor-management problems and got
them back to full production.[7]

Almost immediately after V-J Day, Woods got wind of the fact that
General Clay wanted him to go to Germany to serve in the army of occu-
pation. George didn't want that, so he worked feverishly for several days
until he was granted leave on August 15, 1945. (He was actually mustered
out of the army on November 9.) Meanwhile, as Louie returned to New
York, he rented a yacht and pondered his experiences while sailing off the
coast of New England. Then he returned to private life and First Boston.
His horizon had been expanded beyond the world of utility financing and
government bonds. It would never be the same.

Woods's short-term interest was sparked by the prospects of a merger
with Mellon Securities. Woods and Denton had talked about this on
many occasions. It would bring major industrial financing to First Boston
and Woods's expertise to Mellon Securities. When the merger was con-
summated after the war, Richard Mellon and his sister took a 20 percent
interest in First Boston in the form of nonvoting stock. The capital of
First Boston was increased from roughly $14 million to $25 million. To integrate the two organizations, a coordinating committee was established
consisting of Woods (chairman), Coggeshall and Lanston, representing
First Boston, and Hugh MacBain, for Mellon Securities. This merger made
it possible for George Woods to spread his wings.

Macomber and Pope, aged seventy-one and sixty-seven, were induced to remain in service for another year beyond January 1, 1947, but Woods and Coggeshall, who had served as Pope's deputy in overseeing corporate sales and trading, were elevated to the newly created posts of executive vice-presidents.[8] Addinsell remained chairman of the executive committee until, in 1948, he became chairman of the board. In 1948, Woods became chairman of the executive committee and Coggeshall became president. In 1951, Woods was elevated to chairman of the board. The team of Coggeshall and Woods lasted until Coggeshall retired in May 1962. Woods became president of the World Bank on January 1, 1963.[9]

As noted earlier, at Harris, Forbes and First Boston, George Woods spent his entire career on the buying or underwriting side. James Coggeshall, Jr., who went to First Boston from the First of Boston branch of the 1933 merger, was on the selling or trading side. Of course, when Woods became chairman of the executive committee and Coggeshall became president in 1948, they shared, with Harry Addinsell, overall leadership responsibilities, but the emphasis for Woods was always on buying; and for Coggeshall, selling.[10]

Even when George Woods became chairman of the board, he did not do the day-to-day running of the company. It was Coggeshall who more nearly acted as chief executive officer.[11] Woods and Coggeshall had a remarkable division of responsibilities: "One of the most remarkable I've ever run into in the business world,"[12] recalled Edward Townsend, who worked intimately with Woods for sixteen years. "Two more dissimilar men you couldn't very well find." But the pair had a happy, symbiotic relationship. Woods took care of putting the pieces together with jewel-like precision and Coggeshall did the "going out and seeing people."[13] Coggeshall, a Harvard man, contacted the bankers and insurance executives who formed the underwriting syndicate. He lined up the dealers. His judgment of the market determined the price of new issues.

It was not a question of dirty versus easy work. Woods did just as difficult things, but they were things congenial to him. After his heart attack in 1954, Woods said, "I've been told certain things and I'm going to do them. I'm going to diet carefully. I'm *not* going to smoke any more. They've told me to do only things I like to do, to avoid things I don't like to do."[14]

There were things with which Woods was very impatient. He did not want to hear other people's personal problems, for example. When Bernadette Schmitt, Woods's regular secretary, was sick for a couple of weeks, Woods borrowed a male secretary. The first morning Woods said, "Now, Brew, I know you have a lot of personal problems, but I don't want to hear anything about them. I've got personal problems, but I'm not going to burden you with mine. Here's my first letter."[15]

If there was a question of going down to Washington to talk to the secretary of the treasury, Woods would ask Coggeshall to do it, or Emil Pattberg, who succeeded Woods as chairman of the board. Several times Townsend went to Washington with either Coggeshall or Pattberg to talk to the secretary of the treasury. Woods did not want to do that. He did not want to pull wires. He agreed that it ought to be done, but he didn't want to do it. He wasn't one to ask for favors.

In long-run corporate planning, Woods was brilliant, and on the occasions he did choose to negotiate, he could be superb. After the Chase and Manhattan banks had merged, for example, and John J. McCloy, who had been president of the World Bank, became chairman of the board, a high-level meeting was called in McCloy's office. Stewart Baker, who had been the head of the Bank of Manhattan, was present. Several others were there, including Edward Townsend and George Woods. It was quite apparent that McCloy and Baker were not seeing things the same way. At one point in the negotiations, McCloy said, "That'll be all right George. We'll do that." Townsend was startled to see Woods jump out of his chair, go over to McCloy, shake his hand, and say, "Thank you very much, Jack. We'll do the best we can for you." Woods passed Townsend's chair and said, "Ed, do the necessary now," and he was out the door. After another hour or two of working out details, Townsend returned to his office to report to Woods. "You were probably a little startled to see me depart so quickly," Woods said, "but the moral of that is, if you have a deal don't hang around until it comes unstuck." If Woods had waited another moment, Stewart Baker might have demurred in some way, and they would have had to reopen the discussion.[16]

On another occasion, when Woods was obliged to appear in a courtroom for cross-examination, he was confronted by a hostile attorney. The attorney asked Woods a complicated question that lasted about ten minutes and involved relationships and numbers. Woods heard him out and then said to the attorney, "That's a pretty complicated question. I guess I need a slide rule to answer it." The attorney replied, "Well, I've got one right here as a matter of fact. I'll let you have it." Woods said, "As a matter of fact, I don't know how to use it. I've never used one." That raised quite a guffaw in the courtroom, but by the time the guffaw had died down, Woods had answered the question in precise detail. He had such a quick mind and was so good with arithmetic that he had worked it all out in his head. The courtroom broke out in applause, and the smart-alecky attorney did not open his mouth again.[17]

George Woods had a knack for gaining people's confidence and this ability was compounded not only by integrity but by a brilliant mind. He had a remarkable gift for seeing the broad picture as well as an ability to do the detailed work to support his visions. He had a prodigious capacity for work. He would call subordinates into his office and touch on one after the other of half a dozen deals. "Have you thought about this?" he would say. "Have you given sufficient consideration to that?" "You'd think to yourself, he's absolutely right," observed Edward Townsend. "That is a bit of a soft spot."[18] Another witness to Woods at work, Martin Rosen, rated Woods very highly, saying, "There is no one who had the sweep from the time point of view or the breadth point of view of the financial life of this country that [George Woods] had."[19]

Perhaps the pinnacle of George Woods's eminence was reached in the financing of Henry Kaiser "when nobody else in Wall Street would touch him."[20] Over a period of ten years (beginning in 1945) Woods raised an astonishing $1.5 billion of private financing for the Kaiser empire.[21] Kaiser interests took more of Woods's time than any other one enterprise for over thirty years.

In 1947, George Woods appeared before the Reconstruction Finance Corporation (RFC) to testify that Kaiser's Fontana, California, steel plant could not expand so long as interest charges were onerous. Woods proposed that the RFC take second position to a group of private bondholders with whom he thought he could place $25 million. The RFC turned him down, but Claude A. Williams, who was looking for steel for the Continental Gas Pipe Lines Corporation, agreed to give Kaiser a $53 million order, including a $10,560,000 advance in cash. This enabled Kaiser, through additional private financing, to pay off the remaining $91 million owed to the government and to buy another blast furnace.

Henry J. Kaiser had begun with heavy construction. He got into dams, then shipbuilding. During World War II, he built ships at an incredible rate. For a while after the war, he built automobiles. Kaiser-Frazer cars were ahead of their time, using frontwheel drives and aluminum engines. They were bulky, however, and Edgar Kaiser could never get enough steel. The Kaiser-Frazer car folded in 1954 after losing over $100 million in nine years.[22]

George Woods entered the Kaiser-Frazer picture when Cyrus Eaton, of Otis and Co., Cleveland, had to give up on Kaiser-Frazer stock. Woods never backed the Kaiser-Frazer automobile, but, in response to a suggestion from A. P. Giannini of the Bank of America, which had a financial stake in Kaiser-Frazer, Woods took on the job of restructuring the company. He avoided bankruptcy for Kaiser-Frazer by merging the ailing automobile company with Kaiser Industries.[23] After that, Woods was regarded as a financial genius. He advised Henry Kaiser, Sr., and Edgar Kaiser constantly on finance and a great deal more. Woods was particularly close to Edgar, both socially and professionally. Edgar died in 1981.[24]

It was partly because of his interest in automobiles that Henry Kaiser bought aluminum plants from the Aluminum Company of America

(Alcoa) when, in 1946, Alcoa was forced by antitrust action to relinquish its monopoly in aluminum. Kaiser, who wanted to duplicate the achievement of Henry Ford, Sr., by flooding the market with a cheap, lightweight, people's car, got into aluminum thinking it might be a substitute for steel in automobiles. Instead, he made a fortune in aluminum products other than automobiles.

In July 1948, together with Dean Witter, First Boston went to the public for the first time. They sold 600,000 shares of the common stock of Kaiser Aluminum at $15 a share. By July 1, 1956, the value of the stock had increased tenfold.[25] Woods "had the confidence of the principal New York bankers to an extraordinary degree," Townsend remembers.[26] But the big breakthrough in banking did not come until 1951, when National City Bank floated the largest bank equity offering up to that time. It was for $40 million. Morgan Stanley, Goldman Sachs, Lehman, and Kuhn Loeb were just under First Boston, and the next tier of ten or so firms were under them. City Bank had said that they would not undertake the financing unless they were absolutely confident that it would be concluded, so all the underwriting had to be negotiated in secret. In fact, when William Brady, of City Bank, called Harry Addinsell, who would retire as chairman of the board later that year, he asked, "Would you walk down the street and see me?" Addinsell, who had known Brady through the Episcopal church, replied that he would be delighted. When he returned from his walk, he immediately called in George Woods and George masterminded subsequent negotiations.

Largely due to the success of the Mellon merger, George Woods was charged with directing the stock offerings of the Aluminum Company of Canada. He was offered a directorship on the board of Alcan. He became a board member of Schenley Distillers, the American Water Works, Campbell Soup, Pittsburgh Plate Glass, Chase International Investment, Commonwealth Oil, the Kaiser Steel Corporation, and Notre Dame University. He became vice-chairman of the Transoceanic Development Corp., a Canadian firm devoted to the equity financing of activities that would supplement the efforts of the World Bank.[27] He was involved with the stock offerings of Haloid, which became Xerox.

On May 18, 1959, it was announced that George Woods would become the first person not a member of the Ochs and Sulzberger families to become a board member of the New York Times. Arthur Ochs Sulzberger later said of Woods: "He was almost like a second father. If there was a problem, we all went down to talk to George. He had a good sense of humor and a wonderful head on his shoulders. . . . I suppose that the single most important contribution that he made [in 1968] was the whole business of taking the New York Times from a private company to a public company, the creation of the two classes of stock, B and A, which entitled and permitted the family to sell enough stock so that the company could, in effect, go public and at the same time retain control of the institution through the B shares. The stock was split 10 for 1. Every shareholder who had an original share of New York Times Company stock received nine shares of A and one share of B. And then the family—the trust, I should say, of which George was one of the three trustees—sold a substantial number of A shares and that was enough to move onto the American Stock Exchange, create the market place for the shares of the New York Times Company, and, at the same time, very importantly, keep the control and protect us from corporate raiders."[28]

Woods stumbled momentarily when, in 1954, he took on the job of reforming the Commonwealth Oil Refining Company. First Boston arranged $24 million in bank loans, sold $16 million in debentures, and purchased $500,000 of common stock for its own account. By the end of 1956, however, Commonwealth was losing $600,000 a month. "We looked at it as a sort of pipe line business," Woods said. We thought "it was like a slow machine: you put something in, pull a handle, and things started happening. We were stupidly wrong. We were in the chemical business and we didn't know a damn thing about it."[29] Woods made himself chairman of the finance committee, scoured the country for a new president, and brought in a firm of engineers to review the bidding and rectify the construction mistakes. For more than a year he devoted about 80 percent of his time to the renovation of Commonwealth. By the first quarter of 1959, it had begun to operate profitably.

Woods had also stumbled earlier, when First Boston became involved in the so-called Dixon-Yates controversy, but that involved politics at the highest levels and prepared him, somewhat, for the ways of Washington and the presidency of the World Bank. The story dates back to 1933, when the Tennessee Valley Authority (TVA) began in the early days of the New Deal. The major objective was to provide inexpensive hydro-electric power for the people of the Tennessee Valley, particularly the farmers in rural areas who were without electricity. At that time, private utilities were unlikely to provide it.

In 1939, virtually all TVA power was hydroelectric. By 1956, however, 70 percent of TVA power came from coal-burning steam plants.[30] Some new plants had been built and many existing private plants had been bought out. TVA had expanded enormously, but it continued to produce low-cost power successfully on a regional basis. The Atomic Energy Commission installations, built since 1946 at Oak Ridge and Paducah, alone used more power than many states. For a while, it appeared that the TVA might even grow beyond the boundaries of Tennessee, an eventuality that private-power advocates found fearful to contemplate.

TVA and private-power forces locked horns over a proposed TVA expansion at Fulton, Tennessee, some thirty miles above Memphis on the
Mississippi River. In his budget message of January 9, 1953, President
Harry S. Truman had included $30 million to begin work on the Fulton
plant, but President Eisenhower, doing a subsequent budget, cut the plant
out. Eisenhower, who wanted to get the government out of the power
business, favored a partnership between public and private power in the
Tennessee Valley, but he wanted private companies exclusively to manage
expansion outside the region.

Edgar H. Dixon was the president of Middle South Utilities, a holding company with private utility companies located on the western border
of TVA. Eugene A. Yates was chairman of the board of the Southern
Company, a utility holding company with subsidiaries bordering on the
southwestern side of TVA. They supported private power. Gordon Clapp
was the chairman of the TVA. He supported public power, at least within
the Tennessee Valley. At issue was the question not only of who would
supply power to Memphis, but also of who would supply additional power
to the Atomic Energy Commission.

The specific Dixon-Yates proposal was that the Atomic Energy Commission contract for private power to be supplied to the city of Memphis,
in Tennessee, and to the Atomic Energy Commission from West Memphis, in Arkansas, just across the Mississippi River. The Atomic Energy
Commission, with the strong insistence of its Republican chairman, Lewis
Strauss, sought to purchase additional power (at higher prices) from private sources rather than from TVA.

TVA support came from both Republicans and Democrats in the
seven Valley states, with the notable exception of Virginia; from Democrats generally; and from Republicans from the Northwest public-power
states. Opposition to TVA came from Republican private-power advocates
centered in New England and the Midwest together with a few Southern
Democrats. In the 1954 Congressional campaign, Adlai Stevenson and
Harry Truman attacked the Dixon-Yates private-plant proposal. President
Eisenhower's support was not strong.[31] The Democrats took control of
both houses of Congress in 1954 as two crucial Senate seats (from Ken-
tucky and Oregon) shifted into the Democrat column.

Into this potential hornets' nest marched the intrepid George Woods.
He called the director of the Bureau of the Budget, Joseph M. Dodge, several times during the week of May 6, 1953, he later testified, to congratu-
late the director on President Eisenhower's commitment to get the government out of business. "God bless you, Joe. I agree with [Eisenhower's
policy] 100 percent, and . . . I want to help you."[32] Woods thought, "It
would be fine if there were untold millions or billions of dollars of securities

sold on the market at a profit to security dealers,"[33] though he felt he was sufficiently honest not to recommend an unsound proposal just to sell securities.

Dodge expressed a desire to obtain the services of an expert on utility financing who could give him a memorandum on whether TVA's projected power demands and costs were reasonable. "I've got just the man for you," Woods replied.[34] He was referring to Adolphe H. (Dad) Wenzell, a vice-president and director who had been with Harris, Forbes and First Boston since 1922. Woods cleared the project with the top officers of First Boston, and Dodge decided to hire Wenzell as a ten-dollar-a-day consultant. Wenzell continued to receive his regular salary from First Boston.

Wenzell later testified that he did not think TVA should be characterized as "creeping socialism," to use former President Herbert Hoover's phrase. "It was galloping socialism."[35] Dodge, himself a past-president of the American Bankers Association, was a Detroit banker. His deputy, Rowland Hughes, was from New York. They were not unsympathetic to Wenzell's and Woods's points of view. They had to be careful, however. Dodge gave strict orders that no one in the Budget Bureau should talk to anyone about Wenzell's assignment. Wenzell never met with anyone from the TVA. When Wenzell needed material from TVA, Bureau of the Budget staff members went for it without letting it be known for whom they were working.

Wenzell handed in his report on September 15, 1953. He included some policy recommendations as obiter dicta, including the recommendation that the entire TVA power system be sold to a new private corporation. A few days after receiving the report, Dodge personally handed copies to President Eisenhower and former President Hoover. On October 19, 1953, Dodge wrote to Wenzell: "It has been examined by two important individuals [Eisenhower and Hoover] whose reaction to your work equaled my own."[36] Despite the completion of his specific assignment, Wenzell continued to sit in (through April 1954) on meetings at which the specific Dixon-Yates proposal was discussed by the Bureau of the Budget, the Atomic Energy Commission, and the First Boston Corporation.

In February 1954, Wenzell drafted a letter to Edgar Dixon from the First Boston Corporation setting forth his opinion as to the probable rate of interest that would be charged and whether the requisite capital could be raised. In March and again in April, Duncan Linsley of First Boston wrote that he concurred.

After acrimonious debate on the floor of the Senate and within the walls of the TVA boardroom, the Dixon-Yates contract was signed by President Eisenhower on November 11, 1954, without concurrence by the TVA board. The matter seemed to be officially settled until February 18, 1955, when Senator Lister Hill of Alabama rose on the floor of the Senate

to announce that Adolphe Wenzell, an officer of the First Boston Corporation, had been advising the Bureau of the Budget on the same Dixon-
Yates deal for which First Boston was arranging the financing.[37] Joseph
Volpe, Jr., attorney for Tennessee, had been doing some sleuthing. He had
had a woman in his office call a personnel clerk at the Bureau of the Budget to ask about Wenzell's service with that agency. The admonition not
to mention Wenzell had not reached the lower echelons. The cat was out
of the bag.[38]

When newspaper headlines on February 19, 1955, confirmed Wenzell's
participation in these meetings, Arthur Dean, of Sullivan and Cromwell,
representing the First Boston Corporation, expressed astonishment that
Wenzell's name had been omitted from official chronologies of the Bureau
of the Budget and that Senator Hill should have thought there was a secret
about it. Nevertheless, there was an aura of a cover-up. As the Wenzell affair made headlines, the Memphis mayor, Frank Toby, reversed his earlier
position and announced that, with the financial help of Walter von
Tresckow, Memphis would build its own power plant rather than rely on
Dixon-Yates. On July 11, 1955, President Eisenhower ordered the Dixon-
Yates contract canceled. On January 9, 1961, by a six to three majority, the
Supreme Court of the United States held that the Dixon-Yates contract
was unenforceable because of a conflict of interest involving Adolphe
Wenzell. Thus, the $1.87 million of out-of-pocket expenses incurred at the
unfinished West Memphis, Arkansas, plant were uncollectible.

At the trial about Dixon-Yates's right to compensation for termina-
tion costs, George Woods stated, "We were doing everything we could to
encourage the idea that we were good people to do this job." He added,
probably with a grin, "I expect that everybody in the United States with
the sense to run a business corporation should do business with First
Boston."[39] But Woods also testified that, as early as May 1954, First
Boston had decided that it would take no fee for its services in connection
with the Dixon-Yates proposal. First Boston had never before refused a
fee. "I hope it will never happen again," Woods testified before the Senate Judiciary Subcommittee on Anti-Trust and Monopoly in 1955[40]—
hearings at which Senator Joseph O'Mahoney, Democrat of Wyoming,
complimented Woods: "Nobody could testify any more fully and frankly
than you have done."[41] Aaron Wildavsky has summarized the results as
follows:

> An important consideration in favor of termination of Dixon-Yates . . .
> was widespread preference for local construction of a power plant. For
> Dixon it had the advantage of removing fear of the Fulton plant and
> striking a blow at TVA expansion. For the Administration and anti-TVA
> congressmen, municipal construction meant an end to demands on the
> federal budget and an acceptable ideological outcome in the form of

local action. For anti-Dixon-Yates congressmen and TVA, it put an end
to private utility invasion of the Memphis area and the unwise involvement of the AEC. For Von Tresckow this solution represented final victory. Construction by Memphis was by no means an optimum solution
for all; but supporters and opponents of Dixon-Yates agreed on one
thing: they regarded this final outcome as preferable to victory for the
other side.[42]

It appears clear that George Woods and others at First Boston were
unaware that budget directors Joseph Dodge and Rowland Hughes had
sought to conceal Adolphe Wenzell's role as advisor to the Budget Bureau.
It probably did not matter to First Boston that Wenzell had offered gratu-
itous policy advice to the Budget Bureau or the Atomic Energy Commission: they simply wanted to support the president of the United States—
a president with whose views they agreed—in any way they could. They
certainly did not intend nor want to get involved in politics at the highest level and were probably astonished at the outcome of the Dixon-Yates
fiasco.

George Woods, describing on the witness stand how he had gone to
Washington in 1953 to help get the government out of the power business, said, "I came down here as a good Republican." "Off the record," in-
terposed Mr. Dixon's attorney with a grin, "Have you changed?"

"On the record," Woods replied, "I have changed."

Notes

1. Eugene Black, Woods's predecessor as president of the World Bank, also
was a former employee of Harris, Forbes & Co. But Black specialized in the sale
of securities.

2. The following account is condensed from Roderick J. Kirkpatrick, *The First
Boston Log*, unpublished manuscript, 1984. It reads, in part (p. 4): "The investment banking field of that day was largely dominated by the Yankee Bankers—
J. P. Morgan & Co., Lee Higginson & Co., and Kidder Peabody & Co., and to a
lesser degree, the firms of German emigre origin such as Kuhn, Loeb & Co., J. &
W. Seligman & Co., Speyer & Co., and Goldman Sachs & Co. Investment banking efforts at that time were directed primarily to railroad financing, and secon-
darily, to the developing industrial complex."

3. The Chicago branch is still known as Harris Trust Savings Bank. Allen
Forbes served during World War I as chairman of a committee of the Investment
Bankers Association of America to consider ways and means to conserve capital,
and as chairman of a committee of three appointed by the secretary of the treasury
to advise the Federal Reserve Bank of New York on all new capital issues. George
Woods once said that Allen Forbes was "the man who made Harris, Forbes."
Forbes relinquished the presidency in 1921 and died two years later.

4. Dean was to serve as best man at the wedding of George Woods in Long
Beach, California, on April 29, 1935. Ramsey would resign in May to become a

 Thomas Mellon, who moved to western
Pennsylvania from Ulster with *his* father at the age of five. The Thomas entered the
Western University of Pennsylvania, now the University of Pittsburgh, at the age
of twenty-one, and studied law. He became a judge and, in 1870 at the age of fifty-
six, a banker. Thomas's son, Andrew, in 1882, following successful ventures in lum-
ber, became sole proprietor of his father's bank. He was joined five years later by his
brother, Richard B. Mellon, as a partner in T. Mellon and Sons. In 1903, the brothers incorporated their bank with a capital of $2 million. By 1947, capital had grown
to over $167 million, deposits to $1,131 million. The Mellon fortune grew as a kind
of revolving fund for the promotion of enterprises and the employment of workers.
The fund was managed by the Mellons but used by other people in all kinds of enterprises. It was a phenomenal family success story. See Frank R. Denton, *The Mellons of Pittsburgh* (The Newcomer Society of England, American Branch, 1948,
printed for the Newcomer Society by Princeton University Press). Andrew Mellon
served as secretary of the treasury from 1921 to 1932 and as ambassador to Britain
in 1932 and 1933. In 1930, he gave to the people of the United States the National
Gallery of Art in Washington, D.C. In his book, *Taxation: The People's Business*, p.
21, he suggested that high rates of taxation do not necessarily mean larger revenue
to the government. More revenue may be obtained from lower rates—a principle
attributed in recent years to Arthur Laffer among others.

6. The corporate headquarters of First Boston have been located at various
places in New York City: 100 Broadway, 15 Broad Street, 20 Exchange Place, and
the Park Avenue Plaza. Annual meetings of the stockholders were held in Boston
(at 1 Federal Street, 75 Federal Street, and 225 Franklin) until, in 1981, the corporate headquarters were moved to the Park Avenue Plaza in New York. Until
1965, one year after Paul Miller became president, the annual reports were issued
in the name of the president, in Boston.

7. Michael Deutch, who served as a consultant to the War Production
Board, once commented, "If I were an employee of a civil service commission and
someone asked me for a list of twenty or thirty names who had a proven spark of
judgement, a temperament, a judicial handling of statistics, and determination, I
would give the name of George Woods without knowing whether he was a plumb-
ing contractor or the chief executive officer of the First Boston Corporation."—
Robert W. Oliver, "A Conversation with Michael Deutch," *Conversations About
George Woods and the World Bank*, Washington, D.C., July 19, 1986, p. 2.

8. Upon hearing of the elevation of George Woods to executive vice-president, John Macomber sent a telegram from Cuba which read: "Your letter, just received, was all that I needed to break me down. Greatly appreciated I assure you. I
suppose time will clear the lump in my throat. To you George, the new executive
chairman, goes my congratulations and the knowledge that this business is in the
best of hands for the future. [I] hope that you personally will have as much pleasure
and happiness in the years to come as I have had over these many years in my association with you. My blessings to Louie and you in the years to come."—George
Woods's personal papers.

9. Emil Pattberg, who succeeded Coggeshall in May 1962, became chairman
of the board when Woods left. In 1964, Paul Miller, a Woods protégé, became
president.

10. The significance of Woods's abilities in long-run corporate finance was
prominently mentioned in Robert W. Oliver, "A Conversation with Simon

Aldewereld," *Conversations About George Woods and the World Bank*, New York City, November 2, 1985. See Chapter 7. In 1946, George Woods was the senior person in the buying department. Dunc Linsley was second-in-command. Then came Adolph (Dad) Wenzell and Nevil Ford, all members of the board of directors. The entire staff of First Boston was about six hundred.

11. Robert Sheehan, "First Man at First Boston," *Fortune*, June 1959, p. 244.

12. "The Reminiscences of Edward Townsend," *George D. Woods Oral History Project*, Oral History Research Office, Columbia University, 1984, p. 53.

13. Sheehan, p. 244.

14. Townsend, p. 55. When Woods became president of the World Bank, he missed Jim Coggeshall's support and attentive personality. Woods, alone, was less than Woods and Coggeshall, the team. Woods probably depended on Coggeshall more than he realized. He was obliged at the World Bank to do some of the things he did not really want to do.

15. Ibid., p. 54.

16. Ibid., p. 15.

17. Ibid., p. 10.

18. Ibid., p. 23.

19. "The Reminiscences of Martin Rosen," *George D. Woods Oral History Project*, Oral History Research Office, Columbia University, 1985, p. 52. Rosen also recalled a negotiating technique Woods had when he was trying to talk someone into buying bonds. He would offer a proposal, and the other person would object to one thing or another. Woods would say, "You're absolutely right. I agree." In the end, he had been so nice and agreed to everything that it was nearly impossible to say no to the financing. Ibid., p. 14.

20. Sheehan, p. 145.

21. Ibid.

22. Robert Sheehan, "Kaiser Aluminum—Henry J.'s Marvelous Mistake," *Fortune*, July 1956, p. 82. See also Robert Sheehan, "Kaiser-Frazer 'The Roughest Thing We Tackled,'" *Fortune*, July 1951.

23. The decision was to avoid bankruptcy if possible. None of the Kaiser companies—except the family company—would have suffered any direct loss from bankruptcy, but the prestige of the Kaiser name was at stake. It was imperative to pay the company's creditors, and it was certainly desirable to give the public stockholders *something*, at least.

Kaiser-Frazer was the first publicly owned company in the Kaiser empire. Over 60 percent of the stock was held by the public. The balance, 37.7 percent, was owned by the family-held Henry J. Kaiser Co., which in turn controlled the eight Kaiser enterprises—aluminum, steel, cement, etc.

With Eugene Trefethen, Kaiser's executive vice-president, George Woods worked out a plan with the following basic features:

1. The common stock of Kaiser Motors was reclassified (the number of outstanding shares being reduced by three-fourths) and was then exchanged, on a seven-for-one basis, for the common stock of the Henry J. Kaiser Co. (HJK Co.). In this exchange, the former stockholders of the HJK Co. wound up with 94.97 percent of Kaiser Motors common; the balance was held by the public.

2. The exchange of reclassified stock left Kaiser Motors the owner of all the stock of the Henry J. Kaiser Co., which in turn controlled the operating companies. The name of Kaiser Motors was therefore changed to Kaiser Industries Corp., to reflect its new character. But first, with the shares of

Kaiser's operating companies as security, some $90 million was borrowed to pay off Kaiser Motors' debts, including the last penny owed by any Kaiser enterprise to the RFC. The plan also preserved the Willys jeep operation, and provided it with additional working capital.

There were many other benefits from the reorganization. There was, for example, a $76 million tax-loss carryover, which could be applied against the profits of HJK Co., and all the companies in which it owned 80 percent or more of the stock. These included Willys Motors, Kaiser Metal Products, and Kaiser Steel.

24. Edgar Kaiser left the University of California in 1929 at the age of nineteen to help run a natural gas pipeline in Kansas. At twenty-five, he supervised the construction of the Bonneville main spillway dam. During World War II, he managed three shipyards, one of which, Oregon Shipbuilding in Portland, was called the world's finest by Admiral Vickary. Edgar was general manager of Kaiser-Frazer from early 1946. He became president in 1949. A second son, Henry Kaiser, Jr., fell prey to multiple sclerosis. See Sheehan, "Kaiser-Frazer," p. 75.

25. Sheehan, "Kaiser Aluminum," p. 82.

26. Townsend, p. 12.

27. "Private 'World Bank' is Organized," *New York Times*, October 4, 1955, p. 47.

28. Arthur Ochs Sulzberger, interview by John T. Mason, Jr., May 1, 1986, transcript, Oral History Research Office, Columbia University, p. 4.

29. Sheehan, "First Man at First Boston," p. 246.

30. Aaron Wildavsky, *Dixon-Yates: A Study in Power Politics* (New Haven, Conn.: Yale University Press, 1962), p. 10.

31. On October 27, President Eisenhower stated that "The TVA authorities have gone over [the proposed Dixon-Yates contract] and said, after incorporation of certain changes they wanted, that it was perfectly satisfactory."—Wildavsky, *Dixon-Yates*, p. 145. In the meantime, however, Eisenhower had replaced Gordon Clapp with General Herbert Vogel, a professional from the Corps of Engineers, beholden to Eisenhower. Vogel was confirmed by the Senate on August 11, 1954. He could still be outvoted by the three-person board, however. Clapp had predicted that an appointee who shared Eisenhower's power philosophy would "tear the TVA Board apart."—Ibid., p. 143. General Vogel continued to serve on the TVA board until 1962, when he was hired by the World Bank.

32. *New York Times*, July 19, 1955, p. 1.

33. Wildavsky, p. 24.

34. Ibid.

35. *New York Times*, July 9, 1955, p. 1, 7; cited in Wildavsky, p. 25.

36. Wildavsky, p. 27.

37. Ibid., pp. 230–231.

38. See Wildavsky, p. 229. To try to quiet the controversy, George Woods arranged to have Wenzell transferred to the World Bank where he was able to avoid Senator Kefauver's subpoena. Rosen, p. 12, said of Wenzell: "He was a fine person. A man, I think, of high integrity."

39. Wildavsky, p. 188.

40. Ibid., p. 195.

41. Ibid., p. 24 n.

42. Ibid., pp. 316–317.

CHAPTER 2

BLACK'S
BANK

Three presidents: Woods with Eugene Black (left) and John J. McCloy

Eugene Black was the third president of the World Bank. He became the executive director for the United States in March 1947, and president two years later.[1] He was president for over thirteen years, during which time the Bank came to be referred to as Black's Bank.

The World Bank opened its doors for business on June 25, 1946, under the elderly Eugene Meyer, former chairman of the United States Federal Reserve Board and publisher of the *Washington Post*, as president. Meyer made a number of significant staff appointments, including that of Chester McLain as his chief legal counsel, but he arranged no loans. A battle for control of the Bank developed between Meyer and his executive directors, primarily Emilio Collado, director for the United States, and Sir James Grigg, director for the United Kingdom. In December 1946, Meyer suddenly resigned, suggesting that he and his staff lacked the authority to manage the Bank. For over two months, President Truman and the secretary of the treasury, Fred Vinson, looked in vain for a replacement. Finally, a former assistant secretary of war, John J. McCloy, a member of the law firm in New York of which McLain was a partner, was persuaded, in March 1947, to take the job. McCloy won the assurance that he, rather than the executive directors, would manage the Bank. As a guarantee, he was allowed to choose his own candidate as executive director for the United States. He chose Eugene Black. He also brought in, as his top manager and vice-president, Robert Garner. McCloy resigned in April 1949 to become high commissioner to Germany, and Black succeeded him.[2]

Eugene Black was born in Atlanta, Georgia, on May 1, 1898. He graduated summa cum laude at the age of nineteen from the University of Georgia and was employed in the Atlanta office of Harris, Forbes & Co. from 1931 to 1933, becoming assistant vice-president.[3] In 1933, he moved to New York City where he was a financial adviser to the Chase Manhattan Bank and its clients. In 1937, he became a vice-president of the Chase Bank and remained there until McCloy's invitation in 1947 took him to the World Bank. As noted above, he became president two years later.

Black was a Southern gentleman in the best sense of the words. He was genial, gracious, and thoughtful. He could tell marvelous stories. He chatted with whoever was in the elevator as he arrived at work. He

bowled and played golf with his staff. He took members of his staff as well
as executive directors to baseball games. He charmed congressional committees. He was a particular friend of Senator Richard Russell, of Georgia,
and Senator William Fulbright, of Arkansas, but he was not unpopular
with anyone in Congress. A story is told of the finance minister who
emerged from a discussion with Black saying, "Damn it, Black turned
down my request for a loan. It's just awful, but I love him nonetheless.
He's a great fellow."[4] Of course, Black was president during the period
when the dollar was scarce and strong and the United States had a surplus
balance of trade.

     Black led the Bank from success to success. He had the prestige of the
bank named for Salmon P. Chase (Abraham Lincoln's secretary of the
treasury), a Rockefeller bank, behind him. He was the grandson of Henry
Grady, a widely known orator and editor of the *Atlanta Constitution* in the
Reconstruction Era; and the son of the former head of the Federal Reserve
Bank of Atlanta. Black made an enormous hit when he was interviewed
by *Fortune* magazine at a *Fortune* lunch in 1956. He was on the cover of
Time and *Newsweek* magazines in the same week, largely because he was
awarded honorary degrees by Harvard, Yale, and Princeton at the same
time. Black's intended retirement was saluted in a column by James Reston entitled, "Another Georgia Peach Slides for Home," in which Black
was compared to Ty Cobb, the great baseball player—another Georgia
Peach who slid for home more than once.[5]

     Among other things, Black was a superb bond salesman.[6] He knew
the market. He knew how to convince institutional investors to buy
bonds—an essential quality, since an important part of the World Bank's
resources is raised by the sale of its bonds in the open market. All member
countries pledge (that is to say, subscribe) to the Bank in varying
amounts; and this, in turn, determines the number of votes to which each
country is entitled.[7] Very little is actually paid into the Bank directly by
governments. Much the greater portion is raised by selling bonds backed
by the guarantees of the subscriptions that can be called up on demand
but remain unpaid unless called.[8] This was the innovative feature of
World Bank financing that attracted the attention of Lord (John Maynard) Keynes, one of the British experts who worked on the Bretton
Woods agreements: the Bank could be truly international because all
member nations would subscribe, but the great bulk of the loanable funds
would actually be put up by the citizens of the wealthy countries who
bought the bonds.[9]

     For a while, in 1947, McCloy, Garner, and Black lived in a house
owned by Nelson Rockefeller. They spent most of their time working at
the Bank during the day and establishing policies for the Bank at night.[10]
One of the first things they had to decide was how loans to foreign gov-

ernments could be made with safety. In the 1930s, there had been many defaults on foreign loans, and they set about trying to see that the same mistakes were not made again.

They agreed that the Bank should not make loans to governments in default on prewar loans. They did not insist that governments pay in full; only that they would seek a settlement with the bondholders' protective council that the council would accept as representing the capacity to pay. That might mean that there would be a reduction in interest rates or a lengthening of maturities or both.

McCloy, Garner, and Black had to publicize the fact that the dollar bonds the Bank might sell were backed, at the very least, by the unpaid but guaranteed subscription to the Bank of the United States government.[11] Before the Bank could even sell Bank bonds to insurance companies, savings banks, and pension or fiduciary funds in the United States, moreover, specific legislation had to be passed by the state governments to make the bonds legal investments. It was a big selling job.

Speeches were made all over the country. "Information conferences" were convened, in which reporters would visit Washington for a day or two at Bank expense to learn about the Bank. William Bennett, bank editor of the *New York Herald Tribune*, was loaned to the Bank in January 1949 for a year (he stayed for twenty-nine years) in part to arrange the conferences and to acquaint investment bankers with the way the Bank operated. He also wrote an information booklet about the Bank, "which was one of the most frustrating jobs I have ever undertaken."[12] Bennett also set about to convince the rating services (Moody's, Fitch, et al.) that they should give the Bank's bonds as high a rating as possible. Moody's relented, agreeing that the Bank was not an ordinary financial institution. They assigned an A (later a triple A) rating because the United States government, in effect, guaranteed the bonds.

On July 15, 1947, the Bank's first bond issue was sold. Questionnaires had been sent to 2,650 dealers asking if they would care to handle the sale: 1,725 replied favorably. Dealer interest was encouraged by a guaranteed commission of over twice that being paid for the sale of comparable corporate bonds.[13] The issue was heavily oversubscribed. McCloy, Garner, Black, and E. Fleetwood Dunstan, director of marketing, did their job well. As Robert Garner once commented, however, when he, McCloy, and Black moved to Washington, "There wasn't a Wall Street man who would touch the bonds with a ten-foot pole."[14]

Soon after Black became president, Morgan Stanley and the First Boston Corporation were chosen to manage the syndicates of dealers. Morgan Stanley had a high standing in financial circles everywhere, and First Boston had a fine system for retail distribution in the United States, established in large part during the Harris, Forbes days. Black, of course, was well aware of the capabilities of First Boston and of the newly appointed chairman of the board of First Boston, George Woods, who participated with Black by speaking several times at information conferences and was in telephonic communication with Black almost daily.

Black also turned his attention to getting currencies other than dollars released for use by European countries and to selling bonds in Europe. In May 1951, the Bank sold bonds in the United Kingdom and, shortly thereafter, in Switzerland, even though Switzerland was not a member of the Bank. He did this in part because Swiss francs were fully convertible and in part because he wanted to lend Swiss francs to Yugoslavia, knowing it would be easier for the Yugoslavs to repay Swiss francs than dollars regardless of the country actually doing the exporting.[15] He kept emphasizing the importance of making the Bank international rather than merely "a dollar bank," an initiative in which he was ultimately successful.

The Bank provides in its articles of agreement that the servicing of loans must be guaranteed by the relevant national government or central bank or comparable agency of the borrowing country. Each loan can be extended only after a written report by a competent committee that presumes the loan will serve directly or indirectly to raise the real, gross national product of the borrowing country; that is, that the benefit-cost ratio must be significantly greater than one and be granted on repayment terms consistent with the nature of the project. It is difficult to see what more could be specified as general instructions for arranging productive loans.[16]

With prescience, Black warned of the dangers of credits such as Export-Import Bank loans geared to the needs of exporters rather than importers and to the requirements of developed rather than developing countries. Black sensed that there is some theoretically maximum rate at which regions (countries) can usefully absorb capital (borrowed funds). If they exceed this rate, they become less creditworthy. If they have an improper mixture of projects and repayment terms, they also become less creditworthy. Brazil and Turkey, for example, were becoming less creditworthy, though credits from various national suppliers obscured this fact, at least temporarily. Black made the point that a government must be aware of its basic creditworthiness, and it is up to the World Bank to offer advice on that subject.

It is also important, Black said in an interview in 1961, to help a country put together a proper investment program or plan, to establish proper priorities, to ascertain how many projects and what total expenditures can be undertaken at one time, to make proper engineering studies of proposed projects, and to see to it that projects are properly carried out. George Martin, of the Bank's marketing department, had been sent to several countries to instruct people in how to establish bond markets. The Bank had established an Economic Development Institute where senior officials were brought in and given training in principles of economic development. When Black was asked in 1961 if he felt the Bank would be more successful if it were the only lending institution for developing countries, he replied, "Yes. Yes, I think so. The strength of the World Bank is our ability to speak frankly to these countries and to insist upon their carrying out their proper policies. . . .

> We haven't got any political axe to grind [Black continued]. As a matter of fact, the World Bank is the only place that anybody can go to get money where there's no selfish motive involved. If they get money from the U.S. government or from the British government or the German government or whatever it is, political and commercial considerations are very likely to be primary objectives, or certainly an important objective. We haven't got either one of those. We're not making loans in order to line up votes for the West in the United Nations. We're not making loans in order to help the manufacturers of any one country get business. . . .
> That's why I think that if all the emphasis were put on the quality of the money and not the quantity, the quantity would be forthcoming. The best example I can tell you is that, when the World Bank started, we had a capital of ten billion dollars and if anybody'd ever told me a few years ago that we could double that capital, I wouldn't have believed it. But when we went to the United States Congress, it just went right through, no question at all; we just doubled our capital. We never could have done that if we hadn't made effective use of the money we had before. I never dreamed we could double our capital. In my wildest fantasy I never believed that could happen. But there wasn't any trouble about it at all, no objection in the slightest. . . .
> We've never turned down a loan for lack of money. Not only have we not turned them down, we've gone out and tried to find loans, tried to make suggestions to countries as to what they might borrow money for. We've gone out and tried to create projects and make suggestions to people.[17]

As Black and development scholars generally thought about the problem of World Bank financing for the lowest-per-capita-income countries, however, they perceived two dilemmas. First, the domestic savings (and, therefore, the domestic investment) rate was so low (because of widespread poverty and the need for consumption) that the poor nations could not grow at all rapidly. They could not take off into self-sustained economic growth. Second, many productive projects such as education and some forms of infrastructure could increase output only slowly and indirectly, so growth in the capacity to repay ordinary World Bank loans, even at subsidized interest rates, was correspondingly low. It was not enough to say that no sound project would be denied Bank financing when the creditworthiness of the poor countries was predicated on their ability to repay in hard currency.

A U.S. presidential commission headed by Nelson Rockefeller had suggested an approach to the problem in 1951: the establishment of an international development authority to make grants or low-cost loans for the development of poor countries. In a formal speech to the Economic and Social Council of the United Nations, Black, as president of the Bank, gave cautious and qualified approval to the idea. In private, he felt that such an authority would tend to undermine the efforts of the Bank. The availability of cheap or free money would dilute the Bank's influence and might result in the financing of projects or programs that had not been properly appraised for suitability and feasibility. Nevertheless, though the Rockefeller proposal was not adopted, the idea persisted. It was under constant consideration by Richard Demuth in the Bank's development services department. Indeed, in October 1958, the United Nations established the Special United Nations Fund for Economic Development (SUNFED) to finance preinvestment studies of potential development.

For his part, Black maintained a friendly but arms-length relationship with the United Nations because the Bank's way of voting is quite different from voting procedures in either the General Assembly or the Security Council. Black did not want the General Assembly to have the power to finance development. He feared that too much would be sought and would be made available on a giveaway basis. The governments of the Third World, acting on their own, would be less likely, Black thought, to use loans or grants productively. The United Nations and the World Bank were conceived differently, at different times, and for essentially different reasons.

In June 1957, David Gordon, of the Bank's staff,[18] wrote a memorandum arguing that multilateral aid, rather than bilateral (e.g., U.S.) aid, greatly increased and available on softer, more flexible terms, was needed if significant overseas development was to occur.

> The case for a multinational framework to administer development assistance rests essentially on its value in minimizing political and psychological barriers to understanding and collaboration, in deflating the issue of "intervention," and in permitting basic development problems to be considered and worked out between the developing countries and ourselves in reasonably objective fashion. . . . A number of American [staff] members of the World Bank, for instance, have found that . . . international sponsorship permits them to gain positions of trust and influence with the local government that they could never achieve working out of the embassy or the ICA mission.[19]

Gordon's arguments had been heard before, but this time, with Black's cautious encouragement and with Senator Mike Monroney running interference, his argument helped to turn the tide. He circulated his memorandum to various U.S. government agencies (the State Department; the Treasury) and, within the Bank, to key people. The reaction initially was skeptical. The United States government would never agree, it was said, but Eugene Black told Gordon, "Let me keep this on my desk, and I'll see what I can do with it."[20]

In October 1957, the Russians sent up Sputnik. There was a concern in Washington about the kind of political waves that event would create throughout the world. A meeting of NATO was scheduled in Paris, and Black called Gordon to say, "I think I've found a use for your memorandum. I've sent it over to Secretary Anderson of the Treasury and told him to read it on his way to the NATO meeting. That may give him some ideas."

Early in 1958, Black called again to say that he had had a call from Secretary Anderson who had some ideas for the new U.S. aid bill that was going to Congress shortly. Anderson felt that some sort of a dramatic breakthrough was needed to counter the Soviets' success. He had several suggestions that he wanted to try out, but Black told him that all were nonsense; they would not have the proper impact. Anderson asked Black what he would suggest, and Black asked Anderson whether he had read Gordon's memorandum. "No, I haven't got around to it, but I will!" The next day Anderson called and asked if he and Douglas Dillon, the undersecretary of state, could come over to see Black. Black invited them for lunch. They talked for two hours, at the end of which they said that they were prepared to support the thrust of Gordon's argument.

Anderson also asked Black if he would be willing to talk to Senator Mike Monroney. Black said he would; he wouldn't take the initiative, but if Monroney wanted to visit the Bank, "I'd be delighted to see him." The next day, Senator Monroney was at the Bank. He agreed that Gordon's memorandum made sense and asked Black to draw up a brief resume of the kind of scheme that would be required. A small committee from the Bank, including Gordon,[21] worked on the proposal at Black's house one Sunday morning. An initial version of the Monroney resolution passed in February 1958.[22] A revised version passed in midsummer. The general view in Washington was that it did not have much of a chance, but it passed overwhelmingly.[23] As soon as Congress and the administration endorsed it, there was an almost immediate, favorable reaction in Europe, so the scheme was off and running.

At first, Senator Monroney thought it could be made to work by making use of the nonconvertible, local-currency funds that had been paid to the United States government under Public Law 480 in exchange for "surplus" agricultural products. Senator Monroney, from Oklahoma, an agricultural state, was a strong supporter of Public Law 480.[24] In his memorandum,

David Gordon had also recommended using available and future local currencies for repayment. This would have obviated the repayment-by-ex-
porting problem, though it might have raised other problems if the local-
currency revenues generated by a given project were inadequate to cover
real costs.

Eugene Black objected. "That's not a loan. I won't be a party to anything as phony an obligation as that." Black insisted that it be a genuine
obligation in foreign exchange; the "softness" of the obligation had to be
introduced in other ways. They explored all sorts of ways before coming
up with the existing formula: foreign currency lending for fifty years at
zero interest, and with only a three-quarters of one percent service charge.

Much revised, the International Development Association (IDA),
with a charter adopted by the Bank's member governments, came into existence in 1960 as a ward of the Bank, which was to administer its funds.
Still, the Bank viewed the new organization with a somewhat jaundiced
eye. How could the Bank associate with this new, openhanded agency and
yet preserve its own reputation as a prudent and meticulous lender? The
dilemma was well pictured in a European financial journal that showed
the World Bank as a demure young lady strolling with a cigarette-smoking
floozy called IDA. The caption read, "A Sister for the World Bank?"

Of course, this "grant-type lending" can be done only at the instigation of the World Bank, through the International Development Association, with funds appropriated periodically by national legislatures, such
as the Congress of the United States. The total appropriation for the five
years beginning in 1960 was $1 billion, though only about $750 million
was actually made available by the (Part I) industrial or wealthy countries.[25] The funds have to be "rationed," not only because the total of potential IDA lending is limited, but also because each project, except for
education and health projects, must pass the same rate-of-return test as
does World Bank lending. Nevertheless, through the "invention" of IDA
financing, the time when the repayment of interest and principal on
World Bank loans would equal the new loans being made by the World
Bank was postponed from the mid-1960s until the 1980s. Other things
being equal, it could have been postponed even longer if IDA financing
had been greater relative to standard World Bank financing. George
Woods, among others, recognized that creditworthiness and absorptive capacity might be impaired if standard World Bank terms were applied indefinitely.

When Davidson Sommers, general counsel of the World Bank, called
upon George Woods to argue in favor of "soft lending," Woods was initially skeptical. Sommers said to Woods, "George, if you were a banker
who had two branches, one of which was making regular loans on the

basis of creditworthiness and the other of which had grant money which you could make available to borrowers who were in trouble, don't you think that would improve the quality of your regular loans?" "I certainly do," replied Woods, "and I am now an IDA supporter."[26]

George Woods was a major adviser to Eugene Black on the marketing of World Bank bonds. He also assisted the Bank in complex and high-level tasks where his negotiating skill and his knowledge of corporate finance were valuable. As Marie Linahan, secretary successively to McCloy, Black, and Woods, said, "Mr. Woods seemed to be very interested in going on missions abroad, and Mr. Black was very interested in having him go."[27]

The first of these occasions occurred in 1952, when Woods went to India to advise the Bank on assisting the private steel industry there. Woods concurred in the recommendation of a Bank mission, actually headed by Black, to lend $31.5 million to expand private steel capacity, the first World Bank loan made directly to a private manufacturing company. Repayment was guaranteed by the Indian government.[28]

The Indian government was in the early stages of its first five-year plan, with emphasis on heavy industry—rather on the model of the Soviet Union. The United States was anxious to help, partly because India was a democracy and partly because of India's geopolitical position relative to China and the Soviet Union. Woods was interested in seeing the world as well as assisting the World Bank. It was a happy conjunction of interests.

The World Bank loaned the Indian Iron and Steel Co. $31.5 million, and nine U.S. commercial banks loaned an additional $14 million. The bankers' loans were arranged by George Woods, who attended the dedication ceremonies in Jamshedpur. The expansion program was carried out by the Kaiser Engineering division of Henry J. Kaiser Company. It covered design, engineering, construction, and procurement of equipment and machinery. The expanded output of ingot steel equaled the combined production of the Russian-built plant in Bhilai in Central India and the West German plant in Rourkela, India.

In February 1954, Woods, as a consultant, led a World Bank mission to India to explore the possibilities of establishing a privately owned and operated "development bank" to finance the expansion of private industry.[29] A steering committee of prominent Indian businessmen was selected by Woods to draft a charter for the corporation—the Industrial Credit and Investment Corporation of India (ICICI).[30] When the charter was drafted, the World Bank loaned ICICI $10 million; another $10 million was raised from private investors in India (70 percent), England (20 percent), and the United States (10 percent); and $15 million was paid in counterpart funds (the local currency raised from sales of surplus U.S. agricultural products under Public Law 480). The ICICI was the third

development bank promoted by the World Bank. Woods was similarly employed in Pakistan, starting the Pakistan Industrial Credit and Investment
Corporation (PICIC) two years later. As will be related, he repeated the
process in the Philippines in 1961.

In his column, "Close Up," Harold R. Bunce noted that "George
Woods has been to India several times since that first visit in 1952 and
has come to be recognized as an authority on the economics of that country."[31] Ellsworth Bunker, ambassador to India, wrote to Woods in 1959,
"Yours has been a major share in helping to change the psychology of the
American businessman and investor toward India, and for this all of us
who have anything to do with our objectives here are most grateful to
you."[32]

When Edward Townsend of First Boston arrived at his hotel in New
Delhi in 1960, he was greeted at the door by the general manager who
wanted "to show you to your suite." Townsend had not ordered a suite; he
had ordered a room with a bath. The suite was on the ground floor. It had
a garden and a breakfast room. It had an enormous living room and a
twenty-by-twenty bathroom, all in marble. It was the most palatial suite
Townsend had ever seen. Townsend immediately began to worry about
how he was going to pay for it, but he reminded himself that George
Woods told him to stay there. "I've just got to accept whatever they offer."
After a week in the hotel, he asked for his bill, but the desk clerk said,
"Oh no, Mr. Townsend, there'll be no bill." It turned out that the owner
was an admirer of George Woods and of anyone who worked for him.[33]

It is crucial to the success of a private development bank that local
promoters be chosen, and that at least some of them will put up money of
their own. It is also important that they be persona grata to their local
government. Moreover, it is important that private investors make a
profit. To accomplish this, George Woods invented a concept called
"quasi-equity." He proposed that the loans of the local government be
subordinated to equity so that lenders such as the World Bank (i.e., not a
local government lender) could lend more without putting too much con-
tractual debt burden on the private development bank. As Martin Rosen
expressed it, "That's the first time in history, to my knowledge, that there's
ever been a loan junior to equity. . . . It's an idea no one had thought of
before."[34]

At a meeting in Black's office on March 28, 1961, Vice-president
Burke Knapp raised the issue of talks he had had about the possibility of
setting up a private development bank in the Philippines. There was already in existence a government-owned development bank, but Knapp
suggested that there was a need for a private development bank on a national scale. He was concerned, for example, that commercial banks were
getting into long-term lending by means of extending one-year credits

renewable more or less indefinitely. Knapp reported that he had received enthusiastic responses from most people, including President Carlos P. García of the Philippines. García thought the development bank might be established in time for the elections in November. Knapp suggested that George Woods be asked to visit the Philippines to investigate the possibilities for a private industrial development bank to raise money in the general pattern followed by the ICICI in India and PICIC in Pakistan.[35]

George Wishart, who was to become Woods's personal assistant, took the minutes of the meeting. Subsequently, Wishart was introduced to Woods in Washington "so that he could have a look at me and see if I was the kind of a person he wouldn't mind going out to the Philippines with." Wishart, who had previously been in the development services department, liked Woods immediately. "Woods," said Wishart, "was always easy to talk to. He was a good listener, too. Yet he was direct in everything."[36]

Woods agreed to be a consultant to the proposed private development bank of the Philippines, and, in July 1961, Wishart preceded Woods to Manila. At the airport in Manila, Wishart met Woods's plane. When Wishart asked if Woods had had a good flight, Woods replied gruffly, "No." What had happened was that Woods had stopped off in Hawaii and when he got to the second leg of his flight, from Hawaii to Manila, he was informed that his first-class flight was overbooked. He didn't have a seat. He was bumped. They then found him a seat in economy class.

In Manila, Woods announced that he would not fly back on that airline. "Come on, we'll send some telegrams." Woods sent two long telegrams, one to the president of the offending airline explaining how he had been treated and asking if the president of that line would look into it; and one to the president of the airline they had decided they would take. Woods asked the second president to ensure that he was not treated "like a load of hay." Later, he had the offending airline investigated: he was sure there had been bribery on the part of the booking clerks in Hawaii. When he became president of the World Bank, he arranged to change the firm that booked flights for the Bank. His experience had had repercussions.

When Woods began to work on setting up a development bank for the Philippines, he called people he already knew and people to whom he had had introductions. Then he called President García. García invited Woods and Wishart to stay for tea, and they found a number of people there to meet Woods. It turned out that García, who lost the subsequent elections to Diosdado Macapagál in November, had already selected a steering committee for the proposed bank. "I'm sorry," Woods said, "that's not the way I work. I want to choose the steering committee myself." "But, Mr. Woods," the president remonstrated, "I've chosen the best businessmen in the Philippines." "I'm sorry," Woods repeated, "I must choose my own." The president gave way, with the words, "All right, Mr. Woods, you must do it your way."[37]

The man Woods asked to be chairman of the steering committee was Francisco (Paquito) Ortigas, Jr., known in the Philippines for his independence. He was a successful lawyer practicing in Manila. Among other things, he was an original trustee of the Ramon Magsaysay Award Foundation. Four other Filipino businessmen were chosen: Jesus Cabarrus, president of the Mining Association of the Philippines; Manuel J. Marquez, president of the Bankers Association of the Philippines and chief executive officer of the Commercial Bank and Trust Company; Aurelio Montinola, Sr., chairman of the Amon Trading Corporation, the Eternit Roofing Corporation, and the Republic Cement Company; and Washington Sycip, of Sycip, Gorres, Velayo & Co., certified public accountants. Woods had chosen two supporters of President García, two supporters of candidate Macapagál, and one independent.

Sycip's father, making conversation, asked Woods at one point how old he was. "I can tell you exactly," Woods replied, "because today is my birthday. I am 60." When Woods and Wishart returned to their hotel, a huge birthday cake awaited them. Woods looked at Wishart and Wishart looked at Woods. "Could you eat any of that?" Woods asked. "Couldn't touch it," replied Wishart. So, with their compliments, they presented the cake to the women in the booking office and became instant heroes.

Woods visited the Philippines, again accompanied by George Wishart, briefly in July 1961. He made a longer visit with Louise Woods in May 1962. Woods wrote to his new friend, Francisco Ortigas,

> On May 23, Mr. Wishart and I met at some length with Mr. Seymour Janow, Assistant Director of AID, the Agency for International Investment [in Washington] and with quite a large group of his associates in the AID organization. . . .
> The most important—and most difficult—question raised at AID has to do with the availability of as much as Ps 37,500,000 [$10,000,000] for the proposed company. . . . The last Ps 7,500,000 [$2,000,000] seems to present quite a problem. I expressed the opinion that the new company would probably be satisfied with a firm commitment that the money would be loaned within a period of 12 or even 18 months. This is a matter that the AID people will have to work out in their own way and in their own good time.[38]

Eventually, AID agreed to make available to the Private Development Corporation of the Philippines a subordinated loan of $27 million at a concessional interest rate to form part of its initial resources.

In June 1962, Woods submitted his final report to Eugene Black. It read, in part:

The new corporation should be established with a sufficient equity base, and with substantial initial resources, to allow it to play a significant role in the economic development of Philippine privately-owned industry. The institution must also be a Philippine institution, that is, one in which Philippine nationals subscribe to and own a majority of the common stock. It is agreed by all that 60% to 70% of the common stock should be held by Philippine investors.

The balance of the equity stock which is not subscribed by Philippine investors (Ps. 7 million to Ps. 9 million) should be subscribed by non-Philippine investors who are desirous of participating in the development of the Philippine private industrial sector.

The leverage money should be available, either free of interest or at a nominal interest rate only, in order to help gear the earnings of the corporation and provide adequate income from the start of operations. In addition, the leverage money should be made available on such terms and conditions as will include certain quasi-equity features and allow the long-term loan to be treated as equity for the purpose of establishing a borrowing base.

Discussions have taken place with the Government of the United States regarding the possibility of the United States making available the long-term loan required.[39]

In the minutes of the meeting of the steering committee of May 15, 1962, it was indicated that the board of directors of the Private Development Corporation of the Philippines (PDCP) would be selected by the steering committee in ninety days. As to the chairmanship, Woods told Ortigas, "You have to be the first president. Otherwise it will look as if you don't believe in it."[40] But Ortigas could stay only until April 7, 1964. His mother was in bad health, and he had many responsibilities in his family business. He was succeeded briefly by Aurelio Montinola, but he, too, stepped down soon after he was elected by the eleven-man board of directors. Montinola was succeeded in turn by Roberto Villanueva, a younger business associate of Ortigas. Villanueva had been a newspaperman with the Manila Tribune. At the time of his appointment he was the president of the Philippine Chamber of Industry. Woods warned him: "This is a different concept of banking. Forget your concept of commercial banking. That won't work. That's a different field altogether. Your time horizons are much longer. You'll have to look at the gestation periods of projects for longer periods."[41]

Villanueva sent some of his professionals for training to the Economic Development Institute of the World Bank in Washington. The staff of the Private Development Corporation of the Philippines grew to over one hundred, eighty or so of whom were MBAs and financial accountants. The staff focused initially on manufacturing, but turned their attention later to agriculture. They captured 85 percent of the Japanese market for bananas, for example.

Villanueva once commented about George Woods, "Everyone felt he was sincere. Nobody left a meeting feeling that he had been short changed or that George would take advantage of him. On the contrary, he felt that, if there were problems, he could go back to George and George would lend a helping hand. . . .

"George had a way of speaking very softly. . . . He had a very analytical mind, and when you asked him questions, he wouldn't just tell you yes or no! He would tell you, 'these are the options. . . . If you ask my opinion, I would take either this or that, but you make your own decision.' He didn't press you or anything. He was a great educator. He believed in sharing his knowledge with other people. And because of that, he was well liked. People would gravitate toward him."[42]

Woods was not exclusively involved with the PDCP project during this period. In February 1962, the World Bank agreed to a $47 million loan to help to finance the Volta River Authority (VRA) in Ghana. Kaiser interests proposed to construct an aluminum smelter that would be the largest single consumer of the power produced by the VRA. George Woods represented Edgar Kaiser. The same month, Eugene Black asked George Woods and four other prominent investment bankers[43] to meet periodically with Black and the officers of the International Finance Corporation to review IFC investments and investment policy. The five were to serve without compensation and would be available to members of the staff for individual consultation on investment opportunities or problems.

Much the most glittering of George Woods's performances for the World Bank occurred, however, in April 1958, four years prior to the successful negotiations in the Philippines. Woods was asked by Eugene Black to help to settle the claims of the French and British stockholders resulting from the unilateral nationalization by Egypt of the Suez Canal.

The Bank and the governments of Britain and the United States had undertaken studies as early as 1953 to build a high dam near Aswan, shortly after King Farouk had been deposed by military officers led by Colonel Gamal Abdul Nasser. The United States and Britain would have had to make sizable grants, however, in addition to loans from the World Bank; and the United States government would not commit itself to finishing the dam once begun.

On July 26, 1956, Premier Nasser announced that the Egyptian government was seizing the property and operations of the Suez Canal. On October 29, Israeli troops invaded Egypt and, on December 2, French and British troops followed.

Almost two years later, at the instigation of UN Secretary-General Dag Hammarskjold, and after Black had reminded the Egyptian government that the settlement of claims was a requirement for World Bank lending, Black offered to help settle the stockholder claims.[44] George Woods and William Iliff, a Bank vice-president, were dispatched to Rome, and then to Cairo, and then to Rome, and so on. At first the British and the French would not meet with the Egyptians, and the Egyptians would not meet with the British and the French. They could not even get the parties into the same town, let alone at the same table. The French and British negotiators would not get closer to Cairo than Rome, and the Egyptians would not budge from Cairo. Occasionally, Woods and Iliff had to retreat to London and Paris. They carried messages back and forth.

Abdel Galeel El Emary, governor of the Egyptian Central Bank as well as finance minister, was helpful. Gradually, over a three-month period, reason prevailed: the negotiators agreed to meet in Rome and then in Cairo. After much talk, pro and con, a price was agreed to. The Egyptians said that the price was too high, but George Woods started to scratch his back, tilted his head, and said, "This is the greatest steal since the Dutch bought Manhattan Island from the Indians."[45] With that everyone laughed. They calmed down and negotiated a settlement of 28,300,000 Egyptian pounds, the equivalent of more than $81,000,000.

On May 2, 1958, Woods wrote to Eugene Black, "I acknowledge with thanks the certified copy of the Resolution of your Executive Directors [commending Woods] with respect to the Suez matter. It was most thoughtful of you and your directors. For my part, I found the problem most interesting and challenging, and thoroughly enjoyed getting to know Bill Iliff and working with him."

One of the many letters and telegrams of congratulations that Woods received came from Mr. J.R.D. Tata, of Tata Industries in Bombay, India:

> My dear George,
>   You may be interested to know that I have heard from a high official source that the Egyptian Government is frightfully pleased with Gene [Black] and yourself. Dr. El Emary spoke to the person in question with feeling about your fair and sympathetic attitude and helpfulness which have been much appreciated. The Egyptians must have a good case in this instance, and the fact that men of your status and influence and coming from your country are prepared to say so and to show understanding and fairness, however unpopular you are in some quarters, is of enormous value in the context of the present world struggle, and I was very happy to learn about it. It did not surprise me by the way![46]

Acclaim, honors, and commendations were heaped upon Black, Woods, and Iliff by the French and the British. Books were written about the historic settlement. The column "Street News," reported:

In injecting himself into foreign financial affairs, [George] Woods has followed in the footsteps of Eugene R. Black. . . . At the age of 57, George Woods has given about as much talent without thought of compensation as any man in the investment banking business.[47]

Woods was indeed following in the footsteps of Eugene Black—although his willingness to serve was not always appreciated, as was illustrated in the AID controversy. Following his election to the presidency in 1960, John Fitzgerald Kennedy set about to alter the purpose as well as the name of the foreign aid administration. In 1948, it had been the Economic Cooperation Administration; in 1951, the Mutual Security Administration; in 1953, the Foreign Operations Administration; and in 1955, the International Cooperation Administration (ICA). Originally concerned with administering Marshall Plan assistance to European countries in need of rehabilitation, successive administrations had expanded the sphere of intended influence to other friendly nations on the perimeter of the containment of communism but concentrated heavily on military rather than economic assistance. Kennedy decided to create a new name for his aid administration, the Agency for International Development (AID), and to reorient the agency away from military and toward economic assistance.

The fundamental task of our foreign aid program in the 1960s is not negatively to fight communism: its fundamental task is to help make a historical demonstration that in the twentieth century, as in the nineteenth—in the southern half of the globe as in the north—economic growth and political democracy can develop hand in hand.[48]

Henry Labouisse was appointed by Kennedy to head temporarily the ICA, as it was still being called. By September 1961, however, Kennedy turned to George Woods, only to be rebuffed by the liberal Democrats in Congress, including Senator Estes Kefauver, who well remembered the Dixon-Yates affair of the early 1950s and quickly mounted an attack on Woods.[49] Arthur Schlesinger, Jr., characterized Woods as "someone conservative enough to reassure Congress but liberal enough to carry forward the program—a business image, as it was put, without a business mentality."[50] But Woods quickly withdrew his name from consideration when opposition surfaced.[51] Fowler Hamilton, a New York lawyer, became the AID administrator. Within a year, David Bell succeeded Hamilton.

On September 22, 1961, John F. Kennedy wrote to Woods:

I am sorry that I was unable to get in touch with you before you left for Vienna to tell you how greatly I appreciate the effort to which you went to make yourself available for Government service in the foreign aid program.

While I regret the circumstances that led to your decision to with-
draw your name from consideration, I fully understand why you came to
the conclusion which you did. I am very hopeful that you will continue
to give us the benefit of your advice and counsel both as to the program
in general and on specific projects, and I would welcome personally at
any time your views on our progress in this area.

Kennedy appended in longhand: "I am extremely sorry about all the
fuss that was created. I hope it was as annoying to you as it was to me. It
was *most* unfair."[52] Eugene Black was free to nominate George Woods to
become president of the World Bank.

Notes

1. See Robert W. Oliver, *International Economic Cooperation and the World
Bank* (London: Macmillan, 1975), pp. 237–241. Also see this work for a detailed
account of the early history of the World Bank, particularly chapters V–IX. See
also Robert W. Oliver, "Early Plans for a World Bank," *Princeton Studies in International Finance No. 29*, International Finance Section, Department of Economics,
Princeton University, 1971; and Robert W. Oliver, "Bretton Woods: A Retrospective Essay," *Discussion Paper No. 105*, California Seminar on International Security and Foreign Policy, Santa Monica, California, June 1985.
2. Black returned briefly to the Chase Bank after his two-year stint before
McCloy announced his intention to become high commissioner to Germany. Mc-
Cloy said he was not going to leave the World Bank, however, until he was satisfied about his successor. Black was in Europe at the time. When Black returned,
pressure was put on the Chase Bank to release him so he could accept the presidency of the World Bank. "I didn't want it. I wanted to make a career in Chase
Bank. I tried every way in the world not to take it. Then after I got it, I came
down here and became very interested in what I was doing. I found that there was
more inner satisfaction in doing this than there was in making money."—"Transcript of interview with Mr. Eugene R. Black, President, by Prof. Robert Oliver,
Brookings Institution, August 6, 1961," *The World Bank/IFC Archives, Oral History
Program*, Columbia University, p. 50.
3. It may be noted that George Woods, though younger, was Eugene Black's
superior at Harris, Forbes & Co.
4. Robert W. Oliver, "A Conversation with Richard H. Demuth," *Conversations
About George Woods and the World Bank*, Washington, D.C., July 18, 1985, p. 4.
5. *New York Times*, February 18, 1962, p. 8E. Black was included with Dag
Hammarskjold, Jean Monnet, Per Jacobsson, and Sir Oliver Franks as being among
the great international pragmatists in the postwar international community.
6. By contrast, George Woods was skilled in buying securities on behalf of investors, most of whom were interested in the long term.
7. At the conference at Bretton Woods, New Hampshire, in 1944, the formula for ascribing voting power was based, roughly, on a formula which took into
account the size of each nation's gross national product *and* the value of its foreign
trade.
8. Since the articles of agreement for the World Bank specify that the borrowing authority of the Bank is limited to 100 percent of the subscriptions, the

Bank has been obliged to raise the total of its subscription from time to time. Each such increase has required legislative action. The Bank began with total authorized subscriptions of $10 billion. In 1991, agreement was reached to increase, over several years, the total from $90 billion to $174 billion. But no calls have ever been demanded by the World Bank against the unpaid subscriptions of the member countries.

9. See Oliver, *International Economic Cooperation*, pp. 151 and 169.

10. Ibid., p. 241.

11. In theory, the obligations of the Bank are guaranteed by the unpaid but guaranteed subscriptions of all countries, but in the early days of the Bank the dollar guarantee of the United States government was stressed. Each government has a veto power over the right of the Bank to sell bonds denominated in its own particular currency. For a period of several years, only dollar bonds could be sold by the Bank: other governments refused permission for the Bank to sell bonds in their markets, largely because they needed to earn hard currencies (e.g., dollars) with their exports.

12. Robert W. Oliver, "A Conversation with William Bennett," *Conversations About George Woods and the World Bank*, Washington, D.C., January 20, 1988, p. 2.

13. The issue consisted of $100 million of ten-year bonds paying 2 1/4 percent and $150 million of twenty-five-year bonds paying 3 percent.

14. Oliver, *International Economic Cooperation*, p. 249.

15. International competitive bidding is normally required by the Bank, regardless of the currencies loaned.

16. Objections to the McCloy-Black-Garner project approach were voiced by Professor Paul N. Rosenstein-Rodan. Professor Rosenstein-Rodan, after teaching in London in 1942, spent three years with the Royal Institute for International Affairs (Chatham House) studying the problems of "underdeveloped countries," a term that he coined. He moved to the World Bank in 1947 and served six years as assistant director of the research or economics department before going to the Massachusetts Institute of Technology. He objected to the project approach as too simple. A loan that seemed to finance a water irrigation project might actually finance something entirely different if the irrigation project would have been financed anyway. The real issue was whether or not the net investment of the entire country was increased by more than a World Bank loan. Of course, this is very difficult to determine. Professor Rosenstein-Rodan believed that a free market in equilibrium was needed to direct investment properly, for which reason he sought to rely on "shadow" prices and interest rates—prices and interest rates that would prevail in a free market in equilibrium. He wanted to take account of "external" economies and diseconomies—costs that are either lower or higher because of the presence or absence of other firms in the market. Above all, he wanted to promote a Big Push for new investment on the grounds that individual projects, particularly small projects relative to the total investment of a country, would be wasted: they would not generate enough total income to allow the project to operate at anything like full capacity. Over time, these concerns were taken into account insofar as practical, but, by and large, the simple project approach continued to be followed by the Bank, at least until lending to encourage the alteration of investment policy began to dominate Bank thinking.

17. "Transcript of interview with Mr. Eugene Black," pp. 37–39. Italics added.

18. Gordon had extensive overseas experience. Educated at Princeton, he had worked for the United States government in Washington during the war and with the Kuomintang government in China on postwar reconstruction and supply prob-

lems. After a brief stint at the World Bank with Robert Garner, he resigned and took a job with the Marshall Plan. He returned to the Bank in 1953 and was sent to Nicaragua and Guatemala as an economic advisor for a year and a half to each country.

19. David Gordon, "The Case for International Administration of Development Assistance Programs," June 4, 1957 (mimeo), pp. 5–6. There is, of course, a long history behind the grant-type assistance that eventually was codified as the International Development Association (IDA) in 1960 as an arm of the World Bank. See *IDA in Retrospect* (published for the World Bank by Oxford University Press, 1982). See also Edward S. Mason and Robert E. Asher, *The World Bank Since Bretton Woods* (Washington, D.C.: Brookings Institution, 1973), pp. 380–389, and James H. Weaver, *The International Development Association: A New Approach to Foreign Aid* (New York: Praeger, 1965). The United Nations had been supporting multilateral, grant-type lending at least since March 1949. It was primarily the United States that was dragging its feet.

20. David Gordon, interview by Robert Oliver, July 24, 1986, transcript, *The World Bank Archives, Oral History Program*. The quotations on pages 44–46 are from this interview.

21. The others included Burke Knapp, Davidson Sommers, Richard Demuth, and Simon Aldewereld. Gordon, as he was able, and various members of the senior staff of the Bank, Demuth and Sommers in particular, continued to work on these ideas. Demuth drafted the articles of agreement of the International Development Association for presentation to the Bank's governors at the annual meeting in 1959.

22. For the substance of the Monroney proposal, see the *New York Times*, February 23, 1958, p. 1. For a cautious response from Black, see the *New York Times*, February 24, 1958, p. 1.

23. Another view of these events has come from Congressman William Stanton. His account reads, "The Republican Administration of Eisenhower, with strong bipartisan support in the United States Senate, literally forced upon the Bank, as I understood it in those days, the existence of the soft-loan window of the International Development Association. . . . [The Bank] had to be talked into it."—Robert W. Oliver, "A Conversation with Congressman William Stanton," *Conversations About George Woods and the World Bank*, Washington, D.C., July 16, 1985, p. 3.

24. Public Law 480 allowed crops which could not be sold at competitive world-market prices to be "sold" to Third World countries (such as India) for local currencies (such as rupees). For a time, some senators thought that agricultural exports could be further enhanced by the additional contributions of governments other than the United States. Lending from neither the Bank not IDA can be tied to the country making the loan, but the comparative advantage of the United States in agriculture in the 1960s was so great that there was a real possibility that the agricultural exports of the United States might have been greater than the dollar contribution of the United States.

25. Australia, Austria, Belgium, Canada, Denmark, Finland, France, Germany, Italy, Japan, Kuwait, Luxembourg, Netherlands, Norway, Sweden, the United Kingdom, and the United States. Funds were also contributed as replenishments by Argentina, Brazil, Colombia, Greece, Iceland, Ireland, Israel, Korea, Mexico, New Zealand, Portugal, Saudi Arabia, South Africa, Spain, Switzerland, the United Arab Emirates, Venezuela, and Yugoslavia. Generally, to be eligible for an IDA loan or credit, a country's per capita income had to be below $300 in 1968.

26. Robert W. Oliver, "A Conversation with Davidson Sommers," *Conversations About George Woods and the World Bank*, Washington, D.C., July 18, 1985, p. 13.

27. Marie Linahan, interview by Robert Oliver, July 19, 1986, transcript, *World Bank Archives*, Oral History Program.

28. The largest plant was operated by the Tata Iron and Steel Company (75 percent of total production). Tata Iron and Steel and the Steel Company of Bengal operated as separate companies but were managed jointly by one agent, Martin Burn. The merged company was known as the Indian Iron and Steel Company. George Woods took a brief leave of absence from First Boston and was in India during the month of June. Discussions of possible steel expansion through financing by the government of India began as early as 1949.

29. A development bank (or a development finance institution) borrows from the World Bank (or from the International Finance Corporation), from the local government, and, perhaps, from private shareholders. It then lends to smaller, innovative, enterprises. The original model was the Latin American Fomentos. It was suggested for Ethiopia by Orvis Schmidt, director of the Western Hemisphere department. The first development bank (in Ethiopia) was owned by the government and was designed to encourage agriculture. The second (in Turkey) was designed to finance private enterprise. William Diamond worked on both.

William Diamond has long been associated with the creation and supervision of development banks. He has written many articles about development banks, the first among them *Development Banks* (Baltimore, Md.: Johns Hopkins Press, 1957). Diamond has a Ph.D. in history at Johns Hopkins. He worked in Washington and Ankara, Turkey, for the Board of Economic Warfare. He was with UNRRA in London and Paris before, in 1947, coming to the World Bank. In 1962, he became director of development banks for the International Finance Corporation.

30. The steering committee (subsequently the board) consisted of A. D. Shroff, a director of Tata and Sons, Bombay; G. D. Birla, managing director of Birla, Calcutta; Sir Biren Nath Mookerjee, chairman of the Indian Iron and Steel Company, Calcutta; Kasturbhai Lalbhai, chairman of several cotton mill companies, Ahmedahad; and Sir A. Ramaswami Mudaliar, chairman of Indo Commercial Bank, Bangalore. Six others were added to the board of directors. By 1958, such a difference of opinion had developed between A. D. Shroff and G. D. Birla that the board of directors of ICICI had to be reconstituted.

31. *New York World-Telegram and Sun*, March 29, 1957, p. 29.

32. Personal correspondence, Ellsworth Bunker to George Woods, October 19, 1959.

33. "The Reminiscences of Edward Townsend," *George David Woods Oral History Project*, Oral History Research Office, Columbia University, 1984, pp. 29–30.

34. "The Reminiscences of Martin Rosen," *George David Woods Oral History Project*, Oral History Research Office, Columbia University, 1985, p. 4.

William Diamond (see note 29) wrote that if "the true equity . . . [were] one hundred, the subordinated loans from the government would amount to a hundred and fifty. Since that debt could be counted as equity, you had in effect an equity of two hundred and fifty. At a ratio of three to one, you have seven hundred and fifty. In other words, out of a total capitalization of one thousand, true debt would amount to seven hundred and fifty. In relationship to the share capital, debt would be nine hundred, so you'd have a leverage of nine to one on the original equity. Without the quasi-equity, the company would have been able to borrow only three hundred. . . . This idea of quasi-equity, which was introduced [by George Woods] in India, remained a key element in all the World Bank promotions of development banks for the next fifteen years or so."—"The Reminiscences of William Diamond," *George David Woods Oral History Project*, Oral History Research Office, Columbia University, 1984, p. 15.

Gradually, the equity investment of the International Finance Corporation replaced counterpart currencies of the local government in computing quasi-equity. The World Bank specified that the debt of the development company should not at the start be allowed to go beyond three times the amount of its equity, a leverage of only three to one. But with the local government debt subordinated to equity upon dissolution and *counted as quasi-equity*, Woods was able to get a nine-to-one leverage.

35. Present were Black, Garner, Knapp, Rosen, Cargill, Lund (IFC), and Wishart. George Wishart, a Scotsman and a lawyer, had first joined the World Bank in 1947. He served in the secretary's department and then, for three years, in the economics department. After nine years away from the Bank, in London, Wishart returned in 1959 to be involved with development banks. He worked on successful development banks in Iran and Taiwan, and an unsuccessful attempt in Central America, before he was asked to accompany George Woods on his mission to the Philippines.

36. "The Reminiscences of George Wishart," *George David Woods Oral History Project*, Oral History Research Office, Columbia University, 1983, p. 9.

37. Ibid., pp. 11–13.

38. Personal correspondence, Woods to Ortigas, May 31, 1962.

39. Personal correspondence, Woods to Black, June 4, 1962.

40. "The Reminiscences of Robert Villanueva," *George David Woods Oral History Project*, Oral History Research Office, Columbia University, 1984, p. 12.

41. Ibid.

42. Ibid., pp. 30–31. A further evaluation of Woods came many years later from Francisco Ortigas, Jr. He wrote: "Here in the Philippines, Mr. Woods was greatly acknowledged as one of the indelible figures behind the creation and growth of PDCP, a symbol of progress of our national economy. To say that he was a corporate draftsman, productive innovator, *un verdadero caballero*, and a vigorous worker is merely to describe how George Woods had become known to many Filipino businessmen.

"The success of the laudable projects of George Woods are easily attributable to his whole hearted dedication, as well as enthusiasm and devotion of some sacrifice for their eventual realization."—Personal correspondence, November 24, 1989.

Washington Sycip, the independent selected by Woods for membership on the five-man steering committee, gave the following assessment of the PDCP: "The Private Development Corporation of the Philippines has served the country for over 25 years now and has financed about 2,000 projects that have contributed to the economic development of the country. More than this, the company has trained many development oriented managers for the Philippines and for many countries in Asia. In fact, Vicente Jayme, the head of PDCP for many years, was appointed Secretary of Finance by President Corazon Aquino. In 1989, Roberto Villanueva, who served as Chairman of the PDCP almost from the start, was asked by President Aquino to coordinate all foreign assistance programs to the Philippines."—Personal correspondence, November 27, 1989.

43. The other four were Hermann J. Abs, director, Deutsche Bank A. G., Frankfurt; Viscount Harcourt, managing director, Morgan Grenfell & Co., London; Andre Meyer, senior partner, Lazard Freres & Co., New York; and Baron Guy de

Rothschild, a partner in de Rothschild Freres, Paris. When George Woods became president of the World Bank, he appointed Dr. Raffaeli Mattioli, chairman, Banca Commerciale Italiana, Milan, as his successor.

44. See Harold N. Graves, Jr., "The Bank as International Mediator: Three Episodes," in Edward S. Mason and Robert E. Asher, pp. 627–643.

45. Mrs. George David Woods, interview by John T. Mason, Jr. (Interview Number 3), February 17, 1983, transcript, Oral History Research Office, Columbia University, p. 100.

46. Personal correspondence, May 17, 1958.

47. *Financial World*, May 14, 1958, p. 29.

48. John F. Kennedy. Cited in Arthur M. Schlesinger, Jr., *A Thousand Days* (Boston: Houghton Mifflin, Co., 1965), p. 592.

49. See the *New York Times*, September 10, 1961, 1:5; and September 20, 1961, 20:5.

50. Schlesinger, p. 594.

51. Cf. Rosen, p. 13: "Woods and I talked at some length about what this would mean if he were named to the job. It would, of course, have required Senate confirmation. He wanted to go ahead with it anyway. I recollect with considerable clarity the day I met him at National Airport when he was going to the White House to meet Kennedy and some of the staff to talk about the job. We drove together into the White House grounds and talked at some length. I kept suggesting that I didn't think he ought to take it. He, I think, agreed intellectually but was impressed with the challenge and the opportunity. I saw him right after the meeting (I just dropped him off at the White House and came back to my office). He came over afterwards. He still was inclined to take the job, although he said they had talked about the political problems. Eventually he didn't take the job. I think it was because the Kennedy administration came to the conclusion that there would be too much flack arising if he were appointed."

52. Personal correspondence, September 22, 1961.

CHAPTER 3

A New President of the World Bank

Woods with President Kennedy

ohn F. Kennedy, personally, urged Woods to accept the job of heading the World Bank. In August 1962, Eugene Black invited Woods to the White House where Kennedy told Woods, in effect: Everything we in the United States have done since the end of the war, including the Marshall Plan, to try to build a peaceful and stable world is threatened by the growing gap between the poor and the rich countries. If that is not solved, it is going to cause the collapse of our policies, including American foreign policy. We have to do something about this, and I think the World Bank, of the institutions available, is the most promising. This is our chosen instrument, and I want you, George Woods, to be the one to make the Bank a bridge between the poor and the rich countries.[1]

Kennedy came to be identified with the notion that the economic development of less-developed countries within the context of a free, pluralistic society is likely, in the long run, to strengthen ties to the United States, and to its Western allies. As Arthur Schlesinger, Jr., summarized Kennedy's thinking about the Third World:

> The purpose of our aid programs must be to help developing countries move forward as rapidly as possible on the road to genuine national independence.
>
> Our military policies must assist nations to protect the processes of democratic reform and development against disruption and intervention.
>
> Our diplomatic policies must strengthen our relations with the whole world, with our several alliances and within the United Nations.
>
> Above all, "this emerging world is incompatible with the communist world order," for the communists rest everything on the idea of a monolithic world, "where all knowledge has a single pattern, all societies move toward a single model, and all problems and roads have a single solution and a single destination." The monolith [is] doomed by the tides of history. "No one who examines the modern world can doubt that the great currents of history are carrying the world away from the monolithic toward the pluralist idea—away from communist and toward national independence and freedom."[2]

* * * * *

On January 1, 1963, George David Woods became the fourth president of the World Bank. He was Kennedy's choice.[3] He was Eugene Black's choice

63

too. Woods was better qualified to head the World Bank than Black had been at the time of Black's own appointment as the U.S. executive director. Woods had had a longer exposure to the problems of developing nations and a wider exposure to U.S. securities markets. Thanks to the missions with which Black had entrusted him, he also had some knowledge of World Bank operations and personnel. The time, moreover, was ripe for an active president. Following prostate surgery in 1961, Black had been slow to recover his former energy and had seemed content to let the Bank run itself.[4]

By 1963, important changes had taken place in the environment of the Bank's operations. At the beginning of Black's terms, the U.S. dollar had been almost the only useful international currency available to the Bank, which meant that, in its resources and its governance, the Bank had been almost a U.S. Bank. Now the Bank had to begin to heed other voices in the shaping of its policies and operations. Not unnaturally, most of the development needs presented to the Bank in the early days had been those of former colonial territories. In its early development lending, the Bank functioned virtually as a replacement for the London capital market. Now, more sources of aid were becoming available. For the first time, because of the International Development Association (IDA), the Bank Group, as it began to be called, had to solicit finance directly from its member governments. The agencies of the United Nations family, which previously had been largely limited to research and the dissemination of information, were becoming more operational, supplying both finance and technical assistance for development projects. Newly independent countries, especially in Africa, were joining the Bank in record numbers, and the developing countries generally were pressing new varieties of needs on the Bank. The Bank was faced with a pluralistic, more competitive, and more demanding world.

Against this background, Woods aspired to make the Bank more useful to more countries, and, with different kinds of lending and more technical assistance, to take into account a wider range of needs. Woods also aspired to maintain the Bank's position of leadership on the world development scene. He not only wanted to maintain the Bank's preeminence in the financial sphere, he wanted to establish the Bank as the intellectual leader of the UN development effort.

Woods was not as outgoing as Black. Woods was brilliant in small groups and delivered formal addresses with more grace than Black, but he lacked Black's ability to put a group at ease. He lacked the ability to be pleasant to people whom he disliked and disagreed with. Once a person had lost Woods's respect, for whatever reason, he could seldom redeem himself. Woods could be blunt, if not rude; direct, if not hostile. On the other hand, Woods was more egalitarian than Black. Woods prided himself in staying at "ordinary" hotels rather than in U.S. embassies or presidential mansions. Perhaps the most significant contrast between Woods and Black, however, was that Black had served with his staff for over thirteen years. Whatever his talents and his experience, Woods was a new president—in the same mold as Black, to be sure, but inevitably different from Black. He was the new man on the team.

Woods favored multinational rather than national economic assistance, and he supported grant-type aid for the lowest per capita income nations. Black had built the reputation of his Bank primarily on loans to finance infrastructure at, or near, commercial interest rates, given the guarantee of the governments of the world.[5] IDA was a horse of a different color. As the *Wall Street Journal* noted editorially on October 23, 1962:

> An offshoot of the World Bank, the separately financed International Development Association began functioning a couple of years ago in a quite different fashion. Unlike the Bank, it makes loans at no interest for as long as 50 years in the underdeveloped areas. Moreover, this easy-loan institution threatens to grow larger than its stricter parent, for that seems to be the way both Mr. Black and Mr. Woods want it.[6]

An article in *Business Week* of October 20, 1962, warned that "Woods' biggest problem is how to increase IDA's capital." The Bank's executive directors, the article continued, "are now studying how to boost IDA's capital up to as much as $3 billion for five years in contrast to $1 billion, $750 million in hard currency."[7]

Eugene Black warned in his farewell speech to the annual meeting in Washington in 1962 that the usable capital of IDA would be exhausted by mid-1963, two years prior to the first scheduled replenishment.[8] He also warned that a group of countries accounting for the greater part of the Third World had more than doubled their external debt over the past five years, while their export earnings had increased by only 15 percent. This trend, if continued, could only result in ever larger loans to developing countries, in interest payments so large that exports would inevitably have to exceed imports,[9] or in outright default. Black and Woods were aware that this was a problem for the future. In the 1980s, it became a reality for many developing nations.

Some of George Woods's tasks were clearly laid out for him: to increase funds for IDA, to identify productive projects in addition to infrastructure, and to maintain a reasonable balance between real increases in gross national products and exports. He had to accomplish this, moreover, while the international financial system was being altered.

The world's dollar shortage was over by 1959. The gold and foreign exchange reserves of Western Europe and Japan nearly doubled between

1952 and 1959, when they reached more than $22 billion of a world total of $57 billion.[10] It would be another two years before the Western Europeans felt secure enough to relax their authorized discrimination against U.S. exports,[11] but the basic balance-of-payments deficit of the United States relative to Western Europe and Japan was already clear enough. "What had changed was that the European countries no longer had an excess—and repressed—demand for U.S. goods. . . . The dollar shortage had been a reserve shortage and had reflected a lack of competitiveness of European products with those produced in America" at existing prices, exchange rates, and levels of aggregate supply and demand.[12] It also reflected the fact that the dollar had replaced the pound as the principal reserve currency, in part because gold and dollars were still interchangeable by foreign central banks at a fixed ratio, because the volume of U.S. output was so great, and because the dollar had been scarce for so long. It was a harbinger of things to come, however, when, in October 1960, the selling price of gold temporarily reached the $38–$40 range in the London market before falling back after John F. Kennedy's brave statement on October 31: "If elected President, I shall not devalue the dollar from the present [gold] rate. Rather, I shall defend its present value and its soundness."[13]

In November 1960, the United States and seven other countries started to sell gold in London to help stabilize the price. (The stock of U.S. gold had declined by $5.1 billion, more than 10 percent, during the three prior years.) The dollar was overvalued relative to gold or, to put the matter another way, the dollar liabilities of the United States had ceased to be "as good as gold." The United States still maintained a small surplus on current transactions, but this was more than offset by net capital outflows, particularly short-term outflows, due, in part, to lower U.S. short-term interest rates. Beginning in 1959 and continuing through the presidential election of 1960 (indeed, through the first Nixon presidency of 1969 to 1973), the dollar tended to be weak relative to gold, the deutschemark, and the guilder. In the United States, people worried about the gold value of their currency and sought to reduce the outflow of capital through such measures as the interest equalization tax on the sales of foreign bonds in the United States. This was a vastly different world from the world in which the United States could export as much merchandise as they chose (subject only to currency restrictions abroad) and export as much capital without concern for balance-of-payments problems.[14] These changed conditions greatly affected the World Bank in general and the George Woods presidency in particular.

At the same time that notions about the balance of payments and the dollar shortage were changing, so also were notions about economic development. In earlier years, under the influence of the Harrod-Domar equation,[15] economists sought to reduce growth theory to a formula: the

real rate of growth of an economy depends upon the rate of real investment divided by the ratio between capital and output. If, that is to say,
new investment rates were 30 percent of real output and the ratio between capital and output were 3 to 1, an economy in equilibrium would
grow by 10 percent after inflation. But, while this may be useful as a defi-
nition, it is not useful for actually explaining growth. A story is told of an
economist who went as an advisor to a small, poor, underdeveloped country. "Tell me, what is your investment rate?" No one knew. "Tell me about
your capital-output ratio." Their eyeballs glazed over. "Well," said the
economist, "let's suppose your investment rate in equilibrium is 10 percent
and your capital-output ratio is $3\frac{1}{3}$, your growth rate will be 3 percent,"
and he handed his astonished audience a bill for $1,000!

At least by the late 1950s, attitudes toward growth and development
had become less mechanistic. The emphasis in the Harrod-Domar equation was on quantitative increases in capital. Edward Denison, who devoted much of his life to studying the sources of growth in the United
States, concluded that education and other advances in knowledge
(human capital) are more important than simple quantitative increases in
already known technology.[16] From there it was not a great leap to the conclusion, particularly in the case of underdeveloped or traditional societies,
that all kinds of things help to explain growth. The absence of war, pluralistic political systems, human rights, a system of welfare, relationships
within the family, schools, the development of agriculture, the market
mechanism, the legal system—all the mores and traditions of the people
help to explain growth, or the lack of it; and these, in turn, are related to,
for example, the climate and the condition of the soil. George Woods and
his advisors were being told by social scientists that development depends
to some extent on almost everything.[17] But institutions cannot be successfully implanted from outside if there is no positive response from inside. Imported machinery may rust in the fields. Turnkey plants may lack
skilled technicians. Irrigation projects may fail because market forces are
misunderstood.

Woods had joined a group that began with Robert Garner, Davidson
Sommers, and William Iliff, and included as senior officers at the beginning of Woods's term Martin Rosen, Burke Knapp, Geoffrey Wilson, Aron
Broches, Simon Aldewereld, and Richard Demuth. It will be useful to
look in more detail at the Bank's senior staff.

Robert Garner, who had gone to Washington with McCloy and
Black, was more responsible than any other individual for establishing in-
ternal Bank policy. He was known affectionately as "Mr. Inside"; Black
was "Mr. Outside"—references to the famous football players at the U.S.
Military Academy during World War II: Doc Blanchard and Glenn
Davis.[18] (Because of the color of his hair, Garner was also known as the

Silver Fox.) As vice-president, Garner pushed for a sister organization
that could participate in loan and equity financing without government
guarantees. In 1956, his dream was fulfilled with the birth of the International Finance Corporation, an affiliate of the World Bank Group, of
which he became president.

Garner retired in October 1961, and Black (and Woods after Black)
assumed the presidency of IFC; but he appointed Martin Rosen as executive vice-president. Rosen was in charge for all practical purposes. He
sought the title of president, but, though he remained at the top of the
echelon, his request was granted neither by Black nor Woods.

When Garner became president of the IFC, Burke Knapp, Davidson
Sommers, and William Iliff[19] became vice-presidents of the Bank. Knapp,
an American from Stanford University, had been recruited by Garner as
a practical economist who understood cost-benefit ratios, absorptive capacity, and creditworthiness. Knapp had been a Rhodes scholar, had
worked in a British investment bank, had been a senior economist on the
staff of the Federal Reserve Bank's board of governors, and, at the time of
his appointment, was director of the office of financial and development
policy for the U.S. Department of State.

Knapp had been third-in-command in the research or economics
department under Leonard Rist, the son of Charles Rist the French economist, and Paul Rosenstein-Rodan, the Austrian economist from the London School of Economics, who left the Bank for MIT after the reorganization of 1952. Once Knapp was on board, however, he ran the show with
the rather poorly disguised pretense that Rist was making the decisions.
Among other things, Knapp hired Andrew Kamarck, John de Wilde, and
John Adler, all experienced international economists. During the reorganization of 1952, Knapp became the first director of the Bank's work in
Latin America and the Caribbean. In 1956, he became a vice-president
and chairman of the staff loan committee, a position he occupied until he
retired in 1978. Under Woods, Knapp was designated senior vice-president with the instruction that he act for the president when Woods was
away. At one point in April 1965, Woods compared himself to a four-
star general, Knapp was assigned three stars, the other members of the
president's council, two stars, and department heads outside of that group,
one star.

Davidson Sommers, another American, succeeded Chester McLain as
general counsel when McCloy and McLain left in 1949. He resigned in
1959 to become senior vice-president and general counsel for the Equitable Life Insurance Company of New York. He was succeeded by Aron
Broches, a Dutch lawyer who had been at Bretton Woods and was serving
as assistant general counsel.[20] William Iliff, from Northern Ireland, had
been one of the principal architects of the Bank's lending policies. He had

played a leading role in a number of international negotiations, including the Suez crisis, but he retired in October 1962 and was succeeded as vice-president by Geoffrey M. Wilson, who had served as alternate executive director for the United Kingdom and then as director of operations for South Asia and the Middle East.

In 1952, Simon Aldewereld, from the Netherlands, became the director of technical operations (project engineering studies). Aldewereld, who joined the Bank shortly before Eugene Meyer resigned in December 1946, became assistant to the treasurer, Crena de Iongh, one of the Dutch representatives at the Bretton Woods Conference. It was Aldewereld's job initially to set up a disbursement system for loans not yet made,[21] but he became Mister Projects and, when George Woods asked him to undertake additional supervision of some aspects of finance, a vice-president.

Richard Demuth, a U.S. lawyer with degrees from Princeton and Harvard, preceded Aldewereld in service to the Bank by a few weeks. Demuth was asked by Meyer, McCloy, Black, and Woods to investigate new ideas such as the general survey missions, the Economic Development Institute, the International Development Association, and the young professionals' program. He was McCloy's assistant, in charge of planning. He represented the Bank at important conferences of other international organizations, including the International Monetary Fund, the United Nations, and the various UN-sponsored organizations. He was in charge of information and external relations and was called the director of development services, an apt title, for he undertook tasks that were unusual.[22]

Under Black, the senior officers were a collegial group: they knew each other's strengths and weaknesses. But they tended somewhat to break apart under Woods.[23] Woods, following Garner, fostered the notion of "creative tension," particularly between the projects department and the area departments; and he added the economics department as the third apex of the creative tension triangle.

Relations were difficult between Woods and Vice-president Geoffrey Wilson, in part because Wilson occasionally sought to correct Woods's manner of speaking. Their attitudes toward work were also different: Woods, personally, took endless pains, while Wilson believed in delegating. At one point, when Bernard Bell and Geoffrey Wilson were briefing Woods about India, Woods seemed strangely uninterested. After about five minutes, he dismissed the pair but called back over his shoulder to Bell, "Bernie, come back later and tell me what really happened." Wilson left the Bank in 1965.

Relations were also tense for a year or two between Woods and Burke Knapp, the senior vice-president and linchpin of the staff. Perhaps Woods was trying to teach Knapp who was in command. Knapp, however, later shrugged off suggestions that he had had a rough time working with

Woods. "Our relationships were never as easy as they had been with Gene Black, but I always remained very happy in my work, feeling that I had a boss who understood what we were trying to do together."[24]

Woods seemed indifferent toward Johnny Miller, head of the Bank's Paris office. Woods went to Paris frequently, but he avoided the Paris office. Once he was with a friend who stopped outside the Paris office and said, "Come on in and look at it." "No, I won't go in," replied Woods.[25] But it was the building, not Miller, of which Woods disapproved. It was very expensive, in a posh neighborhood, furnished with antique furniture. It reeked of money, spent in exquisite taste and luxurious in European, old-money style. Woods considered it a scandal, maybe right for bankers like the Morgans or the Rothschilds but not for an organization that embodied IDA. Woods eventually authorized the construction of new Bank offices at 66 Avenue d'Iena, a few blocks away, which, as an investment, has rewarded the Bank many times over.

Happily, Woods got along well with George Wishart, who had accompanied Woods in the Philippines. At the Bank's Christmas party in 1962, the Blacks and the Woodses were in the receiving line when the Wisharts came through. Woods said to Wishart, "We'll see a lot of each other in the future," and Black said to Wishart, "You know, you can do many things to help Mr. Woods."[26] On the first business day after January 1, Wishart received a telephone call asking him to visit the president's office. When he arrived, Woods asked, "Shall we work together?" Wishart replied, "I'd be pleased to. I enjoyed our times together in the Philippines."

Wishart became personal assistant to the president and had an office with glass doors "so as to let the light into the outer office." People in the Bank said to Wishart, "You don't want that, you'll sit there like a fish in a goldfish bowl," to which Wishart replied, "That doesn't worry me in the slightest. There is a corner with a good armchair which I can move into if I really don't want to be observed all the time."

As his first assignment, Woods gave Wishart the several hundred letters of congratulations Woods had received. Woods said, "I can't reply to all these at the moment; I haven't time." So Wishart, who had a good secretary, dictated brief replies to every letter and sent them in to Woods as drafts. Woods modified them a bit to put a personal touch on them and sent them off.

Meanwhile, Woods announced as a new policy that every letter addressed to him personally, or to the president of the Bank, was to come to him. Under Black, a letter from, say, Thailand would have been sent to the department for Thailand. Wishart would open all the mail addressed to the president and decide to whom it should be directed, including to Woods himself. If it was sent on to a department, Woods insisted that he receive a copy of the reply. This was one way Woods could be kept abreast of what was happening in the Bank. Wishart also went through all the papers that circulated to or from the executive directors. Woods went through all of them himself, but Wishart marked the sentences he thought Woods would particularly want to look at. Woods would go home at night with his briefcase bulging.

The president's suite on the top floor of the building at 1818 H Street had not changed much from Eugene Black's day, though Woods insisted on using the desk that Harry Addinsell had had at First Boston.[27] Wishart and Woods kept three secretaries busy. Wishart brought in Muriel Lee, with whom he had worked before in the Bank; Woods kept Marie Linahan, who had been with McCloy and Black, as his receptionist; and he brought in Bernadette Schmitt, who had been Woods's secretary since his days in the army, to take care of his office and personal papers.

During the fiscal year that started with Black and ended with Woods, a new junior professional recruitment and training program was begun. Prior to that, as staff vacancies occurred or new positions were created, the personnel department sought to find qualified individuals, but much of the training and experience, it was found, could be provided only by the Bank itself. Richard Van Wagenen, dean of the School of International Relations at the American University, had been conducting seminars in international administration. One day in 1961, Van Wagenen invited Don Fowler, director of personnel, and Bill Howell, director of administration, to speak at his seminar. In turn, Van Wagenen sent a particularly good student, Steven Gregory, to Howell with the suggestion that Howell might be interested in hiring Gregory. Howell reacted that this was exactly the kind of person the Bank needed in the younger age-group, and it was a shame that there was no system for hiring a person who lacked only experience.

A year or so later, Howell asked Van Wagenen to have lunch at the Bank with Ray Goodman, his deputy, and himself. They said that a plan had been proposed for bringing young people into the Bank and asked Van Wagenen to come to the Bank and start the program. Van Wagenen took a leave of absence from the university, started the program in November 1962, returned to the university in 1964, was asked to return to the Bank in 1965, and remained with the Bank until he retired in 1977. Together with others interested in the program, Van Wagenen decided to accept a small group of promising young people twice a year who would serve an apprenticeship of two years, receiving a combination of formal instruction and practical experience in projects, country loan and IFC operations, and economics—indeed the entire gamut of work throughout the Bank and IFC. Intellectual capacity and other personal qualities were the prerequisites rather than any particular educational background.[28]

Originally called *junior* professionals, they were renamed *young* professionals at the suggestion of Harold Graves. Geoffrey Wilson originally took them under his wing and gurus such as Robert Sadove, Ken Bohr, and Roger Chaufournier paid particular attention to them. They thrived. Richard Demuth sometimes interviewed them and later claimed he was prouder of the young professionals program than of anything else he had been associated with in the Bank.[29] Some of those hired during the Woods years were Wilfred Thalwitz, Christopher Willoughby, Leif Christoffersen, Kim Jaycox, Joseph Wood, Heinz Vergin, and Rainer Steckhen, who, in 1967, succeeded George Wishart as personal assistant to George Woods.

Early in January 1963, Woods announced that Davidson Sommers had been retained as a part-time consultant to study the Bank's utilization of staff and working procedures. The dichotomy between the various area departments and the project department went back to the reorganization of 1952, when the economists were downgraded, the engineers (and some economists) were separated into a formal engineering or technical operations (projects) department, and area departments were identified by geography. By and large, the area department officers represented the Bank in the field and identified possible projects for which the Bank might make loans. They included loan officers and some economists. In some instances, they lived abroad in the country to which they were attached, for they had to know a great deal about the country—its statistics and the way the economy worked—before they could make sensible suggestions, or evaluate the proposals of the government for projects. Once a possible project had been identified, the engineers and economists could engage in the necessary studies to identify probable benefits and costs.

The difficulty that led to the Sommers study was that the area and project department people did not always agree on when a project was ready for implementation. Sometimes the engineers were too slow or the operations officers too impatient. Sommers suggested guidelines for the projects and area staffs that Woods could implement, though Woods, like Black, would not approve a project unless he supposed that it would be all right from all points of view. As Wishart said, "It wasn't a question of pushing up the amount of lending the Bank was doing."[30]

There was considerable discussion in the weekly senior staff meetings during Woods's first year in office about increasing the funds available to IDA. A meeting in Paris in February had resulted in an absolute impasse, as Burke Knapp reported. The United States had announced its intention to reduce its contribution to IDA to 35 percent and had asked other major powers to increase their contributions correspondingly. The Germans were willing if the French would follow, and the British were willing if the French and Germans would; but the French were unwilling. France,

Germany, and the UK would each have had to increase its contributions to 11 percent unless the United States was willing to contribute 40 percent rather than 35 percent. Woods announced general agreement on $250 million per year as a goal for the first IDA replenishment. He added, however, that he felt the United States was wrong in seeking to reduce its proportional contribution, since a large portion of IDA funds went to India and Pakistan in which the United States had a heavy stake. Woods said that the Bank would remain outside of the discussions regarding IDA replenishments. "It's our responsibility [only] to administer IDA efficiently." He added that in three years the reserves of the Bank would be over $1 billion and consequently the use of the Bank's earnings was an important problem.

John de Wilde told the senior staff about a disagreement in the Development Assistance Committee (DAC) of the Organization for Economic Cooperation and Development (OECD) in Paris: the U.S. team wanted to liberalize the terms of aid while the French and Germans favored a continuation of relatively hard terms. Willard Thorp, a U.S. economist, had agreed to accept the chairmanship of the DAC. Meanwhile, Raul Prebisch, of Argentina, had been named secretary-general of the United Nations Conference on Trade and Development that was scheduled to be held early in 1964. The UN General Assembly, each of whose member governments had one vote, continued to press for infant-industry protection of its developing countries while seeking more concessionary assistance from higher-income countries.

In January 1963, the executive directors of the Bank announced an impasse on the declaration of a dividend out of the earnings of the Bank, but, by March, Woods could tell the senior staff that 90 percent of the executive directors were opposed to distributing a dividend to member nations. The less-developed nations were opposed because the dividend would go primarily to the wealthier countries, and they felt that that was contrary to the purposes of the Bank. The wealthier countries were opposed because they doubted that a dividend would result in increased contributions to IDA and might only increase the pressure for lower interest rates and commissions on Bank loans.

Woods commented that he strongly believed the Bank was, and should continue to be, identified with a capitalist, free-enterprise system. The Bank, he said, should use its resources, in part, to help the development of private enterprises in underdeveloped countries. For example, Woods favored lending to development banks. These banks, which he had helped to invent, were intermediaries, borrowing money from the World Bank and using Bank and locally raised funds to help private enterprises get established.[31]

Dr. Harvey Branscomb, a consultant from the University of Virginia, filed a report on a possible Bank program of loans for education, but Knapp said that education loans would better be described as loans for school construction. Woods had been on some university boards and was afraid that loans for faculty appointments, for example, might, in effect, be shifted to a different purpose. He also felt that loans should be con-fined to the financing of secondary education. At the same time, as noted in the eighteenth annual report:

> The Bank is convinced that the economic progress of the less developed countries will depend largely upon their success in enlarging the skills and widening the outlook of their peoples, which in turn will depend upon providing effective and adequate systems of education.[32]

Agricultural planning was also added to Woods's agenda. The Bank had always been willing to make loans for roads, which served the farmers, and for large irrigation projects. Woods was initially opposed to financing agricultural services such as extension programs to instruct farmers in bet-ter seeds and better crops and better ways to cultivate. He preferred roads to research because they were tangible projects. But one day Woods re-ceived as a visitor Lord Howick (Sir Evelyn Baring). Lord Howick repre-sented one of the two largest financial houses in the United Kingdom, (the other being the Rothschilds). Lord Howick had been governor of Kenya and high commissioner in various African countries. He was him-self an extraordinarily charming person, and he influenced Woods's think-ing about agricultural lending. As George Wishart put it, "In most African countries, agriculture was a sine qua non. If they didn't get agriculture right, they'd never get anything right."[33] So Woods brought agriculture into his plan for more expanded Bank lending.

When Woods decided to make loans for agricultural production, he asked Richard Demuth to head a committee to develop appropriate guide-lines for such loans. Demuth, in turn, asked the head of the agricultural projects department to come up for a discussion, during which the agri-cultural department head burst into a smile a mile wide. He said that that was what he had been wanting to do for ten years. "This will make all the difference in what the Bank can do in agriculture," he said.

Early in 1963, it was announced to the senior staff that five of the newly independent French-speaking African countries would become members of the Bank on July 10: Cameroon, Central African Republic, Chad, Congo Brazzaville, and Dahomey (now Benin). In the Development Advisory Committee of the OECD, the United States had urged that the technical assistance, though not the financing, activities of the United Na-tions be strengthened; the Special United Nations Fund for Economic De-velopment (SUNFED) and the United Nations Development Program

(UNDP) might be merged, a suggestion that was vigorously opposed by India, which wanted more financial backing from the UN. Raul Prebisch would include development as well as trade in the United Nations Conference on Trade and Development (UNCTAD) that he would chair in early 1964. A recent International Monetary Fund mission to Brazil had returned discouraged and disillusioned: Brazil was lagging in implementing its promises with respect to its budget, credit, wage ceilings, and foreign-exchange profits from coffee. George Woods and Pierre Paul Schweitzer, the new managing director of the IMF, had agreed on greater collaboration between their institutions, including the joint use of the dining facilities.

Perhaps the most important change was the addition to the membership of the Bank of the newly independent African states. The Bank increased its total membership by over 50 percent in two years. During Black's presidency, most of the African countries south of the Sahara were dependencies of various European nations and were eligible to borrow from the Bank only with the guarantee of the European powers. Loans were made to the Belgian Congo and to the (British) colonial dependencies of Southern Rhodesia and the Federation of Rhodesia and Nyasaland.[34] Loans were made to independent Ethiopia and Morocco and newly independent Ghana for the Volta River Project.[35] Still, there had been relatively little Bank lending (other than to South Africa) south of the Sahara. Now, as African countries suddenly became independent, a whole new ball game began for the president of the World Bank and his staff. Now, creditworthiness had to be assessed anew, productive projects had to be found, countries had to be visited. The tasks of the staff increased commensurately. In all of this, George Woods, Leonard Rist, now special representative for Africa, and Pierre Moussa, a Frenchman and director of operations for Africa, would play leading roles.

The meetings of the senior staff continued through Woods's presidency, but Woods turned his attention more and more to a president's council. As the number of department heads increased and made the weekly senior staff meetings unwieldy, Woods convened shorter daily meetings of a smaller group that included Burke Knapp, Geoffrey Wilson, Simon Aldewereld, Aron Broches, and Richard Demuth. After he hired Irving Friedman as his chief economist, Woods brought him in, too. He also asked George Wishart to sit in on the council meetings. Wishart asked Woods, "Do you want me to take any record of what they're saying?" "No, it's much better not to have a record. Just sit in and remind me of things if I forget something," replied Woods. "We can't have it too formal or nobody will discuss anything."[36]

In early April 1963, Woods made his first overseas trip as president of the Bank, specifically to meet the governors of the Bank for Britain,

France, Germany, and Italy—his major shareholders, so to speak. He could meet them a great deal more casually when they were not attending annual meetings. In any event, Woods wanted to talk about IDA. According to George Wishart, Woods usually spent an average of three months a year traveling, not only to meet chancellors and bankers but also to see projects and people.

Mr. and Mrs. Woods and Wishart flew first to Rome, where Woods already had many good friends. Wishart asked which hotel Woods desired: "Should we go to the Hassler?" probably the best hotel in Rome. "No," said Woods, "I prefer the Excelsior where I can sit and watch the world go by on the Via Veneto. It's better than a vaudeville show."[37] Woods called upon Guido Carli, the governor of the Italian Central Bank.

They flew next to England, where Woods had lunch with the chancellor of the exchequer. He also called upon the governor of the Bank of England. Unhappily, the Woods party was given an ordinary rental car driven by a chauffeur who thought they were tourists. Turning in his seat, the chauffeur said, "I know you folks want to shop for cashmere sweaters. I know just the place to take you." When they all got to Claridges, Woods said, "Get rid of that car. I never want to see it again." Fortunately, Wishart knew a rental agency close by that supplied high-class cars. He ordered a car that the Woodses used for all their subsequent visits to London.

In Paris, Woods met the governor of the central bank, but he was again troubled by automobiles. The Paris office of the Bank had arranged for a Cadillac, but Woods said, "I'm not going to go around Paris in a Cadillac. I would look as if I'm just another American businessman. I want a Citroen, one of those black Citroens that all the government officials run around in." He got a black Citroen, and later told the Paris office to buy one to replace the old London taxi they had been using.

When Woods went to Germany to see Karl Blessing, the governor of the Bundesbank, Louise stayed behind in Paris to shop. Woods asked Wishart if it was necessary to carry both his U.S. passport and his United Nations laissez-passers passport. "No," said Wishart, "just take the laissez-passer," but when they were going through immigration, they were stopped because Germany was not yet a member of the United Nations. A German official grinned at Woods and said, "We know there's a car for you from the Bundesbank. It's perfectly all right."

Woods subsequently reported to his senior staff that his trip had been informative and successful. He had been impressed by the desire of government officials to be kept fully informed of IDA's policies and operations. He had particularly promised Ludwig Erhard, the German finance minister, to do so.

It was George Woods who proposed to Pierre Paul Sweitzer, managing director of the International Monetary Fund, that there be joint Bank-

Fund banquets for the governors of the Bank and the Fund and their guests at their joint annual meetings.[38] In addition to his responsibility for administering the Bank and presiding at meetings of the executive directors, the president of the Bank, together with the managing director of the Fund, is responsible for arranging the joint annual meetings, for delivering an annual speech, and for inviting and entertaining the participants. In 1963, the week-long meetings involved six thousand people. Later in the Woods presidency, a staff member was appointed to work all year round on arrangements for the annual meetings, but in 1963 Mort Mendels, the Bank secretary, Marie Linahan, one of Woods's two personal secretaries, and George Wishart arranged to see that Woods had the guests he wanted at his table.

In Woods's day, each governor gave a speech setting forth his views of what the Bank and the Fund should be doing. There were many dinners and receptions. Virtually every country decided that it should give a cocktail party and many delegates were obliged to attend several cocktail parties a night. Then there were the dinners. The night before the conference opened, there was a huge buffet supper. When the meetings are in Washington, D.C., as they are two years out of three—usually in September—the secretary of the treasury gives a reception sometime during the week. George and Louise Woods gave two dinners for the governors and their wives, one of them jointly with the managing director of the Fund. In all of this, Louise Woods was in her element. She loved to entertain the wives of the governors. While George was doing the business, Louise was making the friends.

The governors meet as a group once a year. They delegate to the executive directors, who stay in touch with their governments, the day-to-day responsibility for approving or disapproving proposed loans as well as for discussing the guidelines for granting future loans. Most executive directors represent some combination of countries (and therefore governors). The number of votes to which each country (and therefore each governor) is entitled is different depending on the capital subscriptions of each. In Woods's day, only the United States, the United Kingdom, France, Germany, and India were entitled to the five appointed seats prescribed by the articles of agreement. They were entitled, because of the size of their subscriptions, to cast the largest number of votes for their individual countries. Luis Machado, the executive director who had served the longest, on the other hand needed the combined votes of Mexico, Venezuela, Peru, Haiti, Costa Rica, Guatemala, El Salvador, Honduras, Nicaragua, and Panama to qualify for a seat. His total on June 30, 1963, was 6,477 votes, compared with India's 8,250 and the United States' 63,750. On June 30, 1963, there were five appointed seats; thirteen seats were chosen by combinations of countries.

Woods started to prepare his speech to the 1963 annual meeting of the board of governors in June so as to have it well underway before he left for his vacation the week of July 22. As it turned out, his time away from his office lasted a good deal longer than a week. On the way to Seattle, where he and Louise were to be joined by Edgar Kaiser and his wife, Woods suffered an aneurysm. He was in the hospital for two weeks and was recuperative for an additional month. Mrs. Woods called Wishart from Seattle to say that Woods had suffered an aneurysm. She put Woods on the phone to explain what an aneurysm was, and Woods added that he wanted to speak to the man who was writing his speech. He wanted to make a few last-minute suggestions.

It is not recorded who, but one man Woods might have called from Seattle was Nathaniel McKitterick, a former foreign correspondent for McGraw-Hill World News, who had been most recently with the research staff of the committee for economic development. McKitterick wrote many speeches for Eugene Black and, later, for George Woods. He referred to himself as a "a free-lance bureaucrat. The British," said McKitterick, "have defined a bureaucrat as someone who can make the minister look good no matter who the minister is. It is a formal relationship. I consider it professional."[39]

McKitterick's job was to think up ideas for Black's and Woods's speeches and articles. He would do the drafting then present a final copy. McKitterick made copious use of Bank individuals "who had something to say," but he deliberately never gave a draft to either Black or Woods longer than twenty-four to forty-eight hours before the event if he could get away with it.[40]

The Woods-McKitterick relationship ended unhappily. In mid-1966, President Johnson appointed Eugene Black as his special advisor for Southeast Asian regional affairs. Black called McKitterick: "I'm going to Laos, and I want you to come along." McKitterick said that he was working for Woods. "I'll take care of that," said Black. Woods and Black got together for lunch, and, while they were still in the dining room, Black called McKitterick to say, "Come over. George says it will be all right if you go. We'll only be gone ten to twelve weeks." When McKitterick arrived, he found Woods red in the face. Woods was angry.

McKitterick went to Laos, but when he returned, Woods would not answer McKitterick's telephone calls. McKitterick wrote a letter to Woods saying he did not wish to take on any other commitments until he could see if they could continue their relationship. On the last working day of 1966, at 4:30 in the afternoon, McKitterick was summoned to Woods's office, which was dark except for the light above Woods's head. "He read me back the letter I had written and said, 'You will never work for the World Bank again as long as I am here!'" McKitterick wrote a note to Black and said, "Fly now, pay later. I just lost my contract."[41]

Virtually all of Black's and Woods's speeches before 1967 were written in Harold Graves's information department.[42] Woods liked to tinker with the language of his speeches. Black never did. Graves does not recall that Woods ever sought to recast an entire speech, but he did tinker. Graves remembers with anguish a speech Woods was to deliver at an annual meeting. It was typed on a jumbo typewriter (very large type) so it could be read from the podium with a minimum of peering through eyeglasses. There was one page of this final text that gave Woods trouble, and Graves kept revising that page all through the minutes preceding Woods's delivery of his speech. He remembers rushing back and forth through the corridors of the Sheraton Hotel with new jumbo pages. They did four revisions, and at the end, said Graves, "I looked at the original text and at the final revision and they were identical."[43]

Black, according to Graves, could talk very well from his head if it was a matter of exceptional importance, as occasionally arose in the board. He was very good extemporaneously, but his formal delivery "was perfectly awful. I couldn't stand to listen to Gene giving anything I had written for him. I used to leave the hall when he gave his great annual speech, because I couldn't stand to hear Gene read it, but he was a very effective speaker in a small group. He was somewhat like Lyndon Johnson in that way." Graves said of Woods that he "was a better speaker on formal occasions than Black was. He was also effective extemporaneously. He had a colorful flow of speech, a New York rather than an Atlanta color."[44] When Woods talked about a difficult choice between two or more alternatives, he was apt to say, "Well, I guess we can run between the raindrops on that one."

Black was modest about his attainments as a speaker, more than he need have been. His approach to language was: "Let somebody else do this, I don't know how." Of course, one of Black's great merits as a leader was that people knew what he thought. This meant that written directives were seldom needed. Anybody down to the third and fourth level of command in the Bank could tell what Black thought. It was very different under Woods. One of the first things Woods did was to set in motion a series of studies (about agriculture and industry, for example). This had never happened in the Bank before. As Graves put it, "We had paper, paper, paper on all these subjects. . . . We wrote all this stuff down in a big, policy manual, and the Bank has been writing everything down ever since ad nauseam."[45]

In general, the ideas reflected in the speeches of Black and Woods were those expressed in meetings of the senior staff and the committees that were established to study the problems of the Bank. Graves and McKitterick knew the currents of thought that were flowing through the Bank. One or the other was likely to accompany Black or Woods on trav-

els abroad. They could participate in senior staff discussions. Not infre-
quently, a small committee was put together, usually under the chairmanship of Richard Demuth, to discuss a particular speech. The Bank's objectives were in the field of action, in persuading other people to think like
the Bank, so all the material was made immediately available to the person who was assigned to write a speech, an article, or a monograph.

In the case of Woods's first speech to the annual meeting, the ener-
gizer was the economist, Dragoslav Avramovic, who rescued an otherwise
platitudinous speech and transformed it into a pro–developing country
address that challenged the industrial countries to deal with the commodity, debt, and industralization problems. When Avramovic presented
his ideas, Woods's face lit up. He said, "This is what I want to talk about.
You are now the chairman of my drafting committee." Still, Woods's first
speech bore a marked resemblance to Black's last speech. It had much the
same tone and style.[46]

Woods began this first annual meeting speech as Wishart sat below in
case Woods faltered. Woods had asked Wishart to read his speech for him
were he unable to do so. Woods wanted to make it clear to his listeners
that it was *his* speech rather than just a management speech, as might
have appeared to be the case if, for example, Burke Knapp had substituted
for him. He had returned from his aneurysm "looking like a ghost. There
was a lot of comment about how George looked."[47] But he didn't falter.

He acknowledged the new nations that had joined the Bank, most of
them from Africa. He offered a proper tribute to Per Jacobsson, formerly
the managing director of the IMF, who had died since the last annual
meeting, and to Eugene Black. "It was to a large extent his imaginative
leadership which made the Bank what it is today. . . . The Bank and the
Fund . . . became strong and powerful instruments in the world's struggle
against poverty, instability and ignorance. But that battle has just begun,"
said Woods.

Woods welcomed the apparent willingness of the governors to endorse a $750 million contribution to IDA for three, rather than five years,
and he mentioned the continuing usefulness of the IFC. "IFC's ability to
acquire equities has opened substantial new opportunities." He mentioned
the decrease in Bank lending in the fiscal year ending June 30, 1963, but
he denied that the prospect was for a downward trend in the Bank's
operations.

He enumerated three specific problems. Export earnings were not increasing at a satisfactory pace. He called this the commodity problem. A
number of governments were burdened by heavy short- and medium-term
debt. He called this the debt problem. Finally, most countries had difficulty mobilizing resources effectively. He called this the policy problem.[48]
Woods pointed out that most underdeveloped countries had remained

dependent for their foreign-exchange earnings on a limited range of primary products for which world demand at any given moment is inelastic.
His suggested solution was export diversification, though he did not explain how exports could be diversified without running afoul of comparative advantage. His suggested solution to the debt problems was to shift
more debt to the long term, apparently without regard to the payout period of the projects involved. He attributed the policy problem to insufficient savings or to inadequate fiscal and monetary policies. He did not
suggest the carrot of structural adjustment loans in return for adequate fiscal and monetary policies, but that seemed to be implied.

I have the jumbo copy of the speech. It is underlined at various
points.[49] In a passage mentioning the need for lending to agricultural sectors hitherto passed over and for some loans for education purposes, Woods
underlined the words "we must be ready much more often than hitherto to
leave this proven ground and venture out into unfamiliar terrain." He suggested helping to finance storage facilities and farm-to-market roads in addition to large-scale irrigation, flood control, or land-clearance projects.
He wanted to extend credit and technical help to farmers somewhat along
the lines of private development banks in the industrial sector.

He urged that the commodity problem be attacked by investigating
the financing of new industries "of a kind that had not existed before in
the developing country," and he suggested the long-time financing of individual pieces of equipment as a way to attack the debt problem. He said
he was discussing with the executive directors ways and means for providing loans (without the guarantee of a government?) to establish share-
holder-owned enterprises.

He recommended lending for education facilities, though not for
teachers or students. He urged that the Food and Agriculture Organization of the United Nations as well as the United Nations Economic and
Social Council become involved in assisting the Bank to identify projects.

Because of the Bank's strong financial condition, Woods advocated
reviewing the need for supplementing the Bank's resources annually,
though he was not yet ready to advocate appropriating Bank earnings for
the benefit of IDA.

Woods called for increased determination and more effective action
by national governments of both the industrialized and the less-developed
nations. It was an adumbration of a theme he would repeat in later
speeches: The flow of development assistance now comes from more
sources than ever before, it is better coordinated, and, over the last five
years (1959–1963), it has increased by more than 50 percent. However
(Woods emphasized by underlining), "this aid needs to be continued and
on an increasing scale. The terms on which it is provided still need to be
improved."

He made a plea to the industrialized countries to open their markets. "The forthcoming United Nations Conference on Trade and Development will provide a useful opportunity for the developed countries [Woods underlined *developed countries* three times] to reexamine their trade policies vis-à-vis those less developed."

Woods urged a reduction in the time needed for project preparation. He inveighed against the outflow of capital from developing countries. He advocated releasing the energies, talents, and the capital that exist in the private sectors of developed and underdeveloped countries alike. He mentioned the usefulness of arbitration for settling international investment disputes, and returned to the theme of private enterprise:

> A country which is known to be hospitable to private investment will have access over the years to a much larger and more stable pool of capital than its neighbor which relies solely on government-to-government aid. It will have access, too, to a much larger pool of industrial personnel—managerial, administrative and technical—and to a much larger mass of scientific and technological information than it could possibly acquire in any other way. Most important of all, its economy will be stimulated and invigorated by the many different contacts, at many different levels, which a hospitable investment climate will make possible between enterprises and individuals within its own borders and those within the borders of the industrializing countries. None of these advantages [Woods underlined] is likely to be fully available to any nation whose government, however well motivated and however well administered, decides to relegate the private sector to a subordinate role.

It was vintage George Woods. Sir William Iliff, who attended as a guest of the Bank, remarked to George Wishart that it went down well with the underwriters—the bond market. Iliff said that one of the great things was that they felt they could trust George Woods absolutely. They all knew George, and they all knew perfectly well that he was not going to sponsor a give-away program. "You know," said Iliff, "they wouldn't have taken this from most people."[50]

Notes

    1. Robert W. Oliver, "A Conversation with Irving Friedman, I," *Conversations About George Woods and the World Bank*, Washington, D.C., March 1974, pp. 26–27. Other candidates whose names were mentioned included David Bell, Guido Carli, Lord Cromer, Douglas C. Dillon, Thomas S. Gates, Felipe Herrera, William McChesney Martin, Jr., Louis Rasminsky, and David Rockefeller. Davidson Sommers and Burke Knapp might have been considered had it not been for an unwritten rule that existing staff were out of the running.
    2. Arthur M. Schlesinger, Jr., *A Thousand Days* (Boston: Houghton Mifflin Company, 1965), pp. 616–617, quoting Kennedy.

3. Woods seemed a perfect choice for Bank president, and news of his appointment was generally hailed, though the Kennedy administration prudently withheld a public announcement until October 13, 1962, well after Congress had adjourned. Senator Morse, who had not been consulted in advance, and Senator Kefauver, who had, objected. The senators could not have defeated Woods's appointment, of course: the choice is the prerogative of the executive directors of the Bank. But future appropriations for IDA had to go before Congress, and efforts were already underway to change the formula for assigning IDA contributions, the U.S. percentage of the total being substantially reduced. See the *Wall Street Journal*, October 15, 1962, p. 1.

4. Eugene Black had been considered for the post of secretary of the treasury under Kennedy. He declined.

5. Of the twenty-nine new loans negotiated in fiscal 1961/62, less than 10 percent of the total of $882 million was to be for projects other than power, roads, railroads, ports, and coal. See "The Seventeenth Annual Report," *International Bank for Reconstruction and Development*, September 18, 1962, p. 11.

6. *Wall Street Journal*, October 23, 1962.

7. *Business Week*, October 20, 1962, p. 123.

8. For a summary of IDA replenishments through 1983, see *IDA in Retrospect* (published for the World Bank by Oxford University Press, 1982).

9. Developing countries would have a net annual transfer of resources to their creditors!

10. This discussion of the international financial system is largely taken from Robert Solomon, *The International Monetary System, 1945–1976* (New York: Harper and Row, 1977), pp. 26–85.

11. See the articles of agreement of the International Monetary Fund—Article XIV, the Scarce Currency Clause.

12. Solomon, p. 28.

13. Cited in Solomon, p. 35.

14. The Treaty of Rome to establish a European Common Market was signed by France, Germany, Italy, and the Benelux countries in 1957.

15. See Roy Harrod, "An Essay in Dynamic Theory," *Economic Journal*, March 1939, pp. 14–33; and Evsey Domar, "Expansion and Unemployment," *American Economic Review*, March 1947, pp. 34–55.

16. See Edward F. Denison, *The Sources of Economic Growth in the United States and the Alternatives Before Us* (New York: Committee for Economic Development, 1962).

17. See Max F. Millikan and Donald L.M. Blackmer, editors, *The Emerging Nations, Their Growth and United States Policy* (Boston: Little, Brown and Company, 1961). Page 130 reads: "No amount of international machinery can substitute for well developed programs at the national level and for the weaving into these programs of all the various types of external assistance available. In the end, whatever the superstructure for international institutions, these require the method of the consortium, in which the men responsible locally sit down with responsible men from other countries and work out a program for action. The task of the consortium is to bring to bear on a national development program all the instruments available to each donor nation: food and fiber surpluses, hard loans, soft loans, technical assistance, and private capital."

18. Some say the reference was to the Li'l Abner cartoon strip about the skunk-works, where skunks were processed; there was always an inside man and an outside man.

19. Prior to 1956, Iliff had the title, assistant to the president.

20. Sommers and Knapp may have thought that one of them might be promoted to be president of the Bank. Both were enormously popular with the Bank
staff. Sommers, in response to a question on that subject said, however: "I strongly
believe that the President of the Bank and the Managing Director of the Fund
should come from outside. Even if I had not thought that was desirable, I was confident that that was what would happen. Black had only two years more. I was
about 55 years old and thought that if I didn't move, I would probably stay in the
Bank indefinitely. My wife was an invalid, which would not have gone well with
the big entertainment responsibilities in the Bank."—Robert W. Oliver, "A Conversation with Davidson Sommers," *Conversations About George Woods and the
World Bank*, Washington, D.C., July 18, 1985, p. 2.

21. It is specified in the articles of agreement that except in exceptional circumstances, the Bank shall make loans only for specific projects and that it shall
make arrangements to ensure that the proceeds of any loan shall be used for the
purpose for which the loan is granted.

22. Part of Demuth's effectiveness was due to the fact that other Bank people
were not afraid that he would be a bureaucratic threat to them. He preferred to
be a brain truster, an explorer and pioneer, to have high personal standing rather
than a large organization reporting to him. When Irving Friedman was trying to
get supplementary finance accepted (see Chapter 4), Friedman went directly
against the way Demuth operated so effectively. If Friedman had turned the proposal over to Demuth, the probability is high that it would have gone through.

23. Other members of the senior staff when Woods became president in-
cluded (nationalities in parentheses): Peter Cargill, director of operations for the
Far East (British); Raymond Cope, for Europe (British); Pierre Moussa, for Africa
(French); Escott Reid, for South Asia and the Middle East (Canadian); Orvis
Schmidt, for Latin America (U.S.); Robert Cavanaugh, treasurer (U.S.); Harold
N. Graves, Jr., director of information (U.S.); William Howell, director of admin-
istration (U.S.); Howard Johnson, manager of portfolio sales (U.S.); George Mar-
tin, director of marketing (U.S.); Morton Mendels, secretary (Canadian); John
Miller, special representative for Europe (British); Leonard Rist, special adviser
(French); Dragoslav Avramovic, in charge of the economic staff (Yugoslavian);
and John Adler, director of the economic development institute (U.S.).

24. Robert W. Oliver, "A Conversation With J. Burke Knapp," *Conversations
About George Woods and the World Bank*, Portola Valley, California, September 3,
1986, p. 11.

25. Richard H. Demuth, interview by Robert Asher, March 19, 1984, archives
of the World Bank, p. 9.

26. "The Reminiscences of George Wishart," *George David Woods Oral History Project*, Oral History Research Office, Columbia University, 1983.

27. When Woods had been president of the Bank for only a few weeks, Eugene Meyer, the first World Bank president, died. His family telephoned to Mort
Mendels, the Bank's secretary, to say they were presenting Eugene Meyer's desk to
the World Bank to be used by all the presidents of the Bank forever. But Woods
would have no other desk than Harry Addinsell's. Mendels and Wishart found a
suitable site near the proposed Eugene R. Black Auditorium, and the desk was
placed there with a stylish rope enclosure and a plaque stating that it was the desk
of the first president of the World Bank.—George Wishart, personal correspondence, May 23, 1992.

28. Richard Van Wagenen, interview by Robert W. Oliver, July 25, 1986,
archives of the World Bank, Washington, D.C.

29. Demuth called on a lot of graduate schools to induce them to urge their best students to apply. When he was at the University of Cambridge talking to second-year students in the Business School, the first question asked was about the policy of hiring Bank presidents. Is it the policy, the student asked, to go outside of your own staff as happened with Black and Woods?

On October 16, 1963, when Woods was being photographed with the young professionals, he suggested, "Everybody look as though they just had a baby girl."

30. "The Reminiscences of George Wishart," p. 32.

31. The eighteenth annual report of the World Bank (1962–1963) noted that Bank lending to ICICI has provided $90 million in foreign exchange for industrial development projects in India. It has approved financial assistance for 200 industrial projects involving 183 private firms. Lending to PICIC has amounted to $49 million in foreign exchange involving 318 individual loans.

32. Ibid., p. 9. The Bank took two initiatives in education in 1963. One was to sponsor jointly with UNESCO, the Ford Foundation, and the French government a new International Institute for Educational Planning. The other was to recommend standards of design for the construction of schools in Tunisia.

33. Wishart, p. 41.

34. The Kariba Dam loan financed the creation of what was then the biggest hydroelectric reservoir in the world.

35. George Woods represented Kaiser Aluminum in the negotiations leading to the Volta River Project. Kaiser sought a source of inexpensive power (see Chapter 3).

36. Wishart, p. 30.

37. This and the following accounts of Woods's first overseas trip as president are from Wishart.

38. The articles of agreement of the International Bank for Reconstruction and Development, which came to be called the World Bank during Woods's presidency, and the International Monetary Fund, sometimes referred to as the Bretton Woods twins, were negotiated at Bretton Woods, New Hampshire, in 1944, by forty-four nations led primarily by experts from the United States Treasury Department and the British Treasury. See Robert W. Oliver, *International Economic Cooperation and the World Bank* (London: Macmillan and Co., 1975). Membership in the Fund is a prerequisite to membership in the Bank. For the less-developed countries, the Bank is the carrot.

A single governor represents each of the Bretton Woods twins, though the same person may represent both the Bank and the Fund. In the case of the United States, the governor for both the Bank and the Fund is the secretary of the treasury. In the case of the United Kingdom, the governor for the Bank is the governor of the Bank of England, while the governor for the Fund is the chancellor of the exchequer. Between June 30, 1962, and June 30, 1963, the number of governors of the Bank had risen from seventy-five to eighty-five.

39. Robert W. Oliver, "A Conversation with Nathanial M. McKitterick," *Conversations About George Woods and the World Bank*, Washington, D.C., July 24, 1985, p. 1. McKitterick was on the payroll of the Bank in the early 1960s and was a consultant to Woods until 1966.

40. Ibid., p. 2.

41. Ibid., p. 15.

42. Graves joined the Bank in 1950 from a Rhode Island newspaper for which he had been a reporter. He had done a couple of pieces for *Reporter* magazine that Richard Demuth had seen and liked. Graves had known Demuth since 1940: they

both had degrees from Princeton. "Would you be interested in coming to the World Bank and writing speeches for the president and working on his annual report?" asked Demuth. Graves said he would and called at the Bank and talked, especially to Robert Garner, but also to Black and some department heads. It was decided that it was a good idea.—Robert W. Oliver, "A Conversation with Harold Graves, I," *Conversations About George Woods and the World Bank*, Washington, D.C., July 17, 1985.

43. Ibid., p. 12.

44. Ibid., p. 17.

45. Ibid., p. 16.

46. Ibid., p. 12.

47. Graves, II, July 24, 1985, p. 24.

48. These were the three problems identified by Dragoslav Avramovic.

49. Occasionally words in the speech are changed. For example, in his discussion of the IFC, Woods crossed out the word "private" from the sentence which read: "The corporation obtained wider private participation in its investments than in any previous year." He penciled in EYE-DEO-LOGICAL above the word *ideological* at one point. He substituted *similarity to* for *analogy with* in the sentence, *There is an obvious analogy with the role of the industrial finance companies in many countries.*

50. Wishart, p. 45.

President John F. Kennedy addresses the annual meeting of the Bank and the Fund on September 30, 1963

George and his younger sister,
Grace, Brooklyn 1907

Henry H. Fowler (seated), U.S. secretary of the treasury, greets Senator J. William
Fulbright as the Woodses look on during the 1965 annual meeting of the Bank
and the Fund

Woods presides over a meeting of the executive directors of the Bank,
December 1966

George Wishart with two members of the Nigerian delegation at the 1965 annual
meeting of the Bank and the Fund.

Woods (third from right) with the other members of the board of trustees of the *New York Times*

Louise Woods greets Susan Griffith in the receiving line at the Bank Christmas party in 1964

A frustrated Woods with J. Burke Knapp and Simon Aldewereld, vice-presidents of the Bank, December 1966

Livingston T. Merchant, appointed executive director for the Bank, July 23, 1965

CHAPTER 4

THE
ROLE
OF THE
ECONOMISTS

The Role of the Economists:
Irving S. Freidman (left) and Andrew Kamarck

B y the time of the 1963 annual meeting, if not before, George Woods had decided that the Bank needed an expanded economics staff. Once Woods had perceived that IDA might finance expenditures whose amortization period could be as long as fifty years with no interest, his concept of development assistance changed. Though IDA loans had to meet the same standards as Bank loans, many more countries could receive help, and the amounts could be greater. The constraint of absorptive capacity was relaxed.

But IDA loans were more difficult to assess than Bank loans. Teams of economists were needed, Woods felt, and development planning based on many kinds of information in all of the Bank's developing countries seemed to be in order. The Bank needed to institute a partnership relationship with its client governments. It needed to become a development-assistance or a development-finance agency rather more than a bank. That changed perception began under Eugene Black, but it came to fruition under George Woods. Black knew he needed more economists, but he didn't quite know how to recruit them. Woods thought that Black was frightened of economists. "But I'm not," he said, as he leaned back in his chair and pushed his glasses up over his eyebrows to the top of his head.[1]

In Paris, at OECD, Willard Thorp, an economist who became chairman of the development assistance committee in 1963, thought that the Bank should do more work on development economics. How should aid be extended and on what terms? How much assistance can poor countries absorb on IDA terms? On what basis do you decide whether a country should be an IDA country or a Bank country? If the Bank did not hire at least twenty more economists, the initiative for such work would go somewhere else, like UNCTAD, to the detriment of the Bank and of objective economic analysis. Andrew Kamarck carried Thorp's message to the senior staff.

Professor Edward Mason of Harvard University, who had been recruited by Richard Demuth to be chief of the Uganda survey mission in 1961, echoed Thorp's advice: more economists, including economists from academia, were needed.[2] Mason also recommended that the economists of

95

the Bank be required to move back and forth, within and to and from the area and technical operations departments and the Economic Development Institute; that they be granted periodic sabbatical leaves; and that they be offered the opportunity to publish more.

Irving S. Friedman, who had been director of the exchange restrictions department of the International Monetary Fund,[3] was chosen by Woods in August 1964 to direct the work of what was to become a greatly expanded economics staff.[4] Woods knew about the systematic country analyses done in the Fund, and he wanted the Bank to have a similar capability.[5] Woods said to Friedman, in effect: I want you to come and develop a country analysis program because I think that IDA has to become more important than the World Bank. I really don't think that most of these countries we're dealing with are the kinds of countries which ought to get a lot of loans from the World Bank. They ought to get loans from IDA. While I'm here, we're going to try to make IDA bigger than the World Bank. I think I know about banks; I know how to decide whether to make a loan or not, but I don't know how to make a decision about IDA. I don't know how to decide whether Pakistan and India and these other countries should have more or less.[6]

Woods relied heavily on Friedman's advice, and most of the executive directors and the senior staff knew this. Friedman was Woods's "fair-haired boy."[7] They were not close socially, but Friedman had access to Woods in his office virtually any time he wanted, and Woods agreed with Friedman's proposals most of the time. They developed a symbiotic relationship that continued even after Woods ceased to be president of the World Bank. It was an exchange of mutual admiration and respect, partly because both were outsiders in a Bank that Eugene Black had built.

Friedman joined the Bank at about the time when Woods decided to inaugurate a president's council to advise him daily. Burke Knapp and Geoffrey Wilson were already vice-presidents when Friedman was hired, and Woods promised that Friedman, too, would be a vice-president. (Pierre Paul Schweitzer, managing director of the IMF, had strongly advised Friedman not to accept the Bank job unless Friedman were promoted, and Friedman was already at the upper limit of his salary scale, ranking just under the managing director and his deputy.) When Woods was reminded that Friedman would be the second U.S. vice-president, however, Woods gave the title instead to Simon Aldewereld, the Bank's director of technical operations. Aron Broches, the Bank's general counsel, and Richard Demuth, director of development services, also had claims to a vice-presidency. Woods suggested that the six senior officers should be considered equal in the president's council; they were all entitled to chauffeur-driven limousines and salaries higher than those of the executive directors.

Friedman chose the title of economic adviser to the president as a way of implying his rank, though that may have been an unfortunate choice of words: some of the staff, with some derision, would say, "There goes Mr. The Economic Adviser to the President." Some testing of a new chief economist may have been inevitable regardless of whom Woods hired, but Friedman seemed to stand apart from his colleagues. He threw himself into the job of reestablishing an economic committee and pushing his own proposals. He never sought to insinuate himself into the staff loan committee, chaired by Burke Knapp, however; nor to propose specific projects in Simon Aldewereld's bailiwick. "When I came to the Bank," Friedman said, "I thought it might be a good idea if a country were to switch from industry to agriculture, [but] I would hesitate to say so on the grounds that I had to wait for them to come up with an agricultural project."[8] He did not seek to alter the Economic Development Institute under the jurisdiction or Richard Demuth. "I was not doing things which the Bank was already doing."[9]

Friedman had a somewhat nasty experience as soon as he joined the Bank. The administration had selected a room for him remote from the president's office. It was the same room he had had when he was a division chief of the International Monetary Fund many years before in the early years when the Fund and the Bank shared the same building. It was a cubby-hole compared to the luxurious rooms that Geoffrey Wilson and Burke Knapp occupied next to the president. Woods was furious, and a new room near him was created.[10]

As Friedman would later explain: "Woods was not a modern manager. He wasn't a guy who went in for tremendous restructuring. He added me on, so to speak. He left other people alone. But how do you work with the people you've got when Woods felt they weren't understanding what he was trying to do? Woods would point out that development should be like the war effort. He had been in the war effort and felt that you ought to tackle this with the same degree of commitment and dedication and verve. He wanted us to work hard, work weekends, work nights. He didn't find this. He found what he called, disparagingly, a country-club atmosphere. How do you change this? He threw the ball right into my hands. That is one of the reasons it became such a fascinating assignment. He said, 'I am giving the assignment to you. You can go out and hire as many people as you want, any kind of people you want, because I am not going to do it with these people. I need new people who will do it. You go out and hire the kind of people that you think will do it, and you will have my support.'"[11]

Friedman was himself a workaholic who would normally be in his office until 7 or 8 P.M. and take a briefcase home at night. He frequently called on Woods in Woods's office at 6 P.M. and stayed an hour or so. He was also an early riser who could get by with little sleep. When he was with the Fund, his colleagues would sometimes complain that he kept them up talking into the wee small hours, though he was always up, bustling about before they were. In 1956, when the negotiations associated with the Suez Canal crisis were underway, Friedman, then with the Fund, collapsed and was on leave of absence for nearly a year.

A major problem in the Fund in the early years (to review briefly a bit of history) had been to achieve currency convertibility. Only the dollar among the major currencies was freely convertible; the European countries suffered from a so-called dollar shortage. The Fund was established to operate under conditions of exchange convertibility, however, and—because of his earlier work with inconvertible sterling balances—Friedman became the director of the exchange restrictions department. In that capacity, he began to ask: "How can you make a judgment as to whether or not a country is making progress toward achieving the preconditions for convertibility without going to the country, without talking to the people, without doing serious economic work, without building an economics staff?"[12]

In 1947, the staff of the Fund was small. Friedman wrote papers in the research department on Iran's and Ethiopia's par values based on the *Encyclopedia Britannica*. He derived many par-value discussion papers from tertiary sources. When he had a department of his own, however, he sought first-hand information about countries. Initially, he was opposed by much of the Fund staff and most of the executive directors.[13] J. W. Beyen, who had been president of the Bank for International Settlements, said, for example: "Friedman is proposing that our countries dance nude on this table. I can assure you that the Netherlands will never dance nude in front of an international body."[14] Gradually, however, as economic conditions throughout the world improved and as Friedman persisted, he was successful. By the late 1950s, the Fund had organized automatic, regular reviews of countries with recommendations for policy, including explicit and implicit criteria by which to judge what was meant by a good performance, a projection of where the country was going, and a judgment as to whether this represented reasonable international behavior worthy of international support.

Meanwhile, in 1949, under the general direction of Richard Demuth, the World Bank had organized a large survey mission to Colombia. Soon thereafter, surveys were published about Cuba (1951), Guatemala (1951), Turkey (1951), and Iraq (1952). They were technical assistance missions, however, not missions for Bank purposes. They were requested by a country's government and organized by the Bank, but the bulk of the personnel were recruited from outside the Bank. The chief economist of the mission was usually a senior economist of the Bank who had the task of pulling the report together, but if the Bank was considering lending to the country concerned, the Bank would send an economic team of its own to prepare a confidential report with recommendations specifically for the

Bank. The Bank had the notion that it should know about a country only if it expected to make a loan to it and only then to the extent that information was needed for the loan. When Friedman moved to the Bank in 1964, the Bank had not had an economic review of Brazil, for example, for several years.

The reorganization of 1952 had reduced the number of economists on the central economics staff to a handful. Burke Knapp became head of the staff loan committee. Some economists joined the area or project departments, while others, like Paul Rosenstein-Rodan, left the Bank. Some, like Gerald Alter and Alexander Stevenson, subsequently became area department directors; others, like Andrew Kamarck, preferred to continue as economic advisers to area departments. Kamarck preferred economics to loan negotiations. A few, like John Adler and Dragoslav Avramovic, continued to study creditworthiness. There was some need for a central economics staff even though Robert Garner had sought to recruit the economists into operations.

Leonard Rist, who had served as director of the economic department, was gracefully asked to become Eugene Black's special representative for Africa. John de Wilde succeeded Rist, though he quickly tired of administration and returned to the Africa area department where, under the overall direction of the Bank, his team published a monumental study of agriculture in Africa. Dragoslav Avramovic followed as an interim replacement while Woods cast about for a permanent economic adviser and director of the economics department.

Avramovic, who joined the Bank in 1953 from Yugoslavia, had become the Bank's expert in commodity and debt studies.[15] Under Friedman, he became the director of special studies. He was out of the mainstream of organized economic work, but he continued his commodity and debt studies and organized a massive mission to Algeria, which, incidentally, raised too high Algerian expectations of Bank loans.

Avramovic felt strongly that commodity agreements should be financed by the World Bank. He discovered that Lord Keynes had supported commodity agreements, and he sought to have his arguments presented to the executive directors. Avramovic became convinced that at least half of the problem of external debt was due to the decline in export earnings when the prices of commodities declined. Rich countries can afford their own program of commodity stabilization; poor countries cannot: they are forced to depend on free markets, and prices in free markets sometimes fluctuated disastrously.

As interim director in 1963, Avramovic wanted the economics staff to grow organically. It had reached twenty or so by 1963, up from a low of five or six. After the reorganization of 1952, the economists joked that if the Bank wanted someone to compute Ethiopia's imports per capita,

they would ask the economics staff to do it. Avramovic wanted the economists all to be fully employed; he wanted to keep the staff at 95 percent
of the demand for work that could be justified in terms of operations. He
objected to jobs being created.[16]

In 1963, Avramovic felt that the esprit de corps of the twenty or so
economists was excellent. Under Friedman, however, the tasks of the
economists were greatly expanded. Economists were hired until, by 1967,
the economics department was second only to the projects department in
numbers.

When Friedman joined the Bank, "there was no Economics Department," as he told me in the first of the recorded conversations I had with
him. "Many a loan officer had a Ph.D. in economics, but he did not want
to be recruited into an economics staff. . . . It would be a demotion in the
Bank to be called an economist," said Friedman. "I wasn't told that there
were no economists in the Bank, but there weren't many. . . . I asked them
to send me a list of the people with Ph.Ds. in economics. If I remember
the figure correctly, there were 150, . . . maybe one-fourth [of the professional staff], but it was a very strong core and with very good Ph.Ds. . . .
When I tried to recruit an economics staff from these people, however, I
found very few who were willing to be regarded as economists. They told
me that being an economist in the Bank was the death of a career."[17]

Woods suggested that Friedman hire someone from within the Bank
to be director of the economics department. Friedman asked various
World Bank people to give him on a piece of paper five names that they
felt were the best economists in the Bank. Andrew Kamarck, whom he
had known in the U.S. Treasury Department, was on everybody's list.
That fit in with Friedman's biases and Kamarck became Friedman's principal lieutenant.[18]

In early 1965, shortly after he became director of the economics department, Kamarck had lunch with Friedman and Woods. Woods said it
was absurd that every Wall Street bank had a report on the economy and
the World Bank did not. Friedman and Kamarck agreed. Kamarck
promised that the economics department would try to prepare a section
on economics for the next annual report.[19] At a subsequent meeting of
the executive directors, the traditional annual report was quickly approved, but the board questioned Kamarck about the economics section
for most of the morning and on into the afternoon. Woods acted annoyed
with Kamarck for being so forthcoming and agreeing with some of the directors' comments, but by the end of the session Woods was pleased.
Thereafter, the annual reports of the Bank and the IDA contained a section on development and development finance. This was the beginning of
what, in 1978 during the McNamara presidency, became the *World Development Report.*

Friedman and Kamarck reconstructed the staff economics committee and put it more nearly on a par with the staff loan committee. There had always been an economic committee that reviewed economic reports and discussed general issues such as external debt, or talked about the creditworthiness of specific countries. Still, as Burke Knapp put it, "As far as operations were concerned, it was a support department."[20] "The retreat of the Economics Department from being closely absorbed in Bank operations [following the reorganization of 1952] did not reduce its contribution; it rather meant that there was so much economics work to do that specific country analysis and project analysis were more efficiently done in the economic divisions of the area departments, while the broad, long-range, global analyses could still be carried out in the Economics Department."[21]

Woods strongly supported Friedman's attempt to increase the scope and the power of the economic committee. Woods insisted that relevant department heads meet with the economic committee as well as the loan committee. He decreed that every loan proposal had to pass a review of the economic committee before it went to the loan committee. Friedman would ask questions such as, What do we think about the development program of the country in question? Is it a feasible program? Is it economically sensible? Is the country appropriate for IDA support? Is it creditworthy for the Bank? Do its development activities merit the support of the Bank? In his words: "We had long discussions about shadow prices and issues of that kind . . . before we would pass a proposed loan on to the Loan Committee. . . . The Economic Committee would have to come up with . . . a recommendation to the Loan Committee and the President that we felt . . . this country was suitable for this proposed loan."[22]

One of Friedman's innovations was to invite the relevant department director of the International Monetary Fund to attend the meetings of the economic committee whenever his country was being discussed. Friedman never sought formal agreement that these IMF directors could participate, but he never had a discussion of a country without the director or the acting director of the Fund being present.

The chief economists in the area and projects departments were members of the committee. They took with them the economists who had been involved. Economists like Mervyn Weiner, in the Latin America area department, or Shigeharu Takahashi, in the agriculture projects department, attended the meetings. They could raise issues that had arisen earlier during benefit-cost analyses. They could discuss economics with fellow economists who had encountered similar or related problems under different circumstances in other areas. The meetings were lively and well attended. They had long discussions, for example, about whether India and Pakistan should receive over two-thirds of the IDA loans.[23]

The traditional idea that the real power in the Bank resided with the chairman of the staff loan committee no longer held true. There was a division of power. Robert Garner had said in 1952 that he was deliberately setting it up so that there would be conflict between the technical operations (projects) and the area departments—conflict that would be resolved in the staff loan committee. George Woods said that there would now be "creative tension" between the economics department and the rest of the Bank. He sometimes talked about the conflict between the area, projects, and economics departments as being like a three-legged stool— stable because there were competing centers of power.

Andrew Kamarck instituted an informal monthly luncheon for all the senior economists in the Bank. This turned out to be very successful in improving cooperation among the economists, and it became a permanent feature at the Bank. The administration department supported the idea strongly and approved adding the cost to the Bank's budget for the first few years. After the monthly luncheon habit was well established, Friedman was invited to become the host. Kamarck also sought to induce the area department directors to have monthly lunches with him. Woods thought that this was a great idea, but Kamarck did not tell Woods that many of the directors refused to attend. Gerald Alter, director for the Western Hemisphere, and Bernard Bell, when he became deputy director of the projects department (both of whom were Ph.D. economists), would attend; but Peter Cargill, director for Asia, would not; nor would Raymond Cope, who was director for Europe and the Middle East as well as second-in-command to Burke Knapp in the loan committee.[24]

Meanwhile, there were mutterings of discontent about the increased power of economists in general and the economic committee in particular. "It used to be simple: we just had to go to the loan committee; now we have to go to the economic committee too."[25] Every country was supposed to be reviewed and a judgment passed on its economic situation, outlook, condition, behavior, and performance before any loan proposal could go before the loan committee, but the area department loan officers would seldom attend meetings of the economic committee. Friedman issued standing invitations, but the loan officers stayed away. It might be suggested, of course, that Friedman, himself, deliberately stayed away from meetings of the staff loan committee.[26] (Leonard Rist, when he was chairman of the economic committee, attended meetings of the loan committee. So did Dragoslav Avramovic and Andrew Kamarck.[27]) Loan officers might have been forgiven for supposing that Friedman was trying to organize a committee composed in part of outsiders (from the Fund) to compete with, rather more than to complement, the staff loan committee.

Friedman was nominally responsible for the professional standards of economics everywhere in the Bank. Woods agreed and said so in writing.

Still, the economists in the projects and area departments looked more to their own directors than to Friedman. Whenever anything unusual came up and neither Friedman nor Kamarck had been consulted, the economists would be told by their directors, "Forget it. Just go ahead and do it the way we tell you to."[28] When Friedman tried to get a population economist appointed, he was turned down by the administration on the ground that it was improper for the Bank to have a population economist. Woods didn't fight for it. He said, "Come on Irving, why care about such things?"

Friedman sought to elevate the status of economists. He thought that the economic advisers of the area departments should be made deputy directors. The principal officer would be a loan officer, but his deputy would be an economist. There would be joint leadership on the operational and the economic side, but Friedman could never get this accepted, even when Woods was president. He was constantly opposed by people who muttered that economists were meant to be advising and that was all.

Friedman was more at home in the Fund than in the Bank, partly because economists were thought better of in the Fund. "I shared the conviction," said Friedman, "that good monetary and fiscal policy was really a pre-condition to sound development. . . . With such policies, it would be possible to avoid significant inflation, multiple-currency practices, and intensive use of trade or payments restrictions." This point of view, much honored in the Bank today, was not valued as much in the project-oriented Bank of Black's, Garner's, and even Woods's day. As Friedman later recalled, "When I came to the Bank, I was much concerned with the fact that in the Bank economics was a secondary profession. . . . I had been impressed as an outsider with how many of my friends who were economists in the World Bank had left their roles as economists. . . . I never stopped being an economist because I left the research department and went into other activities in the Fund. . . . I was still expected to give scholarly papers. I fostered *Staff Papers* [published by the IMF]. We got people to finish their Ph.D. degrees. I got the Fund to finance people going to the American Economics Association no matter what department they were in. They never ceased to be professional economists. When I got to the Bank, I found that the economics profession was highly regarded [because] that was one of the ways in which you became a loan officer . . . [and] ceased being an economist.

"I did everything I could to build the position of the economists and the economics profession within the Bank. The resistance I got was not that the economists weren't good, or useful; but that economists could remain economists and be operationally important was something that seemed to be strange to a number of people there. If you were an economist, you were an adviser. You improved things, but the decision-making and decision-taking responsibility was for people who had left the economics profession.

"I was trying hard to get across the idea that the decisions of the World Bank had to be taken by people who felt they were taking them as professional economists, not on diplomatic, legal, or political grounds. . . . We had meetings in the economic committee on this. We knew what the academic economists were doing and sought to support them. I had numerous conversations with Andy Kamarck about how we might use the World Bank to help such people. But my concern was primarily with whether we were using effectively what was known in the economics profession. The skills and methodology we were developing in the Bank were making economists a vital part of the decision-making process."[29]

Friedman argued that issues like absorptive capacity, capital requirements, development strategy, investment priorities, the encouragement of savings, and the allocation of savings were operational issues. Creditworthiness was not just an arithmetic of export earnings that could be used to service debt: it was a much bigger and deeper concept based on the whole economic outlook of the country. It involved the use of capital and the kind of results that it would produce, both domestically and internationally. Only detailed economic analysis could really give a final judgment on creditworthiness.[30] Woods agreed.

At one point, Andrew Kamarck considered the possibility of asking George Woods to assign all of the area and project economists first to the economics department and second to the relevant area or project department. Kamarck believed that Woods would have done what he proposed, but he decided not to ask Friedman to ask Woods to grant his request. It would not have worked unless the economic advisers in the area and project departments had been willing and eager to come into the economics department. They were not: they preferred the role they had. If they had been forced into the economics department, they might have sabotaged the whole economics program. By and large, they were content to be economic advisers to the area and project departments. They were not the kind of economists whose skills included the more theoretical macro, micro, and statistical work that was increasingly required in the Bank. Economists had to be hired from outside to deal with these issues.

Woods agreed that Friedman and Kamarck could offer salaries up to 10 percent more than the Fund was offering comparable people. Over the five years of the Woods administration, Friedman and Kamarck probably hired over two hundred economists, which alone increased the staff of the Bank by 25 percent. Friedman and Kamarck began to organize divisions. Initially, they agreed to have a division on debt, one on commodities, and one on other functions, including statistics. That was when the statistical tables started to emerge.

Kamarck remembers that, when the economics department was instituted, he realized that he and Friedman had an enormous opportunity. He also realized that they had a limited time. "When you get the go-ahead signal to do something, it doesn't last forever; you have to take advantage of it when it's there. . . . We were given an enormous expansion of budget slots, and I knew it was very important to start as soon as possible."[31]

One of the things they did first was to look around for possible talent elsewhere in the Bank. Kamarck wanted someone who would start collecting basic statistical data, to help developing countries produce the kind of data they needed for their economic policies. He sought a person who was good at statistics and had tremendous drive. He found such a person in Emanuel Levy, but Levy was assigned to the Philippines. "You have just the kind of a person we need," said Kamarck to Peter Cargill, who had just become director of the Asia department. Cargill agreed to release him, and Levy inaugurated the work that led to the World Bank Tables. By 1978, these tables comprised five hundred pages. It was the most complete collection of international statistics extant.[32]

The Bank almost from the beginning gathered statistics on the external debt of its borrowers. When the economics department was reorganized under Kamarck however, he recognized that the number of people working on statistics was insufficient: the data were getting more and more inadequate and out of date. The staff was increased and a program was begun of providing technical assistance to the governments of the less-developed countries to improve the coverage and quality of their reports. Cooperative arrangements were negotiated with OECD and the regional development banks (Inter-American, Asian, and African) to set up a comprehensive system of international debt reporting, to be managed by the World Bank. Borrowers from any of the banks were requested to fill out standard forms, and this information was supplemented by a system of reports from lending institutions.

Harold Dyer in the personnel department went through the records of all the people who had applied for jobs in the Bank. He wrote to institutions and people the Bank had worked with asking for suggestions. Kamarck developed a substantial list of names, and Friedman and Kamarck culled the list to find qualified people and to recruit them as quickly as possible. David Henderson, who was in Greece at the time, was a real find. Frank Tamagna, who had been with the Federal Reserve Board, came to the Bank as a consultant. An Israeli, David Kochav, was very good. Isaiah Frank, from the Johns Hopkins School of Advanced International Studies, became a consultant. Bimal Jalan was recruited from India, Meenart Sundrum from Burma, Paolo Pereira-Lira from Brazil. Friedman himself organized within the Bank a brain trust that included Wilfried Thalwitz, from Germany, and Ravi Gulhati, from India. Friedman

attempted to put together a long-term research program centered around
Guy Orcutt, from Yale University, and Irving Kravis, from the University
of Pennsylvania. Woods agreed, though he was suspicious and reluctant.
He would never have countenanced anything like the academic-oriented
programs of later presidents. Woods's idea, which Friedman shared, was
that economics within the Bank was just another part of its operational
activities. At the same time, Woods wanted the Bank to be the acknowledged leader of the world in development economics.

With the first loan to Chile (in March 1948), the Bank had begun to
attach conditions to its lending: it insisted, among other things, that the
Chilean government begin negotiations with the Foreign Bondholders
Protective Association to make a reasonable effort to repay what it had
borrowed. Gradually, thereafter, the Bank employed leverage to induce
member governments to do one thing or another. The conditions under
which some member governments can obtain a loan have become more
and more demanding: today, in return for a structural or a sector-adjust-
ment loan, the Bank may tell a member government how it must conduct
its monetary and fiscal policy.

From the beginning, some loan negotiations have been conducted in
an adversarial atmosphere. Friedman tried to persuade George Woods to
drop the word "negotiations" from the Bank's parlance, but he never succeeded. "With whom," Friedman asked, "are we negotiating? They are all
our member countries. They own us. We are negotiating with our own
stockholders. We ought to be thinking, How do we help this country
achieve social and economic development?"33

Friedman's point is well taken, though in reply it might be said that
the bondholders who had loaned money to the Bank were negotiating to
insure that their funds were wisely used. That was a purpose of the staff
loan committee. Representatives of the Bank sit on opposite sides of the
table from representatives of the borrowing government. The one executive director who does not speak when the proposed loan is finally submitted to the board for approval is the executive director for the borrowing country.34 The Bank was full of expressions like *arm's length*. Friedman
deplored this. "You're damn right I don't want to deal with countries at
arm's length. I want to be sitting in their laps or side by side."35

What Friedman seemed to be proposing, in effect, was that the Bank
should be ready to extend long-term loans that would not only contribute
to, but optimize, a nation's development, given all the externalities involved. This would have raised all the issues of absorptive capacity and
creditworthiness—within the context of sensible fiscal and monetary policies—but would have required a crystal ball of unimaginable clarity. Perhaps this is greatly to overstate Friedman's realistic aspirations, though he
was on record as proposing to move in that general direction so that the

Bank could be transformed from a bank into a development, or a development-assistance, agency. (Actually, it was George Woods who used the words *development assistance agency;* Friedman suggested *development finance agency.*)

Friedman argued, "You could not offer advice without a willingness to share the responsibility for what was going on in the country. The moment you are an adviser, you can't step away and say, 'This is not my responsibility; I deal at arm's length with the country.' That is why the difference in viewpoint is a very profound one. This is not a minor thing.

"My feeling was that if you undertook to advise a country, and if they followed your advice, you had the responsibility of trying to find the development capital. . . . One of my earliest recommendations to George Woods was that we ought to have consulting groups for at least 25–30 countries. . . . If you think the development program is reasonably good and you have accepted an advisory role with the program, . . . you go out and advocate on behalf of the country; you provide the manpower and the studies for this kind of work."[36]

Friedman persisted until he had arranged annual reviews for all of the borrowing member countries. "As long as you start talking to countries about their development programs and policies and advise them on policy, by heavens you are a development agency. You would find yourself being an adviser to the whole world, not only to the country but to every financial agency assisting, and eventually also to the private sector. The private sector would start looking to [the Bank] because [the Bank] would know a lot more about the country than anyone else outside of the country itself, and they would regard [the Bank] as more objective than themselves, just as the commercial banks of the world look to the Fund. Just as the Fund had a judgement on a short-run balance-of-payments, the world would begin looking to the [World] Bank as being the development agency. . . . Woods just loved it. He said, 'Oh, this is exactly it.' He just raved really at that time."[37]

From annual reviews of the borrowing countries, Friedman went on to a proposal that was more controversial. It was called the supplementary finance scheme. It involved the World Bank's ensuring that a country would have access to sufficient investment funds to carry out its development program even if, for some reason for which the country was not responsible, it had an unforeseen decline in its available investment resources. It would have done for the World Bank something similar to the compensatory finance facility of the IMF in the area of short-term finance.[38] In the 1960s, however, there was a basic difference between compensatory and supplementary finance.

Compensatory finance is based on the notion that countries can get into balance-of-payments difficulties in the short run, but the difficulties will be offset by surpluses, generated if necessary by currency devaluation, in the longer run. Compensatory finance is about export earnings. The Fund computes normal export earnings by a statistical formula. When the country's earnings fall below this norm, the country is eligible to draw on the Fund. Supplementary finance, on the other hand, would have included a plan on how the investment program was to be financed—from loans or aid from external sources, and how much of this was to come from the Bank or IDA. Then, if the country was not at fault (because of a crop failure, a mine cave-in, the loss of a foreign market, or an external loan failing to be made for some reason external to the country), the Bank would pick up the slack—probably by financing some other project included in the original overall program.

It is perfectly possible that a country might have been eligible for one form of finance and not the other. It would have been difficult at times to evaluate the reasons why the country needed additional funds to carry out its investment program, but it would not have been impossible. In a sense, the ultimate question involved the implementation of IDA itself. What are the normal flows of development assistance? How should external assistance be allocated among countries? Before a country could have been judged eligible for supplemental financing, however, there would have had to be agreement about the development program being insured.

The supplementary finance suggestion originated in the United Nations Committee on Trade and Development (UNCTAD) in 1964, the year Friedman joined the Bank. It was offered by the British. The Bank was asked to examine the merits of the idea and then, if they thought it worthwhile, to come up with a proposal to implement it. It was one of Friedman's first assignments, and he tackled it with vigor. For a year or so, he spent at least 30 percent of his time on supplementary finance, much of it defending his scheme against critics.[39]

One of the most dogmatic opponents was Marcus Fleming, who represented the Fund in UNCTAD. Fleming denounced supplementary finance on the grounds that it was no business of the World Bank. The World Bank was not supposed to advise on monetary, fiscal, and exchange rate policy. That was for the Fund. He asked why Friedman, who had had a good deal to do with the compensatory finance facility, was now doing things that were going to undercut the Fund and weaken its influence. At one point, Frank Southard, the deputy managing director of the Fund, called Friedman and accused him of betraying the Fund. "You used to be one of its strong advocates, and now you're trying to build up the Bank through supplementary finance." Friedman replied, "If the Fund feels so strongly, why don't they increase compensatory financing and try to make compensatory financing an adequate substitute for supplementary finance?"[40]

Friedman argued strongly that his supplementary finance scheme was a proper function of the Bank and was not competitive with the Fund.

The time needed by a developing country to repurchase from the IMF (unless it borrowed new funds to repay the IMF) was often much more than three to five years. Projections involved a developing country's strategy, planning an investment program for some years, the lifetime of projects, and so on.

The Germans suggested that projects be done jointly by the Bank *and* the Fund. The country assessment would be a joint activity conducted from both the short-term monetary and the long-run development point of view. The Bank quickly accepted this suggestion, but the Fund continued to insist that the Bank should have no role in compensatory *or* supplementary finance.[41]

There were many Bank and UNCTAD meetings on this subject over the four years following 1964. The Scandinavians, Germans, British, and Swiss became strong supporters. A majority in UNCTAD, both of the developed and the developing countries, supported it. The French held back, primarily because they favored international commodity agreements as a way of dealing with fluctuations in export earnings, and they influenced the former French colonies in Africa. Those countries eventually came around, however. Only the United States, the IMF, and some senior people in the Bank held back.

Anthony Solomon, who was assistant secretary of state for economic affairs, was influenced by an economic argument of Professor Mason's: it is good to have volatility in the export earnings of developing countries, for that means that the market mechanism is working. Shortfalls in export earnings indicate that the wrong investments have been made or that countries will have to adjust to changes in the terms of trade. Within the World Bank itself, it was argued that the supplementary finance scheme was a threat to project lending and evaluation; it would lead to program or balance-of-payments lending. Some senior staff were fearful that funds to offset shortfalls in export earnings would have to be raised in lieu of normal project loans. Friedman tried to suggest that this was an argument for increased IDA, rather than Bank, lending. George Woods favored the supplementary finance scheme precisely because it provided an additional reason for increasing the scope of IDA. It was discussed by the development assistance committee in Paris, and the conclusion there was that if supplementary finance would only result in a diversion of resources already available to developing countries, it was not worth setting up a new mechanism. The ultimate question was: Would governments put up new, additional resources to fund supplementary finance? The answer seemed to be no, and that killed it.

Meanwhile, George Woods was reversing his earlier position on IDA. In 1963, he had indicated that he would remain passive about the size of IDA: he would administer IDA to the best of his ability but would not lobby the industrial, wealthier countries for contributions. That changed after Douglas Dillon stepped down as treasury secretary in April 1965, to be succeeded by Henry Fowler.[42] Under Eisenhower in 1959, Secretary of the Treasury George Humphrey negotiated the original funding for IDA. Under Kennedy, Douglas Dillon led the negotiations for the first replenishment, due to begin in 1964. But Secretary Fowler asked Woods to negotiate the second replenishment because the United States was in balance-of-payments difficulties as a result of the large outflow of capital that put the dollar under downward pressure, even though the United States still had a trade and current-account surplus. To give an example in illustration of the situation, the United States was in the midst of discussions about Roosa bonds, which would have raised dollars in Europe.

Woods agreed to undertake the second replenishment due to begin in 1967, recognizing that it was a new function for the president of the Bank to go around cap in hand, so to speak. Woods gave Friedman the task of determining how much IDA should seek. Friedman was already at work on his supplementary finance scheme, but the approaches dovetailed nicely. It was a natural transition from discussions of shortfalls in projected investment resources to the question: What ought to be the normal flows of development assistance?

There were all sorts of estimates. The OECD had a figure, the UN had a figure. The figures varied all the way up to $10 billion a year. Friedman hit on a new approach:[43] he would ask the Bank's country economists to estimate how much more capital the developing countries could usefully use if they could borrow for fifty years at zero percent interest. Basically he was asking about the rate at which the less-developed countries (LDCs) could absorb (usefully use) capital. He was asking people with a great deal of experience in the field. He was eschewing models that depended on capital-output ratios and import elasticities, about which academic economists could only conjecture.[44]

Friedman questioned the country economists in the Bank and then took the answers to the corresponding desk officers in the Fund. Collectively, they came up with a figure of $3–4 billion a year *more* (in 1965 dollars), at least half of which, they felt, should be concessional (IDA-type) money. Friedman suggested to Woods that they seek half of that amount, leaving a billion dollars for other concessionary lenders to finance—whether it was the regional banks, such as the Inter-American Bank, or national programs. Woods never really expected to get a billion dollars a year in IDA money, but he and Friedman wanted to establish that the size of the problem of concessional aid was $1 billion. They particularly wanted to make it clear that $250 million a year was too little.

This intellectual debate about the overall $1 billion need for concessionary aid occurred in 1965–1966.[45] During the Black years, the stance of the Bank and of all the major high-income countries was that the Bank was lending as much as the LDCs could usefully use—that absorptive capacity was the ultimate constraint on lending. Under Woods, the Bank Group said that a great deal more could be done if more good projects could be identified, *particularly if they could be financed by IDA*. Woods changed the thinking in the Bank; he ultimately changed the thinking of the major donor nations. It was probably his most important victory. It was certainly a major paradigm change.

That Woods did not consult with member governments about the $1 billion figure resulted in a furor. That was deliberate. The first time the governors of the Bank read about it was in a letter from George Woods. Many of them never forgave Woods. They felt he was putting them on the spot. But that is exactly why he did it. He wanted to put them on the spot. He had confidence in his economic team and he believed in IDA. Still, the memory of some governors' resentment was still fresh a decade later.

After the $1 billion figure was announced, Woods asked the British chancellor of the exchequer and the German minister of finance if he should go to Europe to talk about IDA replenishment. They all replied without hesitation, "Don't come to see us until you can tell us what Joe [Henry Fowler, secretary of the treasury] thinks; unless we know what Joe thinks, it doesn't do any of us any good to talk to you."[46] Woods went to see Fowler, who said, "I will give you the earliest possible reply." But Fowler became ill and had to have an operation. His work began to pile up and the Treasury Department delayed answering Woods's question for at least six months. Woods, meanwhile, was becoming more and more agitated.

By the time Woods and Friedman went to Europe, the ministers said, "How come you waited for the Americans? Why didn't you come to see us earlier? You are an American-dominated institution." Woods was, of course, eager to get on with the negotiations. Nothing occupied his mind in the same way as did the IDA replenishment. At that time (1965–1966), Woods was devoting 90 percent of his energies to IDA. He told Friedman, "Irving, what I want to succeed in doing as president is to see that IDA becomes more important than the World Bank. There is no future in the World Bank Group unless IDA becomes more important than conventional lending." IDA replenishment was for him the central theme —the mission he had as president of the World Bank. But the replenishment got caught up in international politics.

The U.S. basic balance-of-payments deficit continued in spite of predictions by economists from the Brookings Institution that higher inflation rates in Europe would gradually ease the downward pressure on the dollar (exchange rates were fixed at the time). The Europeans, the Germans in particular, were running a large export surplus and were obliged by the articles of agreement of the IMF to support the dollar through purchases by the Bundesbank, the German central bank, of dollars in ever larger amounts. The central bank of France was also obliged to buy dollars, though it was then exchanging "surplus" dollars for gold at $35 an ounce, gradually reducing the stock of gold held by the U.S. Treasury. Meanwhile, enthusiasm in the United States for foreign aid of any kind, multinational or bilateral, was waning. John F. Kennedy had been assassinated and a new team was in the White House. Civil rights and the poverty program occupied center stage in the U.S. political consciousness. The Vietnam War would follow. George Woods could hardly have chosen a worse time to propose that the second replenishment of IDA should be increased from $200 million to $1 billion a year.

The Treasury Department accepted Friedman's country-by-country analysis of the need for an increase of that magnitude, but it had to find a way to sell the increase to Congress. The Treasury came up with the idea of a balance-of-payments "safeguard," meaning, in effect, that IDA funding be tied to exports. The articles of agreement of the World Bank (and therefore of IDA) specified that loans could not be tied to the exports of any country, but that had not hitherto been a problem for the Bank: U.S. exports, purchased through Bank loans (as Bank procurement figures showed) traditionally had exceeded the U.S. dollar contribution to the Bank. IDA looked like a different story, however. The United States was projected to contribute 40 percent or so to IDA, while U.S. exports looked as if they would amount to only 20–25 percent as a direct result of IDA. This troubled the Treasury Department; and it would trouble Congress even more. The Congress was prepared to be generous so long as jobs were created, or appeared to be created, but if money were sent overseas without inducing a corresponding outward flow of goods, that was bad.[47]

At first the Treasury blatantly sought to tie IDA lending to exports. While Friedman was away for a few days in Princeton, Livingston Merchant, the executive director for the United States, and Richard Demuth came up with a new (read *old*) proposal on the balance-of-payments aspects of the second IDA replenishment. The proposal was that the United States would agree to contribute its "fair" share (40 percent) to IDA, but the funds would be in two pools. If the exports of U.S. goods were not as great as the IDA contribution, the remaining funds would not be used. Since it was predicted that the U.S. exports from IDA funding would amount to only 20–25 percent of the total, this would have amounted to a huge reduction in the U.S. contribution. Furthermore, it would have tied the U.S. contribution to the exports of U.S. goods in clear violation of the articles of agreement of the Bank and IDA.[48]

After it was pointed out to Woods that such a procedure would violate the spirit, and probably the letter, of the articles of agreement, he was terribly disturbed. "I don't think he ever forgave Demuth that incident, because he didn't know about balance of payments, and it never occurred to him that anyone, knowing his strong views about untied aid, would maneuver him into such a position."[49]

In the meantime, the word had gone back to the Treasury that George Woods had agreed with the two-pools approach. Fowler and the people who were handling congressional relations were terribly pleased. They immediately ran with the ball and started to talk to people about this new approach. Some of it leaked to other countries. The first reaction the Bank got from abroad was that no one in the Bank would dare to have a meeting on IDA replenishment if he came up with this tied-loan proposal. It would be regarded as sheer chicanery. But Friedman worked out a modification of the two-pools approach: to the extent that the U.S. share was not offset by exports, it would be used later than the other contributions; and the Bank would not seek a third replenishment until all the funds of the second replenishment had been used.[50]

The French, having known about the original U.S. proposal, said that the new proposal was a fake. You have no intention of using the last portion, they said. When you get to that portion, we will be told that it is a burden on the U.S. balance of payments, and, in one way or another, the funds will be frozen. At the meeting in Paris when the Bank first proposed the two-pools, balance-of-payments solution, the French attacked the United States on the grounds that this was only a disguised way of reducing the U.S. contribution. Burke Knapp and Irving Friedman were leading the Bank delegation at the time, and the French charged that the Bank was just playing the U.S. game.[51]

It should, perhaps, be added that France and the United States had disagreed about much of international monetary policy ever since General de Gaulle had become president of France in 1958. De Gaulle's financial adviser, Jacques Rueff, believed fervently in restoring an international gold standard and opposed such things as special drawing rights on the International Monetary Fund. Rueff was opposed to inflation and sought to force the United States to deflate by getting the French to buy gold from the United States whenever French dollar reserves permitted. Rueff wanted the United States to have balance-of-payments problems; he wanted to discipline the United States. In 1971, with the Smithsonian accord, President Nixon finally succeeded in inducing Japan and the Europeans to increase the value of their currencies so as to reduce the prices foreigners had to pay for U.S. exports, but inflation continued in the United States, and in 1973 the dollar was set free to float.[52]

The point was that the Congress and the Treasury were concerned that IDA was not paying its way through exports. At one time, in 1966, the U.S. capital market was effectively closed by the Treasury to new sales of World Bank bonds. The Treasury urged the Bank to look elsewhere for funds to borrow. In 1963 and 1964, George Woods refused to allow the past earnings (reserves) of the Bank to be used to finance IDA. If this were done, Woods claimed, we were likely to educate congressmen to the idea that, if the United States did not contribute its fair share to IDA, the Bank could simply bail out IDA by using past earnings. Woods later changed his mind, but relations between Woods, on the one hand, and Congress and the Treasury Department, on the other hand, remained strained.[53]

It would have been understandable had Woods felt that he had fallen into a snake pit. The United States, which had been enthusiastic about IDA in the late 1950s, was reversing its position in the 1960s because of balance-of-payments problems—an area Woods understood only imperfectly. Woods began his tenure as president of the World Bank with high hopes that he could significantly increase IDA lending by identifying projects that would improve the creditworthiness of the World Bank Group, and his natural ally, the United States, was turning against him. Furthermore, largely because of the problems of the forthcoming second replenishment, the executive directors were stirring restlessly. They insisted on longer meetings and were asking more questions. Ralph Hirshtritt, who had been alternate executive director for the United States in 1964–1965, observed some years later: "I don't think Woods . . . took seriously the fact that the US was not going to participate unless it got balance-of-payments safeguards."[54] But Woods (and Friedman) persisted.

It is now impossible to know the extent to which Woods was acting alone on the IDA replenishment issue and the extent to which he was following the advice of Irving Friedman. Both men had strong, aggressive personalities. Both had visions of what the Bank should be. Both were ambitious and a bit stubborn. Without a college education, Woods had risen to the top of the First Boston Corporation and then to the presidency of the World Bank, a position that would not have attracted most investment bankers. Friedman had quickly risen to the highest levels in the International Monetary Fund. Both men were brilliant, but they were essentially loners: neither had close friends or allies, at least in the World Bank. Like Richard Demuth, both were idea men, but both had difficulty in translating ideas into political action.

Woods went outside the Bank to find his economic adviser. He could have turned to John de Wilde, Dragoslav Avramovic, John Adler, or Andrew Kamarck, but they probably would have remained economic advisers to Geoffrey Wilson, Simon Aldewereld, or Burke Knapp. They might not have been aggressive in enunciating new, independent proposals. Woods probably also wanted as his economic adviser a person with whom he felt comfortable in conversations about technical matters. Friedman himself commented, "I managed to explain things to Woods in such a way that he did not feel he was a nincompoop because he didn't know the Two-Pools Theory."[55]

"I suspect there were other people in the Bank who had that facility, but I had it. I would have thought that Jerry Alter could have done the job. I would have thought that Andy Kamarck could have done the job. [Woods] was not that interested in how I managed the economic work and staff. That became a primary concern of McNamara, but not of Woods. He was interested in the economic committee and what it did. He was a stalwart supporter of it, but I don't think he ever asked detailed questions about its organization."[56]

In our conversations, Friedman spoke at length about his discussions with Woods. "I really had a tremendous amount of freedom of action and a tremendous feeling of support which everyone in the Bank recognized," he said. "They always knew, if they were dealing with me, that they were dealing with someone who, in the end, the president was going to support if I made an issue of it. The organizational techniques, the structures, the management methodology seemed to be something he didn't care much about. He was more interested in my views about substance. For example, he would have long discussions with me about inflation, though I never succeeded in getting him to put some paragraphs in his annual speeches on inflation (this was in the '60s): how inflation was going to become a great menace to economic and social development. . . . [But he] loved to talk about it. He loved to chat about absorptive capacity and development strategy pricing. He thought this was fascinating stuff."[57]

About his difficulties, Friedman was candid. "In front of Woods, people, who simply refused to cooperate or collaborate in practice, would never disagree with anything that had to do with me. Then when it came to implementation, they simply refused to collaborate," he said.

"I didn't want to seem as someone who was trying to build an empire consisting of things that already existed. My job was to innovate and bring about a new dimension in the Bank. I was very empire building in that regard."[58]

Kamarck said: "Irving was responsible for the relationship with the president and defending the economics complex against the rest of the Bank. He contributed strategic ideas to what the economics department and what the Bank should do. He was there not simply as the economic adviser to the president, but as a person whose job it was to look after the economic work of the Bank. When Woods brought him to the Bank, the role he wanted Irving to consider was advising Woods on what the Bank as a whole was doing outside of the economics complex: the strategy, the policy of the Bank as a whole. This was something that Irving was very good at, and this was very important to Woods."[59]

"The idea of thinking in terms of billions of dollars a year [for IDA] came from George Woods, and when it first came forth, it was regarded with horror. . . . But, over the years, IDA did become a multi-billion-dollar agency. This came out of the Woods era. Irving had a big role in that, and that is over and beyond what the economics complex had to do."[60]

In its way, however, India was to provide Woods with an even greater challenge.

Notes

1. See Robert W. Oliver, "A Conversation With Irving S. Friedman, I," *Conversations About George Woods and the World Bank*, Washington, D.C., March 1974, p. 29.

2. See Edward S. Mason, et al., *The Economic Development of Uganda* (Baltimore: published from the International Bank for Reconstruction and Development by the Johns Hopkins Press, 1962). Mason prepared a ten-page, single-spaced memorandum dated December 16, 1964, to George Woods and Geoffrey Wilson entitled, "Some Thoughts on the Economic Work of the Bank." His memo addressed seven specific propositions: the Bank is not getting top-quality candidates from leading graduate schools in the United States; economists in the Bank quickly lose contact with, and standing in, the economics profession; career opportunities for economists are unnecessarily narrow; communication among economists in the Bank is difficult; a special effort is needed in the Bank to address the central problems of development; the Bank is badly understaffed with economists; and the mission of the economics department is unclear.

In elaboration of these points, Mason (p. 6) mentioned, inter alia, that "the establishment of IDA carried with it the strong implication that if a country is incapable of servicing additional debt, the Bank has an obligation to find out why this is so and to assist the country in overcoming its difficulties. To overcome difficulties frequently means changing policies and institutions and the Bank may find itself in the position of using what leverage it has to bring these changes about." Mason also argued that, "The establishment of consultative groups tends to place the Bank in the position of expert adviser to other providers of development financing and such advice to be effective requires a careful assessment of development priorities."

3. Irving Friedman received his doctorate in international relations from Columbia University in 1940. He had written his dissertation about China, but went to work for the government of India's trade commission in New York under Sader Singh Malik, a Sikh who was in the civil service and later became the first Indian ambassador to France. Malik was one of the very few recipients of the Victoria Cross, an internationally seeded golf and tennis player, and winner of a double first at Balliol College, Oxford. He adopted Friedman as a sort of younger brother. From 1941 to 1946, Friedman served in the division of monetary research of the U.S. Treasury Department. In the war years, Friedman headed the Treasury's Asian division of monetary research. He joked that they must have asked him because he knew the difference between Calcutta and Bombay! He worked on sterling balances and was sent on a lengthy mission to China and India during the war.

Soon after the Bretton Woods Conference, Friedman went to the International Monetary Fund and served briefly under Edward M. Bernstein in the research or economics department. He was close to people like B. K. Nehru and I. G. Patel of India and Mohamed Shoaib, who later became Pakistan's minister of finance and then a vice-president of the World Bank. He was chief of the Canada division of the IMF from 1946 to 1948 and policy assistant to the managing director from 1948 to 1950. Largely because of his experience with sterling balances, in 1950 Friedman became director of the new exchange restrictions department, a post he held until Woods contacted him in June 1964.

Consulting his friend, Anjaria, the executive director in the Fund for India, about going to the World Bank, Friedman remarked, "If I take this job, I'll be able to bring about closer relations between the Fund and the Bank." Anjaria bent his head as if he were reading something very near to the table. He shook his head dolefully and said, "The one thing we don't want is cooperation between the Fund and the Bank. We in India can only survive because the Fund and the Bank do not cooperate with each other." Friedman did not know what he meant until he saw the differences between the two institutions. Then he understood what it meant to be an Indian able to walk from one building to the other to try to get support for a proposal that the other thought was impossible.

In 1970, during McNamara's Bank presidency, Friedman was succeeded by Hollis Chenery, a noted international economist who had been at Harvard University before becoming a senior economist and adviser to the Agency for International Development. After a year's sabbatical at Yale University and Oxford, Friedman returned to lecture briefly in the Economic Development Institute before moving to Citibank where he became a senior vice-president and senior adviser for international operations.

Friedman died of a heart attack on his way to the hospital on November 20, 1989. He was seventy-four.

4. Alec Cairncross, who had helped to establish the Economic Development Institute in the Bank and who, in 1964, was the economic adviser to the British Treasury, was approached by Woods as a possible alternative to Friedman, but Cairncross was unavailable. See Friedman, II, New York City, June 21, 1985, p. 12.

5. The articles of agreement of the IMF and the International Bank for Reconstruction and Development (IBRD, or World Bank) were drafted at the conference held in Bretton Woods, New Hampshire, during July 1944. The Fund was designed originally to make short-term loans to countries having temporary balance-of-payments problems. A pool of currencies and some gold were contributed (subscribed) by the member countries in accordance with quotas based on the volume of foreign trade and national incomes of each country. In the case of countries having fundamental (long-term) balance-of-payments problems, the required remedies were a decrease in aggregate national demand, typically through lower public spending, and/or devaluation of the currency. Because of the devaluation of the dollar and the oil crisis of the 1970s, the Fund has been altered somewhat. See "Sisters in the Wood," a survey of the IMF and the World Bank, *Economist,* October 12, 1991, pp. 56ff. See also Robert W. Oliver, *International Economic Cooperation and the World Bank* (London: Macmillan, 1975).

The Fund and the Bank evolved differently. From the moment that John J. McCloy agreed to accept the presidency of the Bank only under the condition that he be allowed to run the Bank in the tradition of U.S. business, the executive directors of the Bank became less important than their counterparts in the Fund. It was only under Woods that the executive directors began seriously to question Bank policy. It was particularly true in the days of McCloy and Black, but it remains somewhat true today that, in the Fund, the executive directors constitute a forum for discussions of international monetary problems. The board may ask for the recommendations of the staff. The managing director may urge in turn that a staff recommendation be changed, but he primarily acts as a bridge between the staff and the board. His responsibility is only to select the staff. He is responsible for the calibre of the work and the integrity of the people but not for their specific recommendations. In the Bank, on the other hand, the president of the Bank gives the line to his staff. His staff are his principal lieutenants and his principal advisers. The leadership of the Bank is a presidential-type leadership. There is a high premium for agreeing with the president of the Bank. Under Black, many in the Bank wore black homburg hats because Black wore a homburg hat. In the Fund, the leadership is more collegial, both at the board and the staff level. In the Fund, Per Jacobbson, the managing director in the early 1960s, tried for three years to choose a successor to Edward Bernstein as director of the economic research department, but he could not persuade the executive directors. Jacobbson wanted an Englishman, and the executive directors did not see why it had to be an Englishman.

When Friedman first went to the Bank, he was told by Burke Knapp, "We don't bother with [the executive directors] the way you do in the Fund. We respect them, but they are not what they are in the Fund."—Friedman, V, p. 19. See also Friedman, I, pp. 2ff; and Friedman, IV, p. 32.

6. Friedman, III, Washington, D.C., July 15, 1985, p. 6. Years later, after Friedman had become a senior vice-president at Citicorp, Friedman asked his close friend Andrew Overby if he had recommended him (Friedman) for the job of Woods's chief economist. (Overby was then employed by First Boston, but he had been deputy managing director of the IMF under Camille Gutt and Per Jacobbson.) Overby told him, "George called me up one day and said, 'I'm going to ask Irving Friedman to come over and talk about this. What do you think of the man?' Of course, I recommended you, but the suggestion didn't come from me. I don't know where it came from."—Friedman, II, p. 11.

Friedman was influenced in his decision to take the job by his college-age daughter Barbara, who asked, "Dad, do you really want to spend all your life just helping the richer countries of the world rather than the poorer countries? Don't you think it would be nice if you would spend some of your time helping the poorer countries?"—Friedman, I, p. 25.

7. According to Richard Demuth, "Irving [Friedman] was [Woods's] one effective appointment as a senior officer, and so he backed him because Irving was his man. Whether he thought Irving was right or wrong, he backed him."—Robert W. Oliver, "A Conversation with Richard H. Demuth," *Conversations About George Woods and the World Bank*, Washington, D.C., July 18, 1985, p. 2.

8. Friedman, I, p. 20. See also Friedman, III, pp. 9–12.

9. Friedman, IV, Washington, D.C., July 22, 1985, p. 4. According to Andrew Kamarck, "The Bank was a bit of a closed shop. Practically all the senior people were people who had come up in the Bank. At various times in the earlier history of the Bank, people were brought in at a high level and almost invariably this had failed. . . . Either they didn't have the experience or the judgment or whatever it was to live up to the Bank, and there was a tendency on the part of the Bank people to gang up against the outsider. You had that very strong element in the Bank, and Irving ran into it almost immediately.

"Then there is the fact that Irving came from the Fund, and relationships between the Bank and the Fund are not all that good most of the time. There are exceptions, but most of the Bank people don't think much of the Fund people, and most of the Fund people don't think much of the Bank people. . . . Consequently, when Irving came, he came into an environment in which people were not going to go out of their way to cooperate with him. In fact, if they could do it without too much harm to themselves, they were going to do their best to do him in.

There is no question about that."—Robert W. Oliver, "A Conversation with Andrew Kamarck, I," *Conversations About George Woods and the World Bank*, New York City, November 2, 1985, pp. 14–15.

10. Friedman, II, p. 2.

11. Friedman, I, p. 30. Ironically, much the same thing was said about Friedman's management style. "Irving was a terrible administrator," reported Andrew Kamarck. "Irving is very creative. Like George Woods, he has a creative mind. He's an innovator. He's not afraid to kick over apple-carts. It doesn't bother him to come up with an idea that is going to completely disrupt all the existing work and change everybody's assignments or pull them off or wreck what they are doing if there is something he thinks is important to be done. All of this is very valuable, but you need somebody alongside of somebody like that to hold the organization together."—Kamarck, I, p. 17.

12. Friedman, I, p. 10.

13. According to Andrew Kamarck, "Eddie Bernstein, who had been head of the research department, and Irving were involved in an early fight in the Fund. I think Irving was absolutely on the right side. Bernstein represented, more or less, the British point of view, whereas Irving, with the help of Andy Overby, represented the American. The British and Bernstein's point of view was, more or less, that the Fund was there for a country to draw on whenever it felt it needed it; whereas Irving and Andy Overby's point of view—the U.S. Treasury's point of view most of the time—was that the Fund was there to provide resources, yes, but it was also there to improve the performance of the borrowing country—so that aid should be conditional."—Kamarck, I, p. 17. This early fight left bruises. When Frank Southard became deputy managing director of the Fund, for example, he let it be known that the Fund was not unhappy to see Friedman go to the Bank.

14. Friedman, I, p. 12.

15. Avramovic was with the Yugoslavian Ministry of Finance from mid-1948 until 1951 when he went to a university and then to the economics department of the World Bank. Martin Rosen, then an economist with the World Bank, was with Avramovic in Yugoslavia in 1948 when Stalin's tanks confronted Tito's tanks. Unbeknown to Stalin, Tito's tanks were out of gas, a fact that Rosen quickly reported to the Bank. A loan was hastily arranged.

16. George Woods liked Avramovic. Avramovic had helped to inspire Woods's first annual speech. But Avramovic was too mercurial. At one point in 1968, Avramovic quarreled vociferously with Friedman in a corridor within earshot of Robert McNamara. McNamara virtually ordered Friedman to fire Avramovic. Friedman refused, but McNamara was never cordial to Avramovic thereafter. Avramovic left the Bank in January 1978.

17. Friedman, I, pp. 23–24. In 1963, the Bank division with the greatest number of economists was the transportation division of the projects department.

18. Kamarck had gone to the Federal Reserve Board from Harvard University, where he graduated summa cum laude and received his Ph.D., and was borrowed by the Treasury Department. At Treasury, he served with Harry White, assistant secretary of the treasury and a principal author, with John Maynard Keynes, of the Bretton Woods agreements. Kamarck knew Irving Friedman in the Treasury and Burke Knapp at the Federal Reserve Board. After serving in Italy and Germany in allied control commissions during World War II, Kamarck returned to Treasury and became head of staff and chairman of the interdepartmental staff committee for the cabinet-level National Advisory Council. In 1948, he returned to Rome as U.S. Treasury representative and head of the finance division of the Marshall

Plan mission. In 1950, he joined the Bank at Burke Knapp's urging. In the 1952 reorganization, he became economic adviser to the department of Europe, Africa, and Australasia. When the Africa department was formed in 1962, he became economic adviser to that department. When Woods called in 1965 to ask Kamarck to return to the Bank as chairman of the economics department—the job had previously been referred to as head of the economic staff—he was at UCLA on leave as a Regents Professor. Kamarck accepted Woods's invitation.

19. See "Trends and Outlook in Development Finance," in the 1964/65 annual report for the World Bank and IDA, pp. 52–63.

20. Robert W. Oliver, "A Conversation with J. Burke Knapp," *Conversations About George Woods and the World Bank*, Portola Valley, California, September 5, 1986, p. 3.

21. Ibid., p. 4. Knapp felt that the 1960s could be thought of as the economic phase after it had moved out of the project infrastructure phase of the Bank's history. He also felt that the economic phase was a natural, organic evolution and would have occurred regardless of who was president of the Bank. Kamarck, too, recounted how analytical work devolved to area departments. He wrote:
"The main meaningful economic work was done in the area and projects departments. The residual economic staff [not economics department] did useful work, but it was minute compared to the whole. For example, in the early years of the Bank the determining creditworthiness assessment was of *dollar* creditworthiness. We looked at the ability of a country to earn dollars to determine whether it could receive a loan and the magnitude of acceptable lending to the country. The decision of the Bank to abandon this approach and instead look at the total balance of payments was made in the economic committee based on a memorandum I wrote as economic adviser to the Europe, Africa, Australasia department. Because we economic advisers thought this was good sense, the rest of the Bank went along with it. The economic staff had little input other than one vote in the staff loan committee."—Personal correspondence, February 13, 1990.

22. Friedman, II, p. 24.

23. One of the first things that McNamara did when he became president was to abolish the economic committee. In its place he substituted a program review committee that sought to project lending for several years ahead—rather like the program Friedman had proposed in his supplementary finance scheme. See later in this chapter.

24. Kamarck, I, p. 16.

25. Friedman, II, p. 31.

26. For his part, Burke Knapp never attended a meeting of the economic committee.

27. Kamarck has commented: "As head of the economics department I was a member of the loan committee, and I did attend its meetings. Sometimes it was an uneasy experience. Sometimes when Cope was chairing the meeting when Knapp was away, he would try to get me to raise an economic issue for the loan committee to discuss and decide. At times, I would be asked to brief the meeting on what the economic committee had discussed, although it was more the responsibility of the area department director to have taken this into consideration. At such times, I had to be very careful how I worded what I said. If I said anything that sounded like loan operations decisions, Cope would try to make an issue of it. Knapp was always very fair and the other area department directors, including Cargill most of the time, were no real problem or were even helpful."—Personal correspondence, February 13, 1990.

28. Friedman, III, p. 22.

29. Ibid., pp. 26ff. Kamarck has written (personal correspondence): "In the Chronology in the Mason-Asher book on the Bank that includes some fairly trivial items, the creation of the new economics department and my appointment as director are left out." Neither Irving Friedman nor Andrew Kamarck is mentioned in Edward S. Mason and Robert E. Asher, *The World Bank Since Bretton Woods* (Washington, D.C.: Brookings Institution, 1973).

30. Friedman may not have been aware of an earlier statement in the Bank staff's *The World Bank, Policies and Operations* (Washington, D.C.: International Bank for Reconstruction and Development, 1960), pp. 35–36: "The Assessment of repayment prospects involves an exercise of judgment after consideration of a multitude of factors. The availability of natural resources and the existing productive plant within the country are the obvious starting points, but equally important is the capacity of the country concerned to exploit its resources and operate its productive facilities effectively. The judgment required therefore involves, among other things, an evaluation of the effectiveness of the government administration and of the business community, the availability of managerial, supervisory and technical skills, the scale and character of investment, and the economic and financial policies which are likely to be followed, particularly as they affect the level of domestic savings, the flow of foreign private capital, and the economic and financial policies which are likely to be followed. The probable impact of all these factors upon the country's future balance of payments must then be assessed in the light of such considerations as the likely prospects for the country's principal exports and imports and the effect of population increases.

"But creditworthiness is not determined by economic forces alone; within fairly wide limits it is determined, also, by the intangible factor of the country's attitude towards its foreign debts. A country which shows a willingness to maintain debt service at the expense, if necessary, of sacrifices in consumption standards is plainly a better credit risk than a country, even with a potentially somewhat stronger economy, which does not treat its foreign obligations with equal seriousness."

Woods and Friedman might have countered that not many of the area and project economists had the academic background needed to carry out this directive. They were too specialized. In any event, Woods wanted the economists from the area and projects departments to compare notes about creditworthiness and other economic issues with each other in the economic committee.

31. Kamarck, III, New York City, November 3, 1985, p. 1.

32. When I was in the economics department on leave from the California Institute of Technology in 1970 and 1971, Emanuel Levy and I were together on a mission to Indonesia, under the general direction of Wouter Tims, a Dutchman, an economist and an econometrician. I prepared a working paper on Djakarta, the capital city of Indonesia, for the division of urbanization, and Levy led a team of statisticians who were helping the Indonesians improve their statistics-gathering procedures. It was while I was in Indonesia that I heard the story of a person sent to one of Indonesia's outer islands to count heads and gather other simple statistics. The islanders, who only vaguely knew that they owed allegiance to the government of Indonesia, supposed that the head counter was there to get them to pay taxes, and he never returned.

33. Friedman, I, p. 17.

34. The same practice is generally followed at the staff level. Rarely is anyone permitted to go on a mission if they are a national of the country about which information is being gathered.

35. Friedman, I, p. 18.

36. Ibid., pp. 21–22. According to Friedman, the only person in the president's council who shared Woods's vision of a greatly enlarged economics staff was Richard Demuth, who also shared Woods's vision of the transformation of the Bank into a development agency. That was partly because he had had a great deal to do with IDA. "He must have done a lot of hard thinking [about] IDA and the poverty problems as against just the development problems," said Friedman (I, p. 28). As for George Woods's vision of what he hoped to accomplish at the Bank, Friedman said, "I honestly don't know where he got it." It is possible that he got at least part of it as a poor boy growing up in Brooklyn.

37. Friedman, I, p. 34.

38. In 1963, the IMF established a permanent facility to lend funds to governments of countries experiencing a temporary shortfall in export earnings for reasons largely beyond the members' control.

39. See Robert W. Oliver, "A Conversation with Ravi Gulhati," *Conversations About George Woods and the World Bank*, Washington, D.C., November 19, 1985, p. 4. See also Andrew M. Kamarck, "Development Plans and Export Earnings," *Foreign Trade Review*, Vol. 1, No. 12, July-September, 1966, pp. 123–133.

40. Friedman, IV, p. 7. At the time, the Fund was not expanding compensatory financing; shortly thereafter, however, the Fund decided on a big increase in its compensatory financing.

41. "We could never convince the Fund of the usefulness of our supplementary finance measures. On the other hand, they could never convince us that the existing IMF facility met the kind of objections that sponsors of this proposal in UNCTAD had. There was no meeting of minds in the Fund and the Bank."—Gulhati, p. 8.

42. See the "Reminiscences of Henry H. Fowler," *George D. Woods Oral History Project*, Oral History Research office, Columbia University, 1984. See also Chapter 7.

43. This was not exclusively Friedman's idea. Friedman, Barend deVries, and Kamarck spent a Sunday afternoon walking along the old canal near the Potomac talking about how to do the study. They agreed that the model approach of working out estimates of capital needs based on a few basic assumptions was not sufficiently realistic to base policy on. The way they decided to do the study (by tapping the experience and knowledge of the Bank people who worked with countries) came up in the course of the conversation.

It is also noteworthy that Robert McNamara, a few days after he became president of the World Bank, requested the president's council to give him "a list of all the projects or programs that you would wish to see the Bank carry out if there were no financial constraints."—William Clark, "Robert McNamara at the World Bank," *Foreign Affairs*, Vol. 60, No. 1, Fall 1981, p. 168.

44. A group of academic experts, including Jan Tinbergen, Hollis Chenery, and Alan Strout, had been at work in the development assistance committee of the OECD, estimating capital requirements using what came to be called the reduced minimal standard model, used by most country economists today. Chenery published his results and won the academic high-ground. The Bank study was not published but it affected policy decisions and policy orientations of all the governments concerned. So everybody won. (Chenery presented the full range of the results of applying his model. He forecast that LDC imports of capital needs would range between $6 billion and $18 billion a year for five years.)

Friedman never allowed his country-by-country study to be published. He would have had to publish project, and, therefore, growth projections for the developing countries individually, and he felt that that would be politically unwise.—Friedman, I, p. 58.

45. The economic section of the annual report of the World Bank and IDA for 1964/65, p. 62, contains the famous paragraph: "A preliminary Bank inquiry, carried out country by country and based on the judgement and experience of the Bank's country specialists and area economists, suggests that the developing countries could effectively use, on the average over the next five years, some $3 billion to $4 billion more of external capital per year than has been provided in the recent past."

In Paris, at OECD, Willard Thorp suggested to George Woods that he could agree that the $1 billion concessionary assistance of the United States be given through IDA rather than through the U.S. foreign aid program, but Woods rejected that suggestion. He wanted the U.S. concessionary aid program to be over and above the $1 billion to be raised for IDA. He insisted that bilateral concessionary aid programs should be increased, as well as IDA programs. Friedman made this clear in his reminiscences: "We were interested in getting more money for IDA," he said. "We knew that we were asking for less than what was needed and could be used."—Friedman, I, p. 58.

46. Friedman, I, p. 61.

47. This, of course, is mercantilist reasoning. From a standard-of-living point of view, it is imports rather than exports that are important. Congress would have been well advised to accept a reverse Marshall Plan, with no exports being sent abroad at all!

48. Friedman later discovered that this scheme had been suggested by Berhard Zagorin, who had been the Treasury Department's representative in India and the alternate executive director for the Bank and who was, at that time, the U.S. executive director to the Asian Development Bank. Ralph Hirshtritt, who had been the temporary alternate executive director for the United States to the World Bank from May 1964 to September 1965 when John Bullitt was executive director, commented in an interview, "We probably would have done it in a way where it wasn't contrary to the charter [articles of agreement] of IDA. We had good lawyers."—Robert W. Oliver, "A Conversation With Ralph Hirshtritt," *Conversations About George Woods and the World Bank*, Washington, D.C., November 22, 1985, p. 9.

49. Friedman, I, p. 70.

50. See Chapter 7.

51. For insight into some of the objections of other countries, see Friedman, V, Washington, D.C., July 23, 1985, pp. 22–27.

52. See Robert W. Oliver, *Bretton Woods: A Retrospective Essay*, Discussion Paper No. 105, June 1985, Santa Monica, California, California Seminar on International Security and Foreign Policy.

53. See Chapter 7. A factor that mitigated against congressional approval was that the House Banking and Finance Committee felt that too much IDA assistance was going to India. There was also some animosity toward international public servants: some feeling that they lived too well. See "A Conversation with Congressman William Stanton," *Conversations About George Woods and the World Bank*, Washington, D.C., July 16, 1986, pp. 5–6.

54. Hirshtritt, p. 10.

55. Friedman, III, p. 21.
56. Ibid.
57. Ibid., p. 23.
58. Friedman, II, pp. 33–34.
59. Kamarck, III, p. 6.
60. Ibid., p. 7.

CHAPTER 5

INDIA

Woods with Chidambram Subramaniam, minister for agriculture of India,
December 22, 1965

I f there was a developing country about which George Woods felt he
knew something, it was India. As it turned out, however, he understood
large private industries, particularly steel, better than he understood the
Indian government.

Woods sought to influence India through a thirteen-volume report on
the economy prepared under the direction of Bernard Bell, who reported
directly to Woods, and through the leverage of a consortium of North
American, European, and Japanese governments.[1] He was partially successful. To this day, though memories are fading, most Indians are critical
of Indira Gandhi for allowing the rupee to be devalued by 37 percent in
1966, as Bell had recommended,[2] and they still resist some of the other
Bell commission recommendations. Within the World Bank, on the other
hand, the Bell report is still regarded as a major and correct critique of the
policies of the government of India.

George Woods once remarked, "If the only thing I do while I am president of the Bank is to turn India around, I'll be happy."[3] Woods had a
love affair with India. He had gone there first in 1952 as a consultant to
the Bank to advise on the merger of Tata Iron and Steel and the Steel
Company of Bengal. He had returned to help the Industrial Credit and Investment Corporation of India (ICICI) in 1954 in the company of Mrs.
Woods and Mr. and Mrs. Arthur Hays Sulzberger, publishers of the *New
York Times*. They had lunch with Prime Minister Jawaharlal Nehru and
dinner with Sir Benegal and Lady Rama Rau. It was one of the Woodses'
first experiences of being entertained abroad at the highest levels of society.

Included among George Woods's personal papers is a clipping from
the *New York Times* that begins:

Once, when the Roman Empire was dying, and much of classical learn-
ing lay in ashes, and the Dark Ages were descending on the West, there
flourished on the plains of northern India not only the most civilized
culture of its time, but also one of the most creative in history.
There, under the Gupta emperors, 1,000 years before Galileo and
Kepler and Newton, Indian thinkers developed a revolutionary idea
without which modern science could not exist: the concept of mathematical zero, along with the related system of numerals that is called

127

Arabic but was, in fact invented here. By the fifth century, an Indian had discovered the earth's axial rotation. Well before the Renaissance re-illuminated Europe, Indian mathematicians had explored the upland realms of quadratic equations and cube roots, had become the first to assign 3.1416 as the value of pi, and had mastered the concept of infinity. Throughout most of history, in fact, Indian science and Indian culture generally matched and at times exceeded anything anywhere else in the world.[4]

It is not surprising that Woods was beguiled by India's teeming population, its hope for a rebirth of science and technology, its varied climate, its stunning scenery, and its people, divided by caste and dominated by mysticism and eons of tradition. But India is a big country, the more than 900 million Indians[5] are a proud people, and it is far from clear that they wanted to be turned around either by Woods's carrot or his stick.

India began its first Five Year Plan in 1951 when its reserves of foreign exchange, built largely during World War II, were ample.[6] It was supposed in 1951 that India, by the end of the fifth Five Year Plan (in 1976), would require no additional foreign assistance, but that prediction was not fulfilled. As early as 1957, large expenditures on imported machinery combined with a relative decline in the prices of India's exports drained the reserves.

Prior to the first Five Year Plan, Prime Minister Nehru invited Paul Hoffman, president of the Ford Foundation, to visit India and discuss ways in which the foundation could assist India's development. From the beginning, the Ford and Rockefeller foundations worked with the government of India, the United States government, the United Nations, and other international agencies to help India. More and more, however, the Ford Foundation sought to encourage India's agriculture, while Nehru was content to rely on Public Law 480 for food during years of drought.[7]

Jashwantrai J. Anjaria, who had been deputy chief in the Asia division of the IMF, was the chief drafter of the first Five Year Plan. Prasanta C. Mahalonobis, one of India's foremost physicists turned statistician, helped to design the second Five Year Plan, which made the development of heavy industry a primary goal. It placed little emphasis on food or exports.

In 1953, Chester Bowles had written persuasively that India was a bulwark of democracy in Asia; and in 1957 Senators John F. Kennedy and John Sherman Cooper had lobbied successfully in favor of aid to India. But Mahalonobis's plan relied more and more heavily on import licenses and price controls and less and less on the market mechanism, particularly as inflation began to be a problem in the 1960s.[8] The British had left behind a mercantilistic structure of controls and subsidies from well before World War II. They had also trained a well-entrenched bureaucracy dedicated to managing the Indian economy.[9]

By 1958, with the foreign-exchange reserves of India running low, Eugene Black helped to organize the Aid-India Consortium to review India's progress and to agree on financial assistance. The consortium was willing to consider some program (balance-of-payments) lending, in part because the Indians (like the French after the World War II) had an apparently well-conceived development plan. By 1960, however, the Indian economy was strangling in its own bureaucratic red tape. Exports were declining as a percentage of world exports,[10] growth had slowed, there was unused capacity in many industries, and, as in the Soviet Union in the late 1980s, a myriad of controls.

Into this maze, three bankers—also known as the Three Wise Men—stepped in February and March of 1960. They were Herman Abs, chairman of the Deutsche Bank of Frankfurt; Sir Oliver Franks, chairman of Lloyds Bank, London; and Allan Sproul, formerly chairman of the Federal Reserve Bank of New York. They were responding to a suggestion by Eugene Black and a resolution sponsored by Senators Kennedy and Cooper that was passed unanimously by the U.S. Senate.

Abs, Franks, and Sproul were not asked to prepare a formal report; nor was a detailed assessment possible in the time available. But they had opportunities during their visit to observe and discuss economic conditions with leading ministers of India and Pakistan. With their permission, Eugene Black decided to make the contents of their nineteen-page, single-spaced letter to him generally available as a contribution to the public discussion of economic development.[11]

The basic economic problem confronting both India and Pakistan, to paraphrase the letter, was the shortage of foreign exchange: it seemed to require strict import licensing. In both countries, development had been made more intractable by the high rate of population growth and the shortage of managerial talent. In the case of Pakistan, however, the projected emphasis on agriculture and private enterprise in the second Five Year Plan (July 1, 1960, to June 20, 1965) seemed preferable to the continuing overemphasis on heavy industry in India's third Five Year Plan (due to begin on April 1, 1961).

Unusually good harvests during the last three years of India's first Five Year Plan had helped to offset the shortfall of investment, but, though the second plan projected some increase in investment in agriculture, poor harvests followed. Budgetary difficulties had generated inflation, and private import demand had so heavily drained India's foreign-exchange resources that the investment program had to be reduced. Only emergency assistance, largely of surplus grain from the United States under Public Law 480, prevented a breakdown of the plan altogether.

India's third Five Year Plan projected an increase over five years of gross investment from $13.8 billion to $20.9 billion, and an increase in the rate of saving, public and private, from 8 to 12 percent.[12] Unpredictable monsoon conditions introduced an element of chance into these calculations, however; and price controls, the Wise Men warned, could frustrate normal market processes.

It seemed likely that, as the Indian economy moved to progressively higher states of development, new types of imports would be required. Thus, India's export base should be extended well beyond traditional exports if sustainable economic development was to be realized. Inflation might be somewhat restrained by import controls, but import controls impaired foreign exchange by diverting potential exports to domestic consumption. There would be some scope for mopping up excess liquidity by raising interest rates; the relatively low interest rates prevailing have created the illusion that capital is not a scarce resource.

Over the next five years, India needed $4.0 billion in foreign assistance to pay for projects, $1.5 billion in program (balance-of-payments) assistance, and $1.1 billion of food-supply assistance. Bilateral national aid extended by a considerable number of governments with reasonable coordination should make it possible for aid not to be tied to the exports of any particular country. Multilateral aid is the best way of getting the greatest benefit from a given volume of aid. On the other hand, countries receiving aid must recognize that the governments of aid-providing countries must satisfy their legislatures; and legislatures must be assured that the aid-receiving countries' policies are realistic. The role of private investment as a source of assistance for development must also not be forgotten or underestimated.

So ran the advice of the Three Wise Men.

During the third Five Year Plan, the Indian economy grew at a slower rate than in the previous decade. The level of Indian income increased by about 3.2 percent a year during the first three years. Indian industrial production grew at 7.5 percent a year, but agriculture, which provided more than half of India's output, hardly grew at all. The economic picture brightened in the third year of the plan (1963–1964), in large measure because of favorable monsoon rains combined with some increase in the use of fertilizer, but shortages of rain the next year brought the worst drought in half a century. Food grain production declined by 15 percent.

The Indian economy, like the Soviet economy under communism, seemed to respond to targets more than to prices. Ben King, who arrived in India in 1963 to become one of two resident representatives of the World Bank, gave a talk to the Indian Institute of Management's course on marketing and export promotion on December 11, 1963, in which he argued: "When targets are king, people are reluctant to suppose that prices have a function, as for example: on the demand side, to show how much you need of what you are producing; and, on the supply side, to show how much it is costing."[13]

Shortly thereafter, King was taken to task by an anonymous writer in India's *Economic Weekly*, under the heading "Aid and Advise." The article read:

Seventeen years after Independence and after nearly three Plans have run their course, basic questions are being raised by our aid-giving friends. . . . Not that we are witnessing a crusade of *laissez faire*. *Laissez faire* is a bad word even in the West now. The fashionable expression now is "greater use of the market mechanism." Spear-heading the ideological assault on some of the guiding principles of our planning as much as on some of our planning techniques, is the World Bank. . . .

The [World Bank's] 1963 [Annual] Report, reopened some basic issues. It spoke of the conflict between the social and economic objectives of planning. . . . The objective of balanced regional development becomes to the Bank an impediment to obtaining the highest economic returns and leads to "wasteful investments." Further, "Indian planning has tended to neglect the space dimension in economics." We are told we have no comprehensive and well-thought-out policy of industrial location. . . .

More serious is the near-intemperate attack on the system of price and production controls. The fact seems to be that the ratio of advice to aid is increasingly being weighted in favour of advice. . . .

The Bank presumably would wish to be associated in the investment decisions so that choices could be made on the basis of shadow rates of interest, shadow rates of exchange, and other equally shadowy criteria. . . .

One gets the impression that the resident representatives[14] seem to have taken a self-important attitude to their duties here; apparently they seem to have extended their functions to being more than the eyes and ears of the Bank and to have taken upon themselves the role of intimate advisers to the Government on diverse matters—be it on the improvement of our agriculture, on rationalisation of transport policy, or on the alternative economics of different projects; in short to comment on every aspect of our economy. . . .

It is for the Bank to realise that there is a line which divides criticism and advice from interference. . . . While we will take note of their views, the Fourth Plan will be a truly Indian document. What is at stake is the Indianness of our Plans.[15]

This disagreement was one of the early manifestations of a conflict between the Bank and some developing countries. As the Three Wise Men put it in 1960, however, "Countries receiving aid must recognise that the governments of aid-providing countries must satisfy their legislatures, and legislatures must be assured that aid-receiving countries' policies are realistic." Already the International Development Association (IDA) was contributing over 40 percent of its aid to India. Some executive directors were beginning to refer to IDA as the "Indian Development Association," and the Aid-India Consortium was beginning to question the rationality of the third Indian Development Plan. Ben King would have been derelict in his duties if he had remained silent about the questions he was raising. On the other hand, Prime Minister Nehru and most of

India were antagonistic to strings attached to aid, more so because the strings seemed to be directed primarily at India. It was a controversy that would grow more intense over the next several years.

In October 1963, King was writing that a sensible irrigation policy did not exist in India, and there seemed to be no suggestion of a mechanism for choosing the right railway project from among a number of alternatives. Later, he objected to the permissive way the World Bank appraised and financed projects, writing at one point: "The Bank has a great obligation to push for improved performance, sector by sector and sectionwide, rather than in terms of individual projects. . . . The real instrument for improving performance is lending policy and the conditions attached to it."

In April 1964, under the chairmanship of Dragoslav Avramovic, economists Gerald Alter, William Gilmartin, and Peter Wright met to discuss the Indian economy. Research had been done on steel, iron ore, coal, petroleum, power, ports, and transport, but they found that knowledge of these sectors was spotty. Industry was far from solid, education was superficial, and population control nonexistent. The most obvious deficiency, however, was in agriculture. Better analyses were also needed of savings and investment rates, returns to capital, resource allocation, balance of payments, and tax policy. It was suggested that twelve analytical studies were needed, for which extra staff would have to be added.

In May 1964, George Woods called Bernard Bell, whom Woods had never met, to ask if Bell would visit the Bank to see him.[16] "Things on the economic front are not going well in India," Woods said when they met. "The Aid-India Consortium is becoming rather unhappy about the Indian economic performance." Woods felt that neither the Bank nor the other aid givers knew as much about the Indian economy and its problems as it should. He wanted a mission composed largely of people not on the Bank staff to make an extended survey and asked if Bell would head the mission. Bell agreed, and Woods wrote T. T. Krishnamachari (TTK), the Indian minister of finance, in June 1964 to say,

> We are considering, and I favor, the idea of setting up a special and particularly well qualified economic study team for this purpose. If this team is to come up with its findings in time for an appraisal of the Fourth Plan Outline to be completed about a year from now, they will have to start work in India within the next few months. If this is too early from your point of view, we can postpone the commencement, but that could possibly result in complications in arranging further external assistance next year.[17]

TTK replied,

> On receipt of your letter, I have been taking counsel with my colleagues in the Planning Commission to form some assessment of the likely date

when our Fourth Plan would have the kind of shape and size which it should have before it can be usefully studied by a World Bank Mission. While many individual study groups have completed their work, we have not crystallised our ideas on the broad outlines of our Fourth Plan. Recent events in my country have, in fact, delayed consideration of many issues which must be faced before we actually come to the stage of formulating the Plan and it is our judgment that we would not be really ready for a full-fledged Mission to study the Fourth Plan before next spring.

Perhaps, a smaller Mission with *a more limited scope* on the lines of your discussion with Ambassador Nehru coming to India in October or November might be the right answer. I am asking Ambassador Nehru to discuss this matter further with you in the light of the position I have explained above.[18]

Prime Minister Jawaharlal Nehru died in April 1964. Lal Bahadur Shastri succeeded him as prime minister. Shastri was educated in India. He was a man of the soil; a man of the people. He thought like an Indian. He had no ideological commitment to Nehru's economic policies, which were consistent with the bureaucratic structure of British India and the ideology of the Congress party Nehru had led. But Shastri sought to carry out Nehru's program.

The three most important ministers whom Shastri inherited from Nehru were T. T. Krishnamachari (finance), C. Subramaniam (agriculture), and Asoka Mehta (planning). TTK had vigorously supported the third Five Year Plan, including the licensing of imports and the control over industry. When the Indo-Chinese war on the Himalayan border broke out in October 1962, TTK had advocated an increase in military expenditures and a substantially reduced allocation for the rest of the national budget. Nehru had objected: "We must have both defense, and development." In the end, only supplies of raw materials and spare parts were cut from the budget: health, education, and related sectors remained. Inflation followed, though some industries had redundant capacity.

T. T. Krishnamachari and C. Subramaniam were vigorous opponents. In addition to being an advocate for agriculture, Subramaniam was not fond of licenses and controls. Asoka Mehta tended to side with Subramaniam. So, eventually, did Shastri. But the case for agriculture was complicated by the fact that it was the United States, primarily through the Ford and Rockefeller foundations and the U.S. secretary of agriculture, Orville Freeman, who strongly supported increasing agricultural output by raising agricultural prices and building more fertilizer plants. Indians were suspicious of U.S. advice.

Shortly after Bernard Bell had drafted the terms of reference for his forthcoming study, George Woods reviewed them and said, "Among other things, you propose to look at the exchange-rate system and the appropri-

ateness of India's exchange rate. That's not our business, that's the business of the IMF. Stay away from that."[19] Bell replied that he did not think
they could; it was an integral part of the whole problem.[20] Woods suggested that they meet with Pierre Paul Schweitzer, the managing director
of the Fund. When they did, without the slightest hesitation, Schweitzer
said, "Of course the Bank mission has to go into that, amongst other
things. You have all the leverage, we have none. We'd like to hear what
the mission thinks. It's the mission's job to explore the exchange rate."[21]

Ben King later recalled that, as Woods was retiring to his room in the
Taj Mahal Hotel in Bombay in August 1964, Woods asked, "Is there anything else on your mind?" They sat in the lobby on a bench, and King explained that he had understood from colleagues in Washington that Woods
was against any discussion of the Indian exchange rate. King said, "I would
like to make the case suggesting that this is wrong." Woods looked at King
and said, "Well, I certainly hear you. You're quite right, that's what I think,
but I will hear your case." So King made the case as best he could in terms
that he thought Woods would appreciate. Woods was quite tough in his arguing, but he did concede at the end that we could "tip our hat" toward
the subject of the exchange rate to the extent necessary.[22]

The theory of devaluation as a cure for an overt or a suppressed
balance-of-payments deficit is clear enough.[23] Devaluation makes both
imports and exports more expensive in terms of domestic currencies.
Thus, there is a strong tendency for output to shift into exports and away
from imports. Depending upon the forces of foreign and domestic demand
and supply, there is a tendency for the production of exportable goods to
increase and of importable goods to decrease, because the profits to be
made in exportable goods will tend to rise; and in importable goods to fall.

Of course, price is not the only variable that may influence the volume of exports and imports, at least not in the short run. Weather conditions (drought) caused Indian agricultural output to decrease in 1965 and
1966 in spite of the relative rise in the export prices of India's agricultural
commodities (the rupee was devalued on June 6, 1966). Foreign-exchange
reserves and foreign aid temporarily enabled importers to increase the volume of imports even after import prices had risen. In the long run, the
higher relative price of exports is likely to induce a more than proportional increase in the quantity of exports (an elastic supply of exports),
and the higher relative price of imports will tend to induce a more than
proportional decrease in the quantity of imports (an elastic demand for
imports). This is particularly true for India on the export side, though
agricultural output was temporarily constrained by shortages of new seeds,
fertilizer, and irrigation water. (In the long run, of course, the potentially
useful effect on exports of a one-time-only devaluation may be offset by a
subsequent inflation of the entire domestic price level.)

Many government officials and informed intelligentsia in India were impressed by the short-run inelasticity argument that exports would not increase very much as a result of devaluation. The *Economic Journal* published an article by S. J. Patel in 1959 pointing out that exports of tea, jute, and cotton textiles, and miscellaneous items such as hides and skins, leather, coal, spices, and shellac had not increased significantly in the recent past, from which he concluded that exports in general were unlikely to increase in the future.[24] As Manubhai Shah, minister of commerce and international trade, said, "What is the sense of having a bargain sale in a department store when the shelves are bare and when the buyers only want a limited quantity of the goods anyway?"[25] In the short run, Shah was right; but, in the long run, he was wrong, as the Green Revolution has convincingly demonstrated. What was needed was the overall growth of output consistent with comparative advantage, but growth actually became negative in the final year of the third Five Year Plan.

On June 25, 1964, a paper called the *Patriot* attacked the Bank because of the proposed economy survey. A more temperate note was sounded by the *Statesman*, but when George Woods met with TTK in person on August 24, 1964, in New Delhi, he felt obliged to say that he had seen articles in the Indian press that accused the Bank of trying to meddle in matters that were the responsibility solely of the government of India. He hoped that the finance minister would use every opportunity to set the record straight with the press and the bureaucrats of the government. Woods emphatically denied that the Bank sought to shape the fourth Five Year Plan, due to begin on April 1, 1966. TTK replied that he appreciated the attitude of the Bank and had never been under any misconception.

Woods referred to the terms of reference for the survey that would be conducted by the Bell Mission and said the Indian ambassador to Washington, B. K. Nehru, had already approved.[26] Mr. L. K. Jha, private secretary to the prime minister, objected to raising the subject of ownership, public or private, so Woods agreed to delete that subject from future drafts. Woods predicted that the level of assistance by the Aid-India Consortium would continue at existing levels for the fifth year of the third Five Year Plan (1965). He could not predict what the consortium would do about the fourth Five Year Plan (1966–1971), but he stressed that the World Bank needed to be fully informed because the consortium would look to the Bank for guidance and advice. It was one of many occasions when George Woods negotiated directly with a prime minister or a finance minister. Negotiations were one of Woods's many strong points, for he had been there many times before: it was his style from his years at First Boston.

During the summer of 1964, Bernard Bell recruited his team, most of whom arrived in India in the fall of 1964. Half were recruited from outside the Bank staff, including, notably, Sir John Crawford, vice-chancellor of

the Australian National University, David Hopper, from the Ford Foundation, and Wolf Ladejinsky—all well-known agricultural economists.[27]
He included several of the leading members of the staff of the Population
Council as well as Conrad Tauber, deputy director of the U.S. Census Bureau, all well-known figures in the field of population control. In addition,
he selected a number of members of the Bank staff.

By the early summer of 1965, most of the team had completed drafts
of their various reports. In September 1965, Bell completed a thirty-six-
page summary of the mission report. That summary set forth recommendations for action by the government of India, on the one hand, and by
the aid consortium, on the other. Woods agreed with, and accepted, the
recommendations and decided that Bell should present them to the government of India and subsequently to the members of the aid consortium
in their respective countries. Pierre Paul Schweitzer, managing director of
the IMF, was included in the discussions. Woods took advantage of the
fact that Andre de Lattre, who until a few months before had been the director of the international department of the French Ministry of Finance,
became available. Woods asked de Lattre to join Bell and, in October
1965, Bell and de Lattre went to India for initial discussions with the ministers of the government and their chief economic advisors. They discussed their findings in some detail with TTK, who would have to approve any proposal for devaluation of the rupee.

Earlier, on July 14, 1965, TTK had gone on nationwide radio to announce a continuation of existing policies. He rejected new fiscal measures and the devaluation of the rupee. TTK said he continued to favor
import licensing and industrial controls even if that meant less foreign assistance and a smaller fourth plan. Subramaniam and Mehta opposed
TTK, but fiscal policy was clearly in TTK's bailiwick. TTK appeared to
have been annoyed by the Bell mission. He seemed almost to take it as a
personal challenge to his authority. Prime Minister Shastri tended to support TTK, at least for a time. The press was almost unanimous in their
praise of TTK's speech. Later in July, in talks with the business community, TTK misrepresented the Bank and the Fund by talking about the de-
flation that "always accompanied Fund stabilization programs." Meanwhile, I. G. Patel, chief economic advisor to the finance minister, went
to Washington to talk to people in the Bank and the Fund.

In late 1964, officials of the government of India had hoped that the
Bell mission would simply present a more compelling picture of India's development needs, but, as economists on the mission dug more deeply into
India's industrial policy and its implementation and international trade
policies and their implementation, it became more and more clear that
the Indian economy had reached a point of substantial stagnation.
Initially, TTK had opposed the Bell mission altogether. Among other

objections, he felt that it would be an infringement on Indian sovereignty regardless of what it concluded. He finally agreed that a report could be undertaken providing that it would be made available to only two people: George Woods and himself (or the prime minister). None of the Bank staff was permitted access to copies of the complete report.

By December 1965, following the initial discussion with Bell and de Lattre, TTK had become an active opponent of the Bell report. Shortly thereafter, the full text of Bell's summary report appeared in three install-ments in one of the large Indian newspapers, and the leftish Indian press began a campaign against the World Bank and against George Woods and Bernard Bell personally that culminated in an article with four-inch head-lines in two papers: TO HELL WITH BELL. One was the official paper of the Communist party, the *New Age*, and the other was a magazine, *Blitz*, which also published the full text of a letter critical of a USAID fer-tilizer loan to India. As it turned out, *Pravda* had published the same arti-cle about Bell in Russian in Moscow the same day and with the same headline.[28]

The gist of Bell's thirty-six-page summary report may be paraphrased as follows:

The overall growth of the economy during the first four years of the third Five Year Plan has been disappointing. Agricultural output has grown during five years at only 12 percent; 25 percent had been forecast. The mining and factory sector has grown by 45 percent; 70 percent had been forecast. The relatively slow growth of output occurred despite a sub-stantial increase in imports—from $2.3 billion in 1960–61 to $3.1 billion in 1965–66, an increase of $840 million. The gap between imports and exports was financed almost entirely by foreign aid which went, on bal-ance, to support the net increase of population and larger defense ex-penditures. Imports of supplies and raw materials (maintenance imports) have been on target, but imports of capital goods (project imports) have been 15 to 20 percent below forecast. The need for supplies and raw ma-terials was probably underestimated, since there are many signs of unuti-lized capacity. An obvious shortage of fertilizer was apparent in the case of agriculture, and food prices rose accordingly.

It was believed by the agriculture experts on the World Bank team that a rupee invested in agriculture would yield a far higher return than a rupee invested in industry. [This could still be the case in the 1990s in the Ganges River Valley.] In any event, the third Five Year Plan placed too low a priority on increasing agricultural output—on fertilizer and ir-rigation, and the Plan fell short of its targets. Credit was not channeled adequately to the larger number of India's cultivators who are tenants rather than owners. Inadequate steps were taken to provide for the secu-rity of tenure, fair rental agreements, the consolidation of fragmented holdings necessary to achieve effective farm operation, especially in the case of irrigated land. Prices until 1964 were kept below the levels likely to provide financial incentives for the use of fertilizers and other inputs.

Research directed toward the development of improved seed varieties, of more suitable plant protection, of more adequate information on underground water supplies, of more effective farm and water management practices was deficient. In general there was too little appreciation of the power of financial incentives.

The greatest overall shortage was the shortage of foreign exchange exacerbated by the overvaluation of the rupee which worked to defeat import substitution and export expansion which are essential to the development program. The system of import controls has been an inefficient allocator of scarce supplies. Firms which are not themselves producers of desired goods, almost invariably prefer foreign to domestic sources and are frequently successful in obtaining licenses. The subsidy involved has no doubt stimulated investment, but it has not properly directed it.

On the export side, for tea and jute, where the price elasticity of foreign demand is low and where there are a limited number of competing producing countries, special treatment is appropriate, but these are special cases. The system cannot and does not work effectively to promote the development of new exports. A standard, stable rate at an appropriate level would open opportunities to which India's entrepreneurs would respond. There is, in any event, little or no disagreement with the conclusion that, except in the case of tea and jute, no Indian products can be sold in export markets without loss to the exporter. The result has been a belated approach to export stimulation rather than one which is anticipatory.

Since, at the existing effective exchange rate, the demand for imports exceeds the supply of foreign exchange even when supplemented with roughly $1 billion a year in foreign assistance, the government of India has chosen to control all imports. Instances of lost output for want of individual items and the delays in obtaining them are common. The stimulus to holding back excessive stocks is also evident. Import policy, instead of compensating for imbalances in domestic output, has accentuated these difficulties.

Equilibrium should be restored by: 1) a rise in the effective exchange rate (devaluation of the rupee), 2) the freeing of maintenance imports from existing direct controls, 3) a continued limitation of imports of essential finished consumer goods as well as of components and semi manufactures used only in the production of such goods, and 4) the continued direct control of imports of capital goods and of industrial investment through industrial licensing. We emphasize that abandonment of the existing system of direct import controls is not to argue for a reduction in investment in favor of larger consumption.

In both India and Pakistan, defense expenditures represent a significant diversion of resources from development. The Indian economy is large and diversified. Nevertheless, Pakistani natural gas, Indian coal, Pakistani rice and raw jute and Indian manufacturing capacity offer the possibility of mutually beneficial exchange. Successful steps to reduce the tensions and the defense expenditures could make a large contribution to Indian economic progress.

The number of families actually now using one or another of the methods of contraception is estimated to be a maximum of 2 million, or two percent of the number of Indian couples in the reproductive age group. There is no evidence of a decline in fertility rates (births per 1,000 women of child bearing age). At present rates of increase, India's population will be close to 1 billion by 1991.

Strong and stable price incentives to producers of agricultural output must be provided along with adequate supplies of the major physical inputs. These include most importantly fertilizers, irrigation water and improved seed. Farm credit must be made available in adequate amounts and to all classes of cultivation. Extension work must be strengthened, security of tenure and fair rents should be enforced, and the consolidation of fragmented holding should be speeded.

One can question the insistence that foreign investors should generally accept a minority equity position in ventures in which their partners are private Indian interests and always accept such a position where the government of India is the partner. The industrial licensing system appears to have a number of purposes, including to prevent excess capacity in particular lines of production, to direct new investment into types of production regarded as high priority, and to achieve a wider geographic distribution of income. In addition, the licensing seems to have been directed toward encouraging public enterprise, even in the absence of any clearly identifiable purpose, under the assumption that decisions by government administrators are either wiser or more socially beneficial than those made by private entrepreneurs.[29] The system appears to have had largely negative effects.

Roads, dikes, small water facilities and similar works would contribute measurably to the expansion of agricultural output and the reduction of the cost of providing services to the village population. The government of India has not always recognized the need for well planned and effective highway and port facilities development.

We believe some of the basic development strategy of the government is mistaken. We refer to the tendency to make industrial investment choices without adequate consideration of the comparative economic costs and returns involved and to establish import-substituting production at any cost. This neglects the possibility that export production and international trade may be a more advantageous means of meeting import requirements.

We believe that 1) higher priority must be given to agriculture, 2) a better balance is needed between "maintenance" and "project" imports, and 3) a shift in emphasis is required in the direction of production for export and away from import substitution at any cost.

We are confident that, with the necessary and appropriate changes in the government of India's policies and practices and *with a higher level of aid for at least the next five years*, India can significantly accelerate the growth of its economy. Whereas imports of maintenance goods in the most recent years have been in the neighborhood of $1.6 billion per year, the *amount required at this time for the effective use of existing capacity may be $300 million to $500 million higher*. Acceptance of this figure would suggest that during the fourth plan period, some $1.5 billion to $2.5 billion additional foreign exchange, over and above that derived from the growth of export receipts, will be required for maintenance imports.

Service obligations on the debt which will exist at the end of the third Five Year Plan will be $2.2 billion for five years plus whatever debt

becomes payable during the fourth Five Year Plan. Debt service payments during the third plan were $1.2 billion, so some $1.0 billion more
will be required than in the third plan period *and can only be provided by
additional aid.* We judge that the necessary acceleration in India's economic progress will require more aid in the immediate future and that,
without a higher level of aid than in the third plan period, the rate of
progress, irrespective of the policy of the government of India, will de-
teriorate. To the extent that India's debt service obligations can be affected, the amount of new aid commitments can be reduced.

In a nutshell, George Woods, through Bernard Bell, was seeking the
devaluation of the rupee and a loosening of India's import and industrial
controls in exchange for more foreign aid. If the term *structural adjustment
lending* had been in vogue at that time, this program would surely have
qualified.[30] The trouble was that India, which prized its newly won independence more highly, perhaps, than anything else, was not about to be
"bribed" by the proposed quid pro quo. TTK, whatever his faults, had pa-
triotic pride: he bridled at the carrot/stick approach.

Meanwhile, though George Woods and the Bank did their best to be
supportive, tensions increased between India and the United States. The
four-year Public Law 480 agreement negotiated by the Kennedy administration stopped, and President Lyndon Johnson, in June 1965, decided not
to make another long-term commitment to India for continued food support. He sought to keep India on a short leash so as to force Prime Minister Shastri to pay more attention to U.S. advice. Earlier he had forbidden
U.S. representatives to the Aid-India Consortium to pledge amounts of
U.S. assistance. He claimed that specific amounts of IDA appropriations
were to be determined by Congress, and he was not about to make
promises that could not be fulfilled. Privately, he complained that aid to
India was like pouring money down a rat hole.

In September 1965, a major war broke out between India and Pakistan. The United States cut off military aid to both countries. PL 480
shipments were continued to both countries, but some Indian officials al-
leged publicly that all aid had been stopped. Together with the drought,
this rumor accentuated the speculative hoarding of food and increased in-
flationary pressures.

In December 1965, TTK resigned under something of a cloud (unre-
lated to the Bell report) and was replaced by Sachin Chaudhuri, a prominent lawyer. Prime Minister Shastri died suddenly in January 1966, a few
hours after signing the Tashkent Accord ending the short but costly war
with Pakistan. Nehru's daughter, Indira Gandhi, was chosen to succeed
Shastri, to the disappointment of Morarji Desai, who was next in line. Kumaraswami Kamaraj, president of the Congress party, supported Mrs.
Gandhi.

In February 1966, Vice-president Humphrey was sent by President Johnson to India and, in March, Mrs. Gandhi visited President Johnson in Washington. Johnson was favorably impressed by Mrs. Gandhi. In April, Mrs. Gandhi sent Asoka Mehta to negotiate with George Woods over the Bell report and future levels of consortium aid. Mehta, on behalf of the government of India, undertook to reduce and eventually to eliminate all administrative controls over imports, to relax controls over investment and production, to institute an effective program of increasing agricultural production by assigning a much higher priority to agriculture in the allocation of resources, to reduce population growth, and to take steps to mobilize domestic resources in the interests of an accelerated investment program. He also agreed, following discussions with the IMF, to devalue the rupee.

In May 1966, Bell and de Lattre visited Britain, France, and West Germany for discussions with the governments of those countries, explaining and urging the increased aid that the Bell report had recommended and explaining the revisions in economic policy that the government of India had agreed to undertake. In June, Bell, alone, went to Japan for similar lengthy discussions aimed at eliciting government support for increased aid. Meanwhile, in May in Washington, S. Bhootilingham, secretary for economic affairs of the finance ministry of India, was chairing discussions of devaluation and import liberalization that took place in great secrecy. The Ministry of Finance sent a team to the IMF to work out technical details, from which discussions George Woods remained aloof, though informed.

Mrs. Gandhi took few people into her confidence. Most of the top leaders of the Congress party opposed devaluation when Mrs. Gandhi broached the subject—as though it were not already a fait accompli. Devaluation of the rupee was announced on June 6. The new finance minister, Sachin Chaudhuri, was required to explain and defend the devaluation, but his statements were not convincing. The press was lukewarm in their support, as was the Federation of Indian Chambers of Commerce. The monsoon rains, due in July, did not arrive for the second year in a row.

According to Gregory Votaw, chief of the Bank's India division in 1966, and who presumably was present at the meeting, Mrs. Gandhi said to Pierre Paul Schweitzer, "I don't know anything about economic matters. It was not a very good subject of mine at Oxford. But my technicians tell me that you're very concerned about this. I trust you. I trusted your uncle who was one of the great men of our century. What should I do?"

Schweitzer replied, "Well, I mean, it's up to you to decide. But I think you should devalue."

Mrs Gandhi: "By how much?" (The exchange rate was then 4.8 rupees to the dollar.)

Schweitzer: "Six would be good. Seven would be better. Seven and a half would be fantastic."

Mrs Gandhi: "Okay, I'll do 7.5. Whatever you say."[31]

Under the headline, "Mrs. Gandhi Gambles with a Cheaper Rupee," the *New York Times* reported that one gamble the prime minister had taken was that she would win the election, due eight months later:

> Here she must depend largely on the promises she evidently has received from the United States and the International Bank for Reconstruction and Development. For whatever other long-range benefits may stem from devaluation, its chief short-run benefit is expected to be the long awaited first infusion of Western aid for India's fourth Five-Year Plan.
>
> India is unlikely to get what she asked for: $1.6 billion a year. However, there are indications that she will get—probably in two stages—about $1.3 billion. This is an increase of about 30 percent over the annual level of Western aid during the third Five-Year Plan.
>
> Even more important is that $900 million to $1 billion of this—twice the third plan rate—will be in non-project aid for imports of raw materials, spare parts and components. India's liberalization of imports will permit it to use these funds quickly.
>
> The government hopes this massive infusion will allow plants which have been running well below capacity because of the foreign-exchange shortage to boost production substantially. Eventually, they are confident, increased production will bring prices down.[32]

William Gilmartin, the Bank's resident representative in India from 1967 through 1969 and 1972 through 1975,[33] later commented: "The devaluation did not have the beneficial effects on exports that were expected. I think it was the view that the biggest benefit from the devaluation would come by limiting imports. It did that to a certain extent, but in the process it created a great deal of ill feelings. For example, in the textile industry . . . the price of imported cotton jumped considerably. . . . [The Indians] felt that [George Woods] could have done more to insure a large flow of aid to India. I think this unfriendly attitude about Woods continued longer than it continued toward the Bank as such. I don't think the Indians ever quite forgave Woods.

"There was . . . the feeling that more attention . . . should be given to agriculture and that this increased attention would involve a very substantial increase in fertilizer. . . . Woods had the idea of a foreign fertilizer group headed . . . by the Bechtel organization, the idea being that they would work out a program, obtain the approval of the Indian government for this program, and then go ahead with the construction of fertilizer plants on a substantial scale. . . .

"The Indian government objected to this from the outset. I don't think they were prepared at that time to go as far in supporting agriculture as Woods and the Bell mission thought they should. In the second place, they didn't like the idea of foreigners coming in and developing their fertilizer industry. . . .

"After his second India mission [in 1967 to appraise India's fourth Five Year Plan], Bernie Bell was telling Woods about the mission and the agricultural program including the rather favorable prospect of a turn around in agriculture. . . . Woods said that, as far as he was concerned, 'India didn't have an agriculture program.'"

Woods had become disheartened about India just as the Green Revolution was on the horizon. Subramaniam, who had been sympathetic to the Woods-Bell objectives, was determined to bring high-yielding seed varieties and related technology to India. Meanwhile, however, the Woods-Mehta accord had not materialized. Indeed, long-term planning in India was virtually suspended for three years at the beginning of the fourth Five Year Plan, and the focus of economic policy shifted to Morarji Desai and I. G. Patel in the Ministry of Finance. It was they who decreed the continued centralization of the economy through licensing and controls.

Indira Gandhi visited Moscow in July 1966 and joined Leonid Brezhnev in condemning "imperialists bombing and aggression in Asia." This angered President Johnson, who took an even firmer stance over the release of PL 480 shipments to India. The Vietnam War was increasing in intensity.[34] By September 1966, the full extent of the drought had become known, but President Johnson kept India on a shorter leash so far as PL 480 was concerned. Mrs. Gandhi became increasingly worried about the forthcoming election.

On November 7 and 8, the Aid-India Consortium met in Paris and pledged an annual $900 million in nonproject assistance, plus $300 million in project aid—$1.2 billion overall. The total had remained nearly constant, but the composition had shifted substantially toward nonproject or balance-of-payments or program aid.[35] Debt-service requirements were rising faster than export earnings, however: they amounted to 20 percent of exports at the end of the third Five Year Plan and were projected to rise to 25 percent by the end of the fourth. At the same time, the free, foreign-exchange reserves of India continued to decline. The IMF had loaned India $137 million earlier in the year, but, even with that, India's reserves fell almost to $200 million by the end of the fiscal year, 1966/67, the minimum legal limit. It was suggested that debt-service payments due to the major creditors be deferred for the remainder of that fiscal year.[36]

The following February, the Congress party lost six of the seventeen state legislatures. The Congress party president, Kumaraswami Kamaraj, lost his seat in Madras, and party leaders forced Mrs. Gandhi to accept Morarji Desai as her deputy and finance minister. The droughts of 1965

and 1966 had brought on a major recession, largely because of unused industrial capacity. There was widespread unrest.

In June 1967, in a conversation with John D. Rockefeller III, George
Woods remarked, "The devaluation was a flop; India didn't make the policy changes we expected."[37] Import licensing was still in force, decontrol
of industry had been established in only a few sectors, and the expected
changes in fertilizer policy had not yet been forthcoming. Among others,
I. G. Patel recommended that India should never again let its foreign-exchange reserves fall so low as to become dependent on foreign aid. India
was disappointed. So, also, were George Woods and the World Bank. For
Woods personally, it was not unlike a Greek tragedy.

As Gilmartin recalled: "[In February 1968] Woods was to give an address to the UNCTAD conference . . . and the Indian government took
great umbrage with what he had to say. . . .

"His speech was one in support of more aid to developing countries,
and he referred especially to India and said that, because of the decline
in aid India was getting from abroad, 'Hope was turning to despair.' The
Indian government took exception to this statement on the grounds that
India was not so dependent on aid that they would despair without it.
That India would 'despair' over aid levels from one year to another was
ridiculous."[38]

Morarji Desai, the deputy prime minister and finance minister of
India, induced Woods to amend his original text to read:

> We must be frank to say that in many parts of the world, the situation is
> discouraging, even disturbing. Here in our host country, the home of
> one-seventh of all the human race, *in the 20 years of independence sub-*
> *stantial advances have been made in alleviating illiteracy, hunger, illness and*
> *want, but the tasks that remain are staggering in their size and complexity.*
> Those who believe as I do that India is engaged in a labor of deep mean-
> ing for all the developing countries must be gravely concerned by the
> uncertainties that cloud her national life. India is an exceptionally dra-
> matic case because of its size and its location on the troubled Asian con-
> tinent; but it is by no means the only country where *growth needs to be*
> *much faster if hope is not to dwindle toward despondency.*

In the original text, the italicized words were "after 20 years of independence many millions of people have yet to experience more than the
feeblest manifestations of progress," and "hope has dwindled toward de-
spondency."

Desai wrote to Woods on March 4, 1968,

> It was indeed very generous of you that you felt able to amend your
> UNCTAD speech but you also wish to put across in other ways the facts
> we had brought out in our note. I am happy that you shared my anxiety

when I reacted to your original statement in the manner in which I did. My only purpose was to enable you to set the record in its proper perspective.

I was very happy that you were able to come to New Delhi for the Conference and I hope that even after you relinquish your present responsibilities, it will be possible for [you and Mrs. Woods] to come to Delhi for a reunion with your many friends.[39]

Woods had done his best to assist India, even, perhaps, at the expense of a second term as president of the World Bank.[40] He had arranged greatly to increase the nonproject aid to India. He had shifted reserves to India when India's reserves were low. He had fostered debt relief for India. He had been willing to finance public, as opposed to private, industries. Through the Bell mission, he had advocated devaluation of the rupee, however. Perhaps he had tried too hard. As Alexander Stevenson, director of the South Asia department in 1965–1966, recalled, "Some of us, including me, didn't think there would be any magical recovery, because the Indian economy doesn't react quickly to anything."[41] Stevenson also recalled that, after Peter Cargill had become director of the entire Asia department, Cargill left Delhi following the UNCTAD speech while Woods was still there. Woods called William Gilmartin, the Bank's resident representative, asked for Cargill, and was told that he had left after trying to contact Woods. Discouraged, Woods remarked, "Even my own side is letting me down."[42] Observed Kenneth Bohr, who wrote the volume on industry for the Bell mission and was the Bank's representative in India in 1966, "No one appreciates a bunch of people coming in to tell you where you've gone wrong."[43]

Gregory Votaw has well summarized Woods's personal tragedy: "We all recognized that it was extremely important to India's economic development, including its ability to take on and service additional debt from abroad, that somehow or other they get excited about exports. But with this huge domestic market and all their other problems, they didn't really take exports seriously, any more than the United States takes it seriously. . . .

"The issue in India had a lot to do with the exchange rate. Those of us who were trained in economics, particularly the folks in the Monetary Fund, were very, very anxious that the exchange rate issue be discussed with the Indians. I remember the most difficult discussions we ever had with Mr. Woods were over this question. I was not in many of those discussions but even the ones I was in took a lot of time. So that in terms of his total time it must have been day after day for weeks.

"One that I attended I remember him saying, 'Look, of course the rupee should be devalued. But that's not something that I can discuss with the Finance Minister. It's certainly not a discussion which I can initiate. It's like talking to a man about the virtue of his wife! It's just not something you do in polite society.' Yet the technical people in the Bank insisted that he do something in that area. It became obvious that the Fund, whose business it was, didn't quite have the courage to initiate and maintain discussion on that set of issues. So Woods, very, very reluctantly, was persuaded that he and his staff should raise these questions politely and gingerly and gently.

"The tragedy, as I look at all this, is that to this day the Indians involved in those discussions are very angry that Mr. Woods raised that set of issues. I mean, the Indian formal position was that they would handle that within their own good time and in their own manner. They didn't want to be seen as having their arms twisted by foreigners on the question of the exchange rate. Very specifically, they wanted more time to prepare themselves. They felt that had the international community been willing to wait an extra six months, it all would have been handled much more smoothly. I'm not sure how much truth there is in that. There was definitely a sense of their sovereignty being invaded. But what's always seemed to me ironic is that Woods got the blame for this 'interference' even though he had been the only one initially to understand how very sensitive the discussion would be."[44]

On February 14, 1968, Malik Uttam Chaud, chief of the editorial staff of *Minorities View*, New Delhi, wrote by hand to George Woods, in part:

> However unpalatable the views expressed by you to the UNCTAD Session in New Delhi might have been, they needed saying. By all accounts you left your captive audience shaken but impressed. While you censured the advanced nations for too often streamlining their policies to "their own narrow concerns" you did not spare the developing nations nor indeed the institution you head of some well deserved and perceptive criticism. India came in—and with good cause—for a few barbed comments. . . .
>
> Your splendid speech helped to right the perspective and for this reason, despite the seeming harshness of some of its strictures, merits careful consideration. India, at whom some of your most pointed comments were directed, would do well to react constructively to your criticism. You are undoubtedly a genuine friend of the developing countries and your attitude to India in particular has invariably been sympathetic and warm.[45]

Notes

1. The consortium members were Austria, Belgium, Canada, France, Germany, Italy, Japan, the Netherlands, the United Kingdom, the United States, and the World Bank. The Bank served as chairman.
2. The rupee was devalued from U.S.21¢ to U.S.13.33¢. Devaluation has always had opponents in India, but India's finance minister in 1992, Manmohan Singh, a Sikh technocrat, seems to have successfully orchestrated a sharp devaluation, slashed the government's budget deficit, and abolished a wide range of

restrictive licenses on industry, including crippling import licenses. See Edward A. Gargan, "A Revolution Transforms India: Socialism's Out, Free Market In," *New York Times*, March 29, 1992, p. 1.

3. David B.H. Denoon, *Devaluation Under Pressure: India, Indonesia and Ghana* (Cambridge: MIT Press, 1986), p. 59.

4. William K. Stevens, "India, once a Giant in Science, Tries to Rekindle the Creative Fire," *New York Times*, November 9, 1982, pp. C1ff.

5. Eugene Black before Woods, and Robert McNamara after, also were in love with India. Except for China (which was not then a member of the World Bank), India has the largest population in the world; her per capita income of $300 (in 1987 dollars), however, is near the bottom of the scale. India has a land area of roughly one-third that of the United States.

6. The following account relies substantially on Denoon, "Appendix 2A, Chronology of Key Events Related to the 1966 Indian Rupee Devaluation," pp. 53–72.

7. The Agricultural Trade, Development and Assistance Act (Public Law 480) was enacted in July 1954. India signed her first agreement with the United States in August 1956. Under Title I of the act, the president was authorized to sell agricultural commodities for local currencies (counterpart funds). Under Title II, the president could donate supplies freely to meet famine and other urgent relief requirements. This imported food was sold in the open market (for Indian rupees, in the case of India; most of which then belonged to the Indian government). The remainder went into a U.S. deposit with India's central bank and was largely unusable. India's central bank could thus increase credit by an equivalent amount with little danger of inflation. This local currency counterpart was an important source of finance for the Indian government's investment plans. If India produced all its own food, the government would lose this source of noninflationary investment finance.

8. "Because many of the government-determined prices are far below what customers are willing to pay for scarce supplies, government officials, traders, and producers often share in the premiums obtainable above the regulated prices. Because these illegal profits cannot be easily invested in productive enterprises, they often go into the consumption or elaborate laundering schemes. Numerous official commissions have investigated this additional drawback of the controls system, but there is general consensus that corruption is inevitable as long as the Government of India continues to force the sale of goods below market prices."—Denoon, p. 36.

9. Even I. G. Patel (an Indian who had studied at Cambridge University, who had served in the International Monetary Fund in the early 1950s, and who is now head of the London School of Economics) once expressed astonishment at the idea that businessmen might be wiser than government bureaucrats in making investment decisions. "Those entrepreneurs might make mistakes," a source close to Patel once quoted him as saying.—See Robert Oliver, "A Conversation with Bernard Bell, I," *Conversations About George Woods and the World Bank*, Washington, D.C., November 13, 1985, p. 6.

10. See Benjamin I. Cohen, "The Stagnation of India's Exports," *Quarterly Journal of Economics*, Vol. 78, No. 4, November 1964, pp. 604–620.

11. See "Bankers' Mission to India and Pakistan," *News Release*, World Bank, April 20, 1960.

12. In 1965, the gross domestic product of India was $46.2 billion. See *World Development Report, 1989*, p. 168.

13. "Talk to Indian Institute of Management Course on Marketing and Export Promotion," December 11, 1963 (mimeo).

14. The other resident representative of the World Bank in India was Romano Pantanali. His penetrating study of iron ore (mining, processing, rail transport, and port handling) showed the inefficiency of the decisionmaking process for new investments.

15. "Aid and Advise," *Economic Weekly*, April 4, 1964, pp. 630–631.

16. Bernard Bell was educated at the University of Pennsylvania and the University of Paris. He had been chief economist and assistant to the chairman of the board of the U.S. Export-Import Bank from 1946 to 1953. When President Eisenhower decided the Export-Import Bank should stop making loans, Bell left to become a partner of Gass, Bell and Associates and then of Surveys of Research, Inc. As a consultant to the World Bank in 1962, he was the transportation adviser in a mission to Colombia. In 1963 and 1964, he directed the economic work of the Indian coal transport study. This brought him to the attention of George Woods. As a consultant to the World Bank, Bell directed the World Bank's mission to India. He subsequently joined the Bank as the assistant director of the projects department. In 1968, he became director of the Bank's resident staff in Indonesia. From late 1972 to mid-1974, he was vice-president for the East Africa region of the Bank. He then served as vice-president for the East Asia and Pacific region of the World Bank from 1974 until 1977, at which time he retired in accordance with the Bank's mandatory age policy. Since then he has been an economic consultant, primarily to Indonesia, but also to the World Bank and IFC. Bell died on March 28, 1994.

17. Personal correspondence, June 4, 1964, World Bank archives.

18. Personal correspondence, June 27, 1964, World Bank archives.

19. Bell, I, p. 5.

20. Bell had been critical of the overvalued rupee while he was engaged in the coal transport study two years earlier.

21. Bell, I.

22. Ben King, draft of interview, World Bank archives, July 24, 1986, p. 42.

23. See, for example, Richard E. Caves and Ronald W. Jones, *World Trade and Payments*, third edition (Boston: Little, Brown, 1981), pp. 341–362, particularly 352–360. See also Paul Krugman, "A Model of Innovation, Technology Transfer and the World Distribution of Income," *Journal of Political Economy*, Vol. 87, No. 2 (April 1979), pp. 253–266. Writing in the November 1964, issue of the *Quarterly Journal of Economics*, Ben Cohen suggested that "one way of reducing India's export prices is by a devaluation of the rupee, which would also probably have a beneficial impact on other segments of India's balance-of-payments. . . . Devaluation would . . . ease the administrative burden on the import licensing authorities and reduce the inflow of gold and other illegal imports. A general tariff increase or a system of auctioning off import licenses could supplement a devaluation to allow the government to capture some of the private profits made by those fortunate enough to secure import licenses."—Cohen, p. 618. See also Frank Graham, *The Theory of International Values* (Princeton: Princeton University Press, 1948).

24. S. J. Patel, "Economic Prospects and Economic Growth: India," *Economic Journal*, Vol. 69, No. 275, September, 1959, pp. 500–501.

25. Quoted in Denoon, p. 42.

26. Brij Kumar Nehru, son of a cousin of Prime Minister Jawaharlal Nehru and a distant cousin, therefore, of Mrs. Indira Gandhi, was educated at Allahabad University, the London School of Economics, Balliol College (Oxford), and the Inner Temple (London). He was an assistant commissioner for the Punjab from

1934–1939 and under-secretary in the Indian Finance Department, 1940–1944. He became deputy in 1944 and joint-secretary in 1947. He represented India in the UN General Assembly from 1949 to 1952. He served as India's commissioner-general for economic affairs in the United States and became ambassador to Washington in 1961. As such, he was an executive director of the World Bank from 1961–1962. He and George Woods were close friends in Washington and thereafter. Their friendship began in 1952 when George Woods was an advisor to Eugene Black on the iron and steel merger in India.

27. Willard Thorp, head of the development advisory committee of the Organization for Economic Cooperation and Development in Paris, wrote to George Woods personally to ask for a copy of Crawford's report on agriculture about which Thorp had heard "glowing reports."—Personal correspondence to George Woods, November 16, 1966. Personal papers.

28. Bernard Bell, I, pp. 8–9.

29. Was George Woods (or Bernard Bell) violating an agreement with TTK not to raise the issue of public versus private ownership?

30. In recent years, structural adjustment lending has come to connote *program* or *balance-of-payments* (rather than *project*) lending in order to induce the borrowing country to modify some policy such as, for example, running too large a budgetary deficit.

31. "The Reminiscences of Gregory Votaw," *George B. Woods Oral History Project*, Oral History Research Office, Columbia University, 1986, p. 46. Gregory Votaw received an A.M. in history in 1950 at the University of Chicago and a second A.M. in PPE (mainly economics) from Oxford University. He worked in Puerto Rico for three and a half years and in Iran for the Harvard advisory group for sixteen months before he joined the World Bank. He was in Egypt as a consultant to the Bank from October 1962 until February 1963, when he became a regular staff member assigned to India in Washington, D.C. He visited India in the spring of 1963 and, according to Votaw, was told by his mission chief that agriculture was not important in India and they really should not pay any attention to it. Votaw persisted: he became excited about the possibilities of biogenetic research, particularly Mexipac wheat, though, at that time, the agricultural experts in the Bank rejected any thought of that. For them it was all a question of irrigation water and big physical projects like dams. Votaw reminded them that George Woods had been a trustee of the Rockefeller Foundation, which was the organization most active in agricultural research.

32. "Mrs. Gandhi Gambles with a Cheaper Rupee," *New York Times*, June 12, 1966, p. 4E.

33. William Gilmartin received his Ph.D. in economics from the University of California. In the army, in occupied Japan after World War II, he was in charge of the economic section of the HQ agriculture office, mainly preparing the system of land reform that was later imposed on Japan. When he was looking for a job following demobilization in 1946, someone suggested that he try the World Bank. His Japanese experience was of interest to the Bank and he was taken on as a junior economist. In 1952, he participated in the first Bank mission to Japan, before which Japan had been heavily dependent upon U.S. aid. Gilmartin was also in Thailand for two and a half years, during which time the Bank conducted a survey of Thailand; then following his Bank service in East Asia he was transferred to South Asia, spending three years in India.

34. The words of Dean Rusk, spoken the following year, indicate the extent of the U.S. administration's concern: "There is no shadow of a doubt in my mind

that our vital interests are deeply involved in Vietnam and in Southeast Asia.
. . . We are involved in Vietnam because we know from painful experience that
the maximum condition for order on our planet is that aggression must not be permitted to succeed. For if it does succeed, the consequence is not peace, it is the
further expansion of aggression."—Dean Rusk, "Our Foreign Policy Commitments
to Assure a Peaceful Future," *The Department of State Bulletin* 56, No. 1456, May
22, 1967; cited in Frederick H. Hartmann, *The New Age of American Foreign Policy* (London: Macmillan, 1970), p. 261.

Votaw commented: "I think the problem was compounded by the fact that
countries like India did not support the great crusade in Vietnam and went to
some lengths to try to warn the United States against what was happening there
and how their involvement would lead to tragedy."—Votaw, p. 23.

35. Nonproject aid consists of aid used to finance imports or production materials (including components) and spare or replacement parts. Its essential character is that it finances imports used in the operation of existing production and
infrastructure facilities. By contrast, project aid consists of aid used to finance imports of equipment, materials, and services that are used for the establishment of
new or the expansion of existing production and infrastructure facilities.

Bernard Bell estimated that imports into India in the fourth Five Year Plan,
excluding those financed by PL 480, would need to be $16.7 billion as compared
with $11.5 billion in the third plan period. Exports would, he estimated, be less
than $3 billion higher, so the trade gap would be about $3 billion higher—nearly
$6 billion over all. Service on the outstanding debt, including interest and prin-
cipal, would be about $3 billion, so the total gap to be covered by capital inflow
over the five year period was projected to be $9 billion, about $1.5 billion of
which the government of India expected to come from private investment or non-
consortium sources. The remaining $7.5 billion ($1.5 billion annually), which exceeded the $1.2 billion pledged annually by the Aid-India Consortium, was less
than 40 percent higher than the consortium aid commitments of $5.5 billion for
the third plan period. Still, consortium assistance could hardly be expected to rise
by almost 40 percent every five years. The absorptive capacity was there, but exports were not then rising fast enough to match the desired long-term growth of
real GNP.

For the consortium countries, total disbursements (including food) actually
rose to $1.4 billion by 1966/67 and to $1.5 billion in 1967/68, but dropped back to
$1.1 billion in 1968/69. This was well below the $1.7 billion yearly in foreign assistance that Bernard Bell had suggested for the fourth Five Year Plan.

For background on the Aid-India Consortium, see Edward S. Mason and
Robert Asher, *The World Bank Since Bretton Woods* (Washington, D.C.: Brookings
Institution, 1973), pp. 514–517.

36. Debt relief had already been granted since World War II to Argentina and
Chile by the Paris Club and to Brazil by the Hague Club. Debt relief can be extended to both principal and interest payments and can cover debts held by private and public sectors. In the case of India, it could serve both to increase the
amount of net aid and to provide aid in a form quickly usable. The shift from project to nonproject aid was helpful to India, at least in the short run, by providing
foreign exchange untied to Indian projects. It was designed to finance "maintenance imports" rather than "project imports."

37. Cited by Denoon, p. 71.

38. Ibid., p. 18–19. In Denoon's words, "The Indians [in the Finance Min-
istry] were simply adamant . . . that Woods never missed a chance to make a
slighting remark about India."

39. Personal correspondence, Morarji Desai to George Woods, March 4, 1968.
40. It is not clear that George Woods would have accepted a second term as president. See Chapter 8.
41. Robert W. Oliver, "A Conversation with Alexander Stevenson," *Conversations About George Woods and the World Bank*, Washington, D.C., November 18, 1985, p. 31.

Stevenson was a Bank veteran. His career started after Antonin Basch, who had been on the Czechoslovakian delegation at Bretton Woods, called him one day and said, "Why don't you join the Bank?" Sandy, who had just left the U.S. Treasury Department and was at U.C. Berkeley on a demob. fellowship, couldn't afford to wait and joined the economics department. With the reorganization of 1952, he was transferred to operations and became division chief for Scandinavia and then for the whole of Western Europe, supervising the colonial territories ruled by Britain, France, and Belgium. In 1959, he became deputy director in the Asia and Middle East department; and in 1965 director of the South Asia department. George Woods, who had made Stevenson director, merged South Asia and East Asia into a single department under Peter Cargill in 1966 and Stevenson became associate director. Then he returned to the economics department as deputy director under Kamarck. At an annual meeting in September 1967, when Stevenson met the delegation from India in a corridor, some of them said, "You are too good a friend of India."

42. Ibid., p. 22. For an interesting perspective on Indian policies in the late 1960s, see I.P.M. Cargill, "Efforts to Influence Recipient Performance: Case Study of India," and L. K. Jha, "Comment: Leaning Against Open Doors," in John P. Lewis and Ishan Kapur, *The World Bank Group, Multilateral Aid, and the 1970s* (Lexington, Mass.: Lexington Books, 1973), pp. 89–101.
43. After his post in India, Bohr became associated with the urban projects department and then, until he retired, with the operations evaluations department.
44. Votaw, pp. 42–44.
45. Letter in the George Woods papers in the Columbia University Library.

CHAPTER 6

THE
WISDOM
OF
GEORGE
WOODS

Woods with Mohamed Shoaib, minister of finance of Pakistan, on April 20, 1966. Shoaib later became a vice-president of the Bank under Woods.

G eorge Woods was an innovative investment banker and, as president of the World Bank, he sought new ways to assist his clients, the poorer countries of the world. By employing a mix of IDA and Bank loans, he adapted the cost of capital to his clients' needs. By using a combination of IFC and Bank financing, he sought a better mix of equity and debt. By arranging both program and project loans, he hoped to avoid too rigid a reliance on benefit-cost ratios. By advocating loans for education as well as dams, by proposing to finance the Green Revolution as well as irrigation projects, by encouraging the participation of the Food and Agricultural Organization in development planning, he innovated. Within the context of the articles of agreement of the World Bank, the International Development Association, and the International Finance Corporation and the constraints of available funds, he sought the mix that would benefit his clients the most in the long run. With the encouragement of his president's council, Woods transformed the Bank from a relatively passive investment organization into an active development institution. That was the wisdom, some would say the genius, of George Woods.

Simon Aldewereld, the vice-president for finance under Woods,[1] stressed this point. "Gene [Black] was the greatest salesman in the world," he told me. "He could sell a bond to anyone. I once told Gene Black, 'I hope you realize that we lease the building at 1818 H Street because, if not, you are apt to sell it.' George was a buyer, a first-rate corporate finance man. That was the hallmark of his distinguished career in investment banking. From the very beginning of his presidency, he emphasized the need to expand our lending and put more content into it.[2]

"Black and Woods were both executives of the highest caliber. I rate them equally; that's why I said there is a time for everybody. The time had come for the buyer to follow the seller, and, thus, it was logical for George to put his mark on the Bank's development activities.

"He had the concept that, while we were on the right lending track, it was necessary to broaden the scope of lending and to put more substance into it. He brought to bear on our thinking his concepts of how to think about the future, because he was a great banker."[3]

Aldewereld's first major assignment in 1947 was to set up a disbursement system for the loans of the World Bank. The borrowing government,
as Aldewereld proposed, on the basis of a loan contract, would open a gi-
gantic, documentary letter of credit with any commercial bank in the
world in favor of the authorized supplier. The letter of credit stated at the
top: "Reimbursable by the World Bank." After the paying bank was satisfied that the documents were in order, it would pay the money. The result has been that the Bank can process a substantial amount of disbursements to its borrowers with a relatively small staff.

The Bank was governed by two provisions of the articles of agreement: except in extraordinary circumstances, the Bank should make loans
only for specific projects, and it should ensure that the proceeds of any
loan are used for the purpose for which the loan is granted. Aldewereld
took his assignment very seriously. He was aware of the mistakes and
abuses of the international lenders during the interwar period, and he was
as mindful of the small, U.S. investor in World Bank bonds as he was of
borrowers in, say, India.

At the time of the reorganization of 1952,[4] the functions of supervising projects, formerly the responsibility of the treasurer's department, and
of appraising projects, formerly carried out by the loan department, were
merged into a newly created technical operations (projects) department,[5]
and shortly thereafter Aldewereld became its director.

When George Woods became president of the World Bank, he said to
Aldewereld, in effect: I know you are very much involved with projects
and I'd like you to continue doing this. In addition, I want you also to
take responsibility for finance. I have been an investment banker all my
life, and I know this business well. Nevertheless, I want you, Siem, to take
responsibility for financial policy.[6] Aldewereld became the vice-president
for finance and a member of the president's council, second-in-command
by 1965 to Burke Knapp.

When Aldewereld became a vice-president, Bernard Chadenet and
Warren Baum became, respectively, deputy director and associate director for projects, relieving Aldewereld of the supervision of all projects.[7]
With the reorganization of 1972, Aldewereld's responsibilities were directed entirely to finance. (Warren Baum became the vice-president for
the central projects staff and Bernard Chadenet became the vice-president
for administration.) Aldewereld retired in 1974. He had spent twenty-
eight years of his working life with the Bank. "It was a period of great satisfaction," said Aldewereld in 1985. "The nineteen years of the Black and
Woods regime, from 1949–1968, were the most satisfying and fulfilling of
all. I am bold enough to think that was because of our common background: banking."[8]

Aldewereld organized the projects department into several functional
sectors or divisions: agriculture, industry, public utilities, and transportation.

To these, Woods added education and greatly expanded agriculture.[9] More importantly, Woods expanded the concept of development. As Aldewereld said, "[Woods] did not want the Bank to rest on its laurels, but wanted to open new fields of activity: secondary roads (the farm to market roads), telecommunications, to mention some. That was Woods. He did not criticize what had happened in the past, but he expanded and added. He broadened and increased the Bank's activities. He did not suppress one activity in order to create another. He made the Bank's lending activities more comprehensive. Woods did all that without departing from the basic principle that the Bank should remain a sound banking organization.[10]

"If I may characterize Woods," said Aldewereld, "I would put it as follows: he came from a poor background and, therefore, knew what poverty meant. He worked himself up to be a first-rate investment banker. Everything that he achieved in life was because of his own efforts."[11]

Woods believed that the Bank should actively search for new investment opportunities. "Woods recognized," as Roger Chaufournier put it, "that some important elements are left out if it involves too much concentration on bricks and mortar. The human element in education and agriculture is very fundamental."[12] Woods, on occasion, would even make a decision without consulting his staff. Warren Baum recalls that Woods was once considering an airport project in Nepal. Chadenet and Baum asked if they might see Woods to discuss the project with him. Woods agreed, but he opened the discussion by asking, "Do you really think I didn't know what I was doing?" Chadenet replied, "I want to be sure you are aware of all the facts before you firm your decision." Woods listened, but he didn't change his mind. According to Baum, Woods was inclined to go his own way.[13]

One day Woods called Chaufournier to say that the Bank had an economic mission in Italy that had not yet finished its report. The governor of the Bank of Italy had telephoned Woods to ask him to provide Italy with $80 million to get through a difficult foreign payment. "I know they are going to pull out of the difficulty," Woods said. "If I give $80 million to Italy today, I'll get much more back in return. You get down there and get me a project quickly." Chaufournier added, "Woods had this vision of the important things [the Bank] ought to do."[14]

On another occasion, when Woods was considering the El Chacon project in Argentina, he asked Chaufournier in the elevator, "Does that project still stand?" "Well, Mr. Woods," replied Chaufournier, "the rate of return is only about 6 percent." "Little people only think in rates of return," said Woods.[15] Chaufournier added: "[Woods] knew that the rate of return was only a discipline, that there were other dimensions that affected development. He was a precursor of important things to come, and he opened the door for the expansion of . . . activities in the social sector."[16]

Woods had an intuitive understanding of what economists call "externalities." He knew that individual projects are likely to have a higher benefit-cost ratio if they are put in place amid salubrious surroundings and favorable circumstances such as, for example, adequate skilled labor, reasonably full employment without undue inflation, a responsiveness to price changes, and a relative absence of pollution. Indeed, in the developed economies that were seeking to recover from the devastation of World War II, balance-of-payments financing was all that was required for reconstruction. On the other hand, less-developed countries sometimes suffered from such severe structural maladjustment that even the best planned projects could not succeed.

Woods had inherited a Bank in which the technical operations or projects department had enormous power. The area departments could not appraise or supervise a project without getting a decision from the projects department to allocate staff for that purpose.[17] Aldewereld described Woods's innovative ways in terms of expanding the variety and scope of projects, but Woods was also anxious to diminish the relative power of the projects department by creating "a three-legged rather than a two-legged stool."[18] He sought to do this in part by increasing the size and importance of the economics department. As has been noted, he wanted Irving Friedman to be his chief economist in part because Friedman had been in the International Monetary Fund and had top-level contacts in finance ministries. That was important to Woods as he sought to expand IDA.

Woods began to elevate economists to the top levels of the projects and area departments. One such person was Gerald Alter, who succeeded Orvis Schmidt as director of the Western Hemisphere department on May 20, 1964.[19] If Alter, who had been economic adviser in Latin America, had wanted to climb the ladder during Black's regime, he would first have had to become a loan officer. Upon being promoted to director by Woods, however, Alter changed the emphasis of the work in his department: he made needed changes in economic and financial policy the goal—and loans the carrot. Alter was doing what Woods and Friedman hoped the entire Bank would do.[20] The emphasis in the Bank, as Burke Knapp has noted, was shifting to economists and economic analysis.[21]

Perceived absorptive capacity was increasing. This was due, in large part, to the Bank's close relations with borrowers and the increased availability of technical assistance from many outside sources, multilateral and bilateral. The Bank's borrowers could successfully undertake an increasing number of investments, and Woods perceived that this was so. Aldewereld put the matter subtly: "[Woods's] knowledge and experience gradually affected personal and professional relationships. He was a stimulator and a manager of people. He had a great sense of quality, and he tried to convey that sense to others. To my mind, this is the hallmark of a good executive."[22]

Brazil, in 1964, provided an example of the way Woods, Aldewereld, and Alter thought. As Aldewereld recalled, the minister for economics of Brazil called on Woods to request that Brazil, which had been on the Bank's blacklist for several years while Brazil's inflation rate increased, should be restored to favor. President Goulart had been overthrown by Castelo Branco and the military and, the minister argued, the Bank's opposition to loans was "an obstacle standing in the way of our economic development. . . . The ports are in very poor shape; the railroads are losing astronomical amounts of money; the road system needs substantial expansion and improvement. Is there any way to get out of this impasse?" Woods thought for awhile, and then said, in effect: Mr. Minister, we feel that our position of holding back on lending to Brazil is correct. However, it can be argued that if the transport system could be improved, this would result in substantial economic benefits to Brazil. Therefore, despite the Bank's reservations about many of Brazil's policies, I propose that we move ahead by organizing a thorough study of what causes the transport sector to be in such bad condition. We should also investigate what policy and other changes are necessary to achieve a better functioning transport sector. This study should also cover what specific projects should be carried out, how much they would cost, and what their benefits would be. Such a study, because it should deal thoroughly with the physical, economic, financial, and organizational aspects, is bound to be costly. If you agree to the idea of the study, then the Bank would be prepared to contribute a sizable part of its cost. I will ask Mr. Aldewereld to go to Brazil to work out with you and your associates the organization of such a study.[23]

The minister agreed, and shortly thereafter Aldewereld proceeded to Brazil, reaching an agreement on the scope and contents of the study. An international team of twenty experts was formed in October 1964 under Barend deVries who, at that time, was the economic adviser for Latin America. The team, which completed its report in March 1965, focused on policy and procedural problems, many of which were discussed with the Brazilians and resolved to the Bank's satisfaction. The executive directors devoted an entire meeting to deVries's report on Brazil. As a consequence, lending to Brazil picked up considerably. During the period of rising inflation (1959 to 1964), the Bank made no loans to Brazil. Two loans for electric power totaling $79.5 million were made in late February 1965, however, and, in fiscal 1965/66, the Bank made sixteen loans aggregating almost $400 million, roughly matching Bank loans to Italy.

This was part of Woods's strategy: he believed that the Bank should actively search for new projects. Prior to 1963, the Bank had followed the general rule that project preparation was the responsibility primarily of the Bank's borrowers, generally with the assistance of consultants. But

that view was changing, in part because many of the Bank's less-sophisti-
cated borrowers did not have the ability or the trained staff to prepare
proper financial analyses and forecasts. They needed the Bank's assistance.

In November 1963, Vice-president Geoffrey Wilson, presumably on
instructions from George Woods, asked area department heads to respond
in writing to a series of questions on project preparation. What is the extent of the need for advice on project preparation that the Bank is not
now meeting? Is the problem mainly that governments, although in pos-
session of the raw material on which to take decisions, need to be guided,
encouraged, and supported in the decisionmaking process? Do governments need advice, at earlier stages, in project selection, preparatory work,
choice of consultants, drafting terms of reference, and supervision? Is the
need primarily for advice and assistance in the actual engineering of projects? Do the answers to these questions depend to any significant extent
upon the field of activity involved? Assuming that there is a need for
more advice on project preparation, which other competent specialized
agencies are able to provide advice? To what extent should the Bank itself
endeavor to satisfy the need? To what extent would it be desirable to establish regional offices for this purpose? Could resident advisory missions
play an effective role?

Woods was preparing greatly to expand the efforts of the Bank to assist the developing countries in identifying good projects within the
framework of sensible, macroeconomic policies—efforts that continue to
this day. Woods did not actively seek publicity. Indeed, one of Woods's favorite sayings was: "You can accomplish a lot of good if you don't care
who gets the credit."

George Woods was primarily responsible for initiating the active efforts of the Bank to help developing countries help themselves. It was he
who turned the World Bank from a bank into a development institution,
and all subsequent presidents of the World Bank have operated within
that paradigm.

The minutes of the senior staff meetings of late 1963 through early
1966 are replete with illustrations of George Woods's initiatives, particularly in education and agriculture. At a meeting of department heads (affectionately labeled "the lost weekend") convened in Williamsburg, Virginia, in early October 1963, policy papers on education and agriculture
were presented and discussed. Richard Demuth presented the policy paper
on education; David Gordon led the working-party on agriculture.

While Woods was in Pakistan to lead a discussion of a group of donors
for the Indus Valley irrigation works, Geoffrey Wilson, on November 6,
1963, was chairing a meeting of the senior staff on education policy. At
the same meeting, Richard Demuth reported that fourteen underdeveloped countries were supporting a resolution calling on the Economic and

Social Council of the United Nations to take steps, either through the creation of a new commission or otherwise, to review the inflow of capital into the underdeveloped countries.[24] Such a review was intended to systematize pressures for an increased capital inflow and for a UN development fund. Raul Prebisch, the chairman of the United Nations Conference on Trade and Development (UNCTAD), wished to inject the issue of the needs of the underdeveloped countries for capital.

The World Bank under Eugene Black had succeeded in deflecting demands in the United Nations for a greater inflow of unrestricted capital to developing countries by agreeing reluctantly to an International Development Association that would provide grant-type assistance from the wealthier countries on terms over which the wealthier countries retained control. Now the developing countries were again seeking additional sources of assistance that they could control. Indeed, on November 18, 1963, it was announced in a preliminary draft that the Secretary-General of the United Nations proposed to merge the Special United Nations Fund for Economic Development (SUNFED) and the technical assistance program under a new UN development agency.

George Woods decided to meet the specialized agencies of the United Nations half way. The Bank would cooperate with the United Nations Economic, Social and Cultural Organization (UNESCO) in formulating educational projects, with the Food and Agricultural Organization (FAO) in considering agricultural projects, and with the United Nations Development Program (UNDP) in looking at preinvestment reports about potential projects.[25]

On December 4, 1963, it was reported to the senior staff that Geoffrey Wilson would explore with the director-general of UNESCO in Paris the implications of the latter's recent letter to Woods on the subject of UNESCO-Bank cooperation. In particular, he would inquire what staff could be made available to the Bank to work on education projects. The Economic Development Institute, founded in Washington as a staff college for senior government officials, had existed since 1956 and was eminently successful in what it sought to do. But the Bank continued to feel its way in education within the developing countries themselves. Everyone realized instinctively that education that improves the skills of workers is beneficial, but no attempt has ever been made within the Bank to compute benefit-cost ratios for education projects: the benefits are too nebulous and too long term.

The first IDA credit for education was committed to Tunisia—in 1962. In 1963, education officially became a division within the projects department, and the Bank joined with UNESCO to work cooperatively on education projects. The first Bank loan for education was to an agriculture college in the Philippines in 1964. By the time of the Bank's annual report in 1964, IDA credits had been extended for education in Tanganyika and Pakistan. In Tanganyika, two new government schools were in the process of being constructed, and fifty-three others were being expanded and better equipped to provide nearly seven thousand additional places for students. In Pakistan, two agricultural universities were being expanded as well as fourteen technical institutes and three technical teachers' colleges. By the time of the Bank's annual meeting in 1967, Bank and IDA lending for education had risen to over $50 million per year.

In an article in the *Columbia Journal of World Business*, George Woods made clear his dedication to the Bank's investments in education:

> We have chosen to concentrate on technical education and vocational training for industry, commerce, and agriculture at whatever level seems appropriate, including adult education. We have chosen, too, to concentrate on secondary education in general. Finally, we include teacher training in the investments we make, since it is clear that the supply of teachers must keep pace with school expansion. . . .
>
> [When] we came to consider finance for an agricultural school in the Philippines, we informed that government that a regular Bank loan was all that would be available, since the Philippines was not then eligible for the easier terms permissible with International Development Association credits. Actually, of the thirteen educational projects, totaling nearly $110 million, which we have considered in detail so far, three have been financed by regular Bank loans, running from twenty-five to thirty years and, currently, carrying 6% interest, while ten have been financed by IDA credits running for fifty years and carrying a three-quarters of one per cent service charge. . . .
>
> So far, about 68% of the funds we have committed to projects in education have been earmarked for school construction, 30% for equipment, and only 2% for the salaries of foreign specialists. This apparent bias toward bricks and mortar and equipment is misleading. In the first place, most of our investments involve participation with some other qualified agency, a foundation or a bilateral aid agency, which is already providing staff assistance. In the second place, the actual expenditures made with World Bank Group funds are often less important than the reforms and innovations agreed to during the loan negotiations.[26]

The same thing happened with the collaboration between the Bank and the FAO. During the Black years, it had been necessary to find projects that, because of their obvious revenue generating capabilities, would secure the support of the Bank's bondholders. That made the Bank essentially a power and transport projects bank—an infrastructure bank. There was an occasional industry or agriculture (irrigation) project, but the main preoccupation was with power and transport.

Early on, George Woods became dissatisfied with the Bank's approach to agriculture. The creditworthiness of the Bank had been established. IDA had been added because, by then, the efficiency of the Bank was beyond dispute. Woods's preoccupation was not so much with securing finance as with achieving maximum development impact. Woods took the position that if the agriculture projects division could not put together a far more aggressive program in a fairly short time, he would give serious consideration to having the appraisal and supervision of agricultural projects done through a cooperative program with the FAO. Indeed, by the time Woods and Aldewereld visited the director-general of FAO in Rome on November 8, 1963, to put a seal of approval on Bank-FAO collaboration, they received an enthusiastic reception. The way had been prepared by Richard Demuth and others.[27]

The agriculture projects division began to explore the possibility of a rapid expansion of its capability in agriculture. The small division (about twelve people in 1961, mainly agronomists) grew to over fifty people by 1967, and the Bank almost doubled its capacity in agriculture when it joined forces with the FAO. The FAO accepted responsibility for identification, planning, preparation, and feasibility of agricultural projects, and the Bank retained responsibility for appraisal and supervision. Together with the FAO, the Bank increased its lending to agriculture at least tenfold between 1961 and 1968. As Willi Wapenhans, a one-time farmer turned economist, observed in 1988, "It showed the fertility of Woods's mind."[28]

George Woods was well aware of the work of the Rockefeller Foundation, for he had been a trustee of the foundation before he became president of the World Bank. Under the direction of Dr. Norman Borlaug and Dr. George Harrar, the Rockefeller Foundation was largely responsible for initiating what came to be known as the Green Revolution—for which Dr. Borlaug received the Nobel Peace Prize in 1970.

In the early 1960s, food production had been falling behind population growth in much of the developing world, but, by 1968, Pakistan had planted more than a million acres of newly developed wheat seed. Between 1965 and 1972, India expanded its wheat production from 11 million to 26 million tons.[29] Starvation in Asia was less likely, at least for those who could afford to buy wheat. That is why George Woods pushed so hard for the reform of agriculture in Pakistan and India.

Included in George Woods's personal papers is a sixteen-page monograph prepared by Dr. George Harrar, who had joined the Rockefeller Foundation from the department of plant pathology at Washington State College, entitled "Principles for Progress in World Agriculture." The manuscript was presented in 1966 at the 33rd annual meeting of the National Agricultural Chemicals Association in West Virginia.[30]

In 1941, briefly to review a bit of history, the Mexican government asked the Rockefeller Foundation for help in improving corn yields. The foundation sent a small team of specialists. They traveled throughout the country and talked with political, scientific, and business leaders. Their report urged the foundation to respond favorably and to seek increased yields of both corn and wheat by improving varieties, soil fertility, and the control of pests. The U.S. and Mexican scientists found that the main bottlenecks in corn production were inefficient varieties, losses due to pests and pathogens, and inadequate management. The principal problem in wheat production was virulent strains of stem-rust, to which all varieties were highly susceptible. While the plant breeders, plant pathologists, and entomologists were attacking these problems, soil scientists were improving the systems of soil management and water utilization, and advocating the increased use of fertilizers.

Mexico became self-sufficient in wheat production in 1956, just fifteen years after the cooperative program was initiated. The corn gap was closed in 1958. This was possible because of the development of rust-resistant, dwarf varieties of wheat that made highly efficient use of fertilizers.[31]

The government of Mexico provided the incentives that stimulated the Mexican farmers to improve production methods and technologies as new knowledge and materials became available. Incentives included price supports, agricultural credits, subsidies to increase supplies of chemical fertilizers and crop protectants, extension of irrigation systems, and improvements in the network of highways to provide outlets for farm products. It was estimated by Theodore Schultz, professor of economics at the University of Chicago and Nobel laureate in economic science in 1979, that the total cost of the program to both the Rockefeller Foundation and the Mexican government in 1966 was being returned to the Mexican economy at an interest rate of at least 400 percent each year.

Within a few years, the foundation's cooperative program in Mexico attracted the interest of other countries. In 1950 the Rockefeller Foundation embarked on a similar program with the Colombian government. In 1955, work was extended to Chile; and in 1957 to India.

Another example of private philanthropy's assistance to foreign agriculture was begun in 1960 when the Ford and Rockefeller foundations joined forces to establish in the Philippines an international institute to help solve the problems of rice production in Asia. The teams assembled some ten thousand strains of rice from every corner of the world and began the process of crossbreeding. Success came early when a tall, vigorous variety from Indonesia was combined with a dwarf-rice strain from Taiwan to produce IR-8, the first of the "miracle rices."

The International Rice Research Institute has become an important Asian center and has achieved world renown because of its contribution to the improvement in yield and quality of rice. It is engaged in important cooperative activities with Thailand, India, and Pakistan and has relationships also with Indonesia, Ceylon, and Malaysia. This intense focus, through a combination of biology and engineering, resulted in the production of substantial quantities of seeds that yielded five to seven times the national average of most countries hitherto.

Professor Schultz provided an economic rationale for the Green Revolution.

Economists have fallen into the practice [Schultz wrote] of dividing the production agents into two parts, one of which consists of "land, labor and capital (goods)" and the other of "technological change." But what is all too seldom recognized in making this division is that the term "technological change" is merely a bit of shorthand for an array of (new) factors of production that have been omitted in the specification of the factors. . . . A technology is always embodied in particular factors and, therefore, in order to introduce a new technology, it is necessary to employ a set of factors of production that differs from the set formerly employed.[32]

In other words, land without fertilizer is different from fertilized land; land lacking in rainfall is different from irrigated land; new strains of seeds are different from the seeds of yesterday; and labor trained in the latest techniques of farm management (perhaps at experiment stations or research universities) is different from traditional farm labor.

This is not to say that the term "technological change" may not be a useful device for some expository purposes. But it is not an analytical concept for explaining economic growth. To use it for this purpose is a confession of ignorance because it is only a name for a set of unexplained residuals. . . . When these residual values are large . . . it leaves much of real growth unexplained.[33]

Schultz argued that:

The man who is bound by traditional agriculture cannot produce much food no matter how rich the land. Thrift and work are not enough to overcome the niggardliness of this type of agriculture. To provide the abundance of farm products requires that the farmer has access to and has the skill and knowledge to use what science knows about soils, plants, animals, and machines. To command farmers to increase production is doomed to failure even though they have access to knowledge. Instead an approach that provides incentives and rewards to farmers is required. The knowledge that makes the transformation possible is a form of capital which entails investment—investment not only in material inputs in which a part of this knowledge is embedded but importantly also investment in farm people.[34]

Woods outlined his proposed Bank policies on agriculture in a memorandum of January 1964. Crucially important to development, Woods

argued, was the evolution of policies that would give increasingly productive employment to the rural population. An essential condition for such
an evolution is agrarian reform in the broadest sense—including improvements not only in land utilization and, where appropriate, in tenure
arrangements, but also in government agricultural services, in price incentives and other economic policies, in marketing, and in the supply of
credit. A notable feature of Bank lending for agriculture during Woods's
presidency was the explosion of Bank and IDA loans for credit to rural
banks in developing countries—loans that included the financing of irrigation pumps, an important factor in raising the yields of wheat and rice
in India and Pakistan.[35]

Agriculture should be treated as a system, according to Woods, with
each component linked in a chain: research to develop technology, extension to spread knowledge, credit to finance it, and roads to move its
products. For the Bank to assist in providing all these services, however, it
was necessary to relax the Bank's requirement that it should finance only
capital goods and only the foreign-exchange component of those goods.
The articles of agreement of the Bank specify that

> in exceptional circumstances when local currency required for the pur-
> poses of the loan cannot be raised by the borrower on reasonable terms,
> [the Bank may] provide the borrower as part of the loan with an appro-
> priate amount of that currency.[36]

Particularly in the case of Bank and IDA loans for agriculture and education, and particularly with India and Pakistan, Woods sought to finance the whole project (or chain of projects) regardless of whether imported or domestic goods or services were required.

In a memorandum entitled "Foreign Exchange Loans for Local Expenditures," Woods wrote: "There is no economic significance in the distribution between financing the imports required for a project and financing the local expenditures. Both accomplish the purposes of moving
real resources from one country to another and both serve the purpose of
assisting in financing economic development.

"[However] care must be taken to conserve borrowing capacity by in-
suring that borrowing countries make the maximum effort to encourage
savings and reserve their external borrowing capacity for projects of high
priority."[37]

Bank and IDA loans of foreign currencies may be made available to a
borrowing government to finance imported *or domestic goods*, though, if
domestic goods are supplied, the foreign currencies can be put to an alternative use. They are rather like program or balance-of-payments loans
in that the ultimate use of the loan cannot be precisely specified. Woods

was anxious, nevertheless, to see that the chain of projects was not broken.[38]

Woods was particularly anxious to stimulate the use of fertilizers. To accomplish this, he turned frequently to the International Finance Corporation (IFC). The 1966/67 annual report of the Bank and IDA states:

> One of the essentials for the expansion of food production is the increased application of chemical fertilizers. On behalf of the Group, IFC has taken the lead in discussions aimed at establishing new fertilizer plants in the developing countries.[39]

The IFC was the second member of the World Bank Group in point of time. As mentioned above, the inaugural meeting of the IFC took place on July 24, 1956, under the presidency of Robert L. Garner, who had been vice-president of the World Bank since early 1947. The articles of agreement of the IFC authorized an initial capital of $100 million for loans to new or expanding *private enterprises* without the guarantee of any government.[40] In February 1961, it was announced that an amendment would be sought that removed the ban on nonvoting investments in the capital stock of such enterprises. In October 1961, Martin Rosen[41] succeeded Robert Garner as chief executive officer of the IFC.

At one point in early 1961, Robert Garner suggested that the World Bank was cutting into the IFC's business. He argued that the IFC was prepared to make good loans to good private enterprises, but that less expensive money was coming from the World Bank through private development banks.[42] Strictly *private* enterprise, Garner maintained, was within the province of the IFC. After Rosen succeeded Garner, Eugene Black decided to establish in the IFC a separate development banks department, later renamed development finance companies department, that would be responsible for advising the entire World Bank Group. The new unit was announced to the public in late 1961, and Abdel Galeel El Emary, an Egyptian, was asked to be its first director. Within a few months, El Emary's attention was turned to Africa. The African countries were trying to establish an African Development Bank, and El Emary's help was needed. So William Diamond, who had already been deeply involved with development banks,[43] was asked on July 1, 1962, to become director of the development bank's department of the IFC. George Woods became president of the World Bank on January 1, 1963. Thus, although much had started under Eugene Black, the real expansion in the development banking field took place during the five years under George Woods.

At the beginning of 1963, Diamond's became a full-fledged operating department that could write appraisal reports and negotiate loans for the IFC as well as the World Bank's area departments. It stood in the same relationship to the Bank as the Bank's technical operations (projects) departments. In one country after another, development finance institutions were created or enlarged: in Liberia, Turkey, Malaysia, Tunisia, Nigeria, the Philippines, Thailand, Indonesia, Korea, India, Pakistan, Venezuela, Ecuador, and Colombia—all private. Martin Rosen and George Woods felt that development finance companies offered an opportunity for the IFC to work abroad, to participate in large projects, and to induce U.S., European, and Japanese investment corporations to participate with the IFC in financing private development banks in Third World countries.

On June 10, 1964, George Woods formally proposed that the World Bank be allowed to make loans to the IFC of up to four times the IFC's unimpaired subscribed capital and surplus—approximately $400 million. In an earlier memorandum (July 13, 1963), Woods had suggested that the Bank also be allowed to extend loans to *private* shareholder-owned industrial enterprises and development finance companies *without the borrowing government's guarantee of repayment.* He mentioned this idea in his address to the 1963 annual meeting of the board of governors and pursued it in meetings with the executive directors, but the executive directors persuaded Woods that Bank funds might more usefully be channeled through the IFC. Amendments to the IFC's and the World Bank's charters were necessary. Hearings before the Senate Foreign Relations Committee took place in June 1965. The same month, the IFC began to be represented in meetings of the senior staff of the Bank. Following congressional approval of the changes in the articles of agreement and partly because of the newly available credit from the World Bank, by the last year of Woods's presidency (1968), the IFC was able to commit over $50 million, in contrast to only $20 million in 1963/64. In 1968, moreover, the IFC was able to sell to private investors some $24 million of claims it had accumulated, freeing thereby additional funds for commitment in the future.[44]

George Woods innovated in other areas as well. In late 1963 and early 1964, there was much discussion by the senior staff of the Bank of two interrelated subjects: whether Bank loans should continue to be available to the more advanced countries that could easily borrow at market rates of interest; and whether the Bank should transfer some of its earnings to IDA. Japan had continued to be a major borrower (until 1967) from the Bank, long after its economy had regained its pre–World War II capability. Australia and Norway continued to borrow from the Bank as well.

Raymond Cope prepared a paper on the subject of Bank loans to countries with established market credit.[45] Cope suggested that the Bank continue to make loans available when loans at market rates of interest were difficult to obtain. In late 1963, George Woods suggested that Cope's proposals appealed to him because, if the anticipated interest equalization tax became law,[46] countries such as Australia and Japan, which seemed to have been weaned away from Bank borrowing, might again apply on the grounds that the cost of capital in the United States had become unduly high. Woods favored lending to these countries at the rate the market would have charged in the absence of the interest equalization tax. Nonetheless, the Bank began to charge its more industrialized member countries interest rates consistent with the market, and the industrialized countries ceased to borrow from the Bank.

At about the same time, it was decided that neither the Bank nor IDA should discriminate in their charges. The Bank should continue to charge an interest rate to all eligible borrowers slightly higher than the rate at which it could sell its own bonds. By blending Bank and IDA lending, however, the World Bank Group could charge an interest rate somewhere between zero and the rate charged by the Bank.

The articles of agreement specified that commissions on loans made during the first ten years of the Bank's operations should be set aside as a special reserve to cover any losses on loans and guarantees, after which dividends could be paid to the contributing governments. Soon after the original articles of agreement were ratified, provision was also made for a supplemental reserve. But there had been no defaults on either Bank or IDA loans as of 1964, the executive directors of the Bank had voted to eschew dividends, and the annual net income of the Bank was increasing, as Mason and Asher put it, "at an almost indecent rate."[47] Eugene Black had assured the financial community that there would be no financial linkage between the Bank and IDA, but George Woods had made no such commitment.[48] Thus, it was decided that the Bank should transfer to IDA $50 million during fiscal 1964/65. The Bank has continued to transfer some of its net income to IDA ever since. Indeed, by the end of fiscal 1981/82, the Bank had become IDA's fifth-largest contributor.[49] George Woods was doing everything in his power to make IDA's funding greater than the Bank's funding—in part because Woods perceived that Bank debt was growing faster than many developing nations' exports.

George Woods was enthusiastic in his support for the coordination of aid amongst the high-income nations who, like the United States government through its Agency for International Development, provided loans and grant-type assistance bilaterally to selected developing countries.

The Aid-India Consortium (see Chapter 5) had been organized by Eugene Black in August 1958 when it became apparent that India's shrinking holdings of foreign exchange would be inadequate to finance India's second Five Year Plan.[50] In early 1960, Eugene Black had proposed the mission of the Three Wise Men because the India consortium had reservations about India's proposed third Five Year Plan.[51] In early 1962,

after Pakistan had been judged unable to propose projects that could usefully use the funds the Pakistan consortium had made available, that consortium began to be suspect. The coordination of aid continued to be popular, however, particularly in the State Department in Washington, which
worked through the development assistance committee of the OECD in
Paris.

In 1961, when William Diamond was deputy director of the Western
Hemisphere department in the Bank, he, John Adler, and Jerry Alter prepared a memorandum to Orvis Schmidt and Burke Knapp urging aid coordination for several Latin American countries. They got nowhere, but
after George Woods became president, the Bank sponsored a number of
consultative groups of bilateral donors.[52]

George Woods paid a ten-day visit to Nigeria in 1965 after Chief
Adebo complained that the consultative group for Nigeria was not responding adequately to Nigeria's current development plan, following
which, in February 1966, despite a coup d'état in Nigeria, the meetings in
Paris of the consultative group for Nigeria were notably more successful
than previous meetings: the Bank itself, presumably at Woods's urging, declared its intention of committing up to $100 million of new loans for the
coming year.

Perhaps the most ambitious project involving the Bank and a consortium of the governments of Canada, France, Italy, the United Kingdom,
and the United States, as well as the government of Pakistan, was the Tarbela dam project, which was part of the proposal to divide and better use
the waters of the Indus Valley. In August 1951, in an article in *Collier's*
magazine, David Lilienthal, who had been a chairman of the Tennessee
Valley Authority, wrote that the whole Indus system, whose waters served
both India and Pakistan, should be developed as a unit. Eugene Black read
the article and responded enthusiastically. On September 8, 1951, Black
wrote to the prime ministers of India and Pakistan (Nehru and Ali Khan):
"Since the Bank's name has now been publicly mentioned in this connection, I should like to ask you whether you are disposed to look with favor
on Mr. Lilienthal's proposal."[53]

Pakistan responded. India was more reserved, for the headwaters of
the Indus River originated in India and, therefore, by riparian law, belonged to India. Nine years passed before the Indus Water Treaty was
signed in 1960. As part of that treaty, it was envisioned that a huge dam
be constructed in the gorge at Tarbela, near Rawalpindi, west of Kashmir.
For his work as mediator between India and Pakistan, William Iliff was
knighted, but it fell to George Woods to promote the Tarbela dam.[54]

The Pakistanis had made it clear to the World Bank and a number of
friendly countries that, unless they were assisted in the development of
the Indus Valley, the partition of the waters would be insufficient to keep

their population alive and allow for the further development of the country. Preliminary surveys were not promising. Finally, Pakistan's president,
Ayub Khan, and George Woods agreed to the appointment of an independent expert to write a report on the technical feasibility and economic
justification of building a dam at Tarbela. Woods chose Dr. Peter Lieftinck, who was already the executive director for the Netherlands, Yugoslavia, Israel, and Cyprus, in which appointment he continued.[55]

Woods arranged a World Bank loan of $5 million and said, "We want
you to submit a report on the feasibility of Tarbela and the justification
of the dam within one year. You can take some more time in the field
study of water power development."[56] Lieftinck's total report constituted
twenty-four volumes. Lieftinck visited the Tarbela dam site every three
months for four years. He recruited staff members from the World Bank,
one of whom was Bob Sadove, and hired three consultant firms: Alexander Gibbs and Partners, London; Stone and Webster, the United States;
and Illico, a Dutch agricultural development firm. The expected benefit-
cost ratio was favorable: the investment required was estimated at $800
million, a return of 8 percent.

Tarbela was not completed while Woods was president, but the project was ultimately executed rapidly and with reasonable success. The dams
were opened too soon, causing damage from cavitation; and additional
costs were incurred. But, on the whole, the project went well from the
start. Millions of acres were better irrigated than before, and a huge power
plant was built that provides most of Pakistan with power. During the oil
crisis of 1973, when the price of oil rose sixfold, the value of comparable
energy also rose so that the returns became tremendous.

In 1965, the executive directors of the Bank gave final approval to an
International Centre for the Settlement of International Disputes
(ICSID) between investors and foreign governments. As early as 1947,
the Bank, at the particular insistence of Robert Garner, had suggested that
a body of experts be established to recommend equitable settlements of
debts defaulted by various governments. Eugene Black, with the help of
George Woods and William Iliff, was particularly adept as an international mediator: settling the Suez Canal dispute and allocating the waters
of the Indus River.[57] But it was during George Woods's presidency that the
ICSID, to which contending parties to an investment dispute could have
recourse on an entirely voluntary basis, was formally negotiated. As Aron
Broches put it: "The Centre was something new. [Woods] brought this
about, or helped to start to bring it about. It was an achievement of his."[58]

The ICSID did not come fully into being until a little over a year
after Woods's term as president had come to an end, but Woods and
Broches were strong supporters of the convention. It established a legal
framework within which the parties could work. It is administered by the

ICSID as a separate legal entity, not by the Bank, though the Bank makes its facilities available. Some cases are still going on; in some cases there have been awards that have been complied with. In half of the cases where there were final awards, the investors won; in the other half, the developing countries won.

Woods was tough on defaulting government debtors. The default on the Greek public debt caused the Bank to refuse to lend to Greece for many years. Woods was active in pushing the Greek government to settle. The Bank was finally about to make its first loan when the colonels took over from the elected government of Prime Minister Andreas Papandreou (the senior). (Andreas Papandreou, the son of the prime minister and later prime minister himself, had met Woods at the University of California at Berkeley.) The senior Papandreou went into exile in Sweden and wrote a letter to Woods urging him not to proceed with the loan. "I know that you were the one who made Greece eligible for a World Bank loan," wrote Woods. "Nothing would have given me more pleasure than to have signed this first loan with you. But this is a loan that is good regardless of the regime, and, therefore, we have decided to make it."[59]

Woods's innovative activities were primarily in proposing ways in which resources could be better used in pursuit of the Bank's objectives. As William Diamond put it, "He expanded the horizons of the Bank. . . . The new emphasis on economic work was related to this; developing country knowledge and country programs was essential to broader, effective use of the Bank's and IDA's resources. In addition, he was very much involved in launching a new take-off for IFC: by the transfer of industry work, by the new emphasis on development banks, and by making new resources available to IFC. . . . [He] felt that IFC as a $15 or $20 million per year institution didn't make any difference in the world. Before he left it was up to $60 or $70 million and within a year thereafter it was at $100 million, which meant that IFC could begin to visualize an effective future."[60]

The projects of the Bank had increasingly large components of technical assistance. Woods substantially expanded the work in agriculture and education. He backed the Green Revolution and employed the expertise of the FAO and UNESCO.

Woods was transforming the Bank into a development-assistance institution.

Notes

1. Simon Aldewereld, born in Amsterdam in 1909, studied economics at the University of Amsterdam, receiving the equivalent of a master's degree. In 1940

he escaped with his wife to England where he was asked to go to the Netherlands West Indies (to which the Netherlands government had transferred title of many Netherlands assets) as secretary of the Foreign Exchange Commission. With the Japanese invasion of the Netherlands East Indies, he was transferred to New York and asked to do a similar job there. He became deputy to Crena de Iongh, a delegate to the Bretton Woods Conference who became the first treasurer of the World Bank. In 1946, Aldewereld became his assistant.

2. See Chapter 1.

3. Robert W. Oliver, "A Conversation with Simon Aldewereld," *Conversations About George Woods and the World Bank*, New York City, November 2, 1985, p. 27. See also Aldewereld, pp. 32–35.

4. The primary reason for the reorganization of 1952 was to give the loan or operations (area) departments more power, and the research or economics department less power. Three area departments became responsible for loan negotiations, and the technical operations department became responsible for engineering analyses and technical assistance. Most economists were assigned to an area department or the technical operations department. The economics department was reduced to an economics staff. For an insight into this reorganization, see the interview of Paul N. Rosenstein-Rodan, conducted by Robert W. Oliver, the 1961 Oral History Project, Columbia University. Aldewereld commented many years later, "I would have preferred at that time that simultaneously there had been established an economics department, not as a research department, which we had, but as an entity separate and independent from the area departments, which would operationally exercise the same strict judgement on economic policies and future policies of a given country as the projects department did for projects."— Aldewereld, p. 16.

5. The technical operations department was renamed the projects department in January 1965, by which time Aldewereld had come to be known as Mr. Projects.

6. Aldewereld, p. 10.

7. Aldewereld commented, "I was fortunate to attract good people. . . . Men like Bob Sadove. . . . One of the best was Warren Baum. . . . You know the old fable of the sorcerer's apprentice? He was my apprentice, but, in due course, he also became my master. The concepts were mine, but he perfected them. . . . When I retired, he was doing a job on projects which was much more refined. . . . That's why Warren in his book wrote to me 'You started it all.'"—Aldewereld, p. 15.

Warren Baum had earned a master's degree in public administration from Columbia University and a Ph.D. in economics from Harvard. After working for the Marshall Plan and writing a book on the French economy for the RAND corporation, he moved to the World Bank in 1959 as a country economist working on France and Algeria and, later, on Spain and Portugal as well. He became a loan officer in the Europe, Africa, and Australasia department and negotiated loans for many projects. He rose to become a division chief before he was invited by Aldewereld to become the head of the transportation division of the projects department (he had become deeply involved with the Spanish railways). He was the first economist to bridge the gap between an area and a projects department.

8. Aldewereld, p. 33.

9. By 1985, the sectors had become agriculture; education; energy; industry; transportation; population; health and nutrition; water and sanitation; and urbanization. See Warren C. Baum and Stokes M. Tolbert, *Investing in Development* (published for the World Bank by Oxford University Press, 1985).

The changing nomenclature had already, in 1968, added to Bank lore. After George Woods had retired, he was to be presented with a medal at the Mauritanian headquarters at the United Nations in New York. Richard Westebbe, who had worked for the Bank in Mauritania earlier, was present for the ceremony. After Woods's speech, Woods was alone momentarily with Westebbe. Woods asked, "What are you doing now?" Westebbe replied, "I am working in the economics of urbanization." "What the hell is that?" questioned Woods with raised eyebrows.—Robert W. Oliver, "A Conversation with Richard Westebbe," *Conversations About George Woods and the World Bank*, Washington, D.C., January 25, 1988, p. 13.

10. Aldewereld added: "It is not for nothing that the word *bank* appears in the title. It is a bank. Nobody ever should say that it is a welfare organization. It is not a charitable institution, it is a bank. Other people might disagree, but that is my opinion."—Aldewereld, p. 38.

11. Aldewereld, p. 33.

12. Roger Chaufournier, interview by Robert W. Oliver, July 22, 1986, World Bank archives, p. 22. Chaufournier studied law in France but moved into economics, sociology, and political science in England, Sweden, and the University of Illinois. He joined the Bank in 1952 after being a consultant to the Bureau of Labor Statistics. He was hired by Leonard Rist, head of the economics department, but went to work in the new Western Hemisphere department under Burke Knapp. He worked with Robert Sadove on an economic report on Bolivia, was in Peru for four years, becoming head of the mission along with Mervyn Weiner after the first year. Chaufournier was the division chief for Chile when a consultative group was formed. (The first consultative group in Latin America was organized for Colombia in 1963. George Woods was anxious to integrate the economic with the operational work under the umbrella of the Alliance for Progress.) Chaufournier became deputy to Gerald Alter in May 1964, when Alter succeeded Orvis Schmidt as director for Latin America. Later, he became the director for West Africa and then for Europe, the Middle East, and North Africa. He died on March 14, 1994.

13. Warren Baum, interview by Robert W. Oliver, July 23, 1986, Bank archives, p. 47.

14. Chaufournier, p. 24.

15. Ibid.

16. Roger Chaufournier, "The Coming of Age," *Finance and Development*, June 1984, p. 35.

17. See Baum, p. 7, and Chaufournier, p. 41.

18. See Robert W. Oliver, "A Conversation with Barend deVries," *Conversations About George Woods and the World Bank*, Washington, D.C., June 28, 1990. Barend (Bob) deVries moved to Washington in 1949 from MIT. Earlier, he had worked with the Cowles Commission at the University of Chicago. He became skilled in mathematical economics. In Washington, he joined the research department of the IMF, working with Jacques Polak on multiple-currency and foreign-trade problems. In 1951, he went over to work on exchange restrictions with Irving Friedman. Friedman had an exciting group of people, including deVries's future wife, Margaret Garritsen, and a small group of eight to twelve economists with whom Friedman was in close contact. He was sent on missions to Iran, Western Europe, and Latin America. When the Fund sought to move him to the Middle East in 1955 without his consent, he decided to go to the World Bank, joining the Latin American department. He spent six months in Colombia as an adviser in the planning office. When he returned, in 1960, he became the division

chief for Brazil, Colombia, and Ecuador. Later he became the economic adviser for Latin America. For a time, he was an active member of the economics committee under Friedman and Kamarck, and in 1965 transferred to the economics department as deputy to Kamarck. His title was soon changed to senior adviser so that he might have more time for research and Alexander Stevenson became Kamarck's deputy. Then, in 1970, deVries became a de facto economic adviser under Roger Chaufournier in West Africa, Ghana in particular. In 1974, he became again the economic adviser for Latin America.

19. Jerry Alter moved to the Bank in 1951 after working in various U.S. government agencies. He joined the economics staff under Leonard Rist, working primarily with Paul Rosenstein-Rodan and John Adler. He shifted to Western Hemisphere after having spent several years on general studies. By 1958, he was heavily involved in the review and preparation of country economic reports, focusing on creditworthiness. He tried to identify major sector problems and to project the future growth rate and the balance-of-payments outlook. Gradually, his reports began to inquire about the adequacy of a country's investment program. They began to analyze by sectors, which required the participation of the staff of the projects department. By 1964, when Alter became head of the Western Hemisphere area department, he began to seek projects where the Bank could exercise a constructive policy influence.

20. See Robert W. Oliver, "A Conversation with Gerald Alter," *Conversations About George Woods and the World Bank*, Washington, D.C., July 13, 1985, p. 8. Alter had the assistance at various times of Barend deVries, Roger Chaufournier, and Mervyn Weiner as chief economists for Latin America.

21. See Chapter 3, p. 64. As Barend deVries observed, "Woods never destroyed the project complex. This was still strong and continued to be strong, but it didn't have a stranglehold on the Bank anymore. The project complex no longer exists after the reorganization of 1987. If you listen to the engineers, you know the project complex has ended, which, by the way, I think is unfortunate. The ability of the project complex to provide technical assistance to countries and help them organize large projects was a very essential contribution of the World Bank."—DeVries, p. 18.

22. Aldewereld, p. 31.

23. Ibid., pp. 29–30.

24. The fourteen were Argentina, Bolivia, Brazil, Burma, Chile, Ceylon, Ghana, India, Indonesia, Iraq, Liberia, Pakistan, Nigeria, and Yugoslavia.

25. Julian Grenfell has suggested that Woods "won a major battle with the staff of the Bank in bringing the Bank to closer relation with the United Nations. That stands, in my view, as one of his most important achievements."—Robert W. Oliver, "A Conversation with Julian Grenfell," *Conversations About George Woods and the World Bank*, Washington, D.C., July 15, 1986, p. 26. For an interesting discussion of Woods's relations with some of the UN agencies, see Robert W. Oliver, "A Conversation with Irving Friedman, V," *Conversations About George Woods and the World Bank*, Washington, D.C., July 23, 1985, pp. 11–29.

26. George Woods, "Sow Education Aid, Reap Economic Growth," *Columbia Journal of World Business*, Vol. 1, No. 3, Summer 1966, pp. 37ff. See also the annual report for 1966/67, World Bank and IDA, p. 13:

Of the total proceeds of loans and credits for education projects, about two-thirds have assisted education at the secondary level. Commitments at the university level account for just over 15% and the rest is divided more or less equally between other post-secondary education and vocational training. By curricula, about 40% of the funds have been directed toward general education, 30% to technical education and 20% to agricultural studies, most of the remaining 10% going to teacher training. A substantial part of the funds for general education has gone into science laboratories and workshops for existing schools, making possible a more modern and practical curriculum at this level.

Woods spoke often of the need for Bank loans and IDA credits for education. In his address to the UN Conference on Trade and Development (Geneva, March 25, 1964, p. 13) he said, "Efforts to ennoble human beings to realize their fullest potential must be of many different kinds, but somewhere near the root of the process must be education." And off-the-record to the Council on Foreign Relations in May 1964, he said, "We have concluded that the foundation of much of what we want to do is education, so that the Bank, and more especially IDA, will be financing education projects where we find that these are urgently needed as a pre-condition to economic progress."

27. See also Chapter 3.

28. Willi Wapenhans, interview by Robert W. Oliver, Washington, D.C., February 3, 1988. After trying his hand at farming and then receiving a degree in agricultural economics and teaching at the University of Kiesen in Germany, Wapenhans joined the World Bank in January 1961. He became one of the first two economists in the agriculture projects division who had had a broad economic training. When George Woods became president of the World Bank, Wapenhans began to consider ways and means greatly to expand the Bank's capability of agriculture, including working with the FAO. He also spent about half of his time from the end of 1962 to the beginning of 1967 as the principal economist studying the Tarbela project for the Indus Basin. He was deeply involved in the Jaickel tribal project in Malaysia, which turned Malaysia into the largest producer and exporter of palm (vegetable) oil in the world. (Malaysia's exports in the early 1960s had been almost solely rubber and tin.) In 1967, Wapenhans became deputy head of the agriculture projects department. With the reorganization of 1972, Wapenhans became director of the projects department for Europe, the Middle East, and North Africa (EMENA). In 1975, he became vice-president of EMENA and, in 1976, vice-president for East Africa. He returned to EMENA in 1984 and, with the reorganization of 1987, became the senior vice-president for external affairs and administration. He returned again to EMENA in 1990 as regional vice-president.

29. See Lester R. Brown, By Bread Alone (New York: published for the Overseas Development Council by Praeger Publishers, 1974).

30. J. George Harrar, "Principles for Progress in World Agriculture" (New York: Rockefeller Foundation, 1966), pp. 10–15. For a detailed discussion of the early work of the FAO and the Rockefeller Foundation in Mexico, see Arthur T. Mosher, Technical Cooperation in Latin American Agriculture (Chicago: University of Chicago Press, 1957). Concerning Woods's favorable opinion of the Rockefeller Foundation, see Friedman, V, p. 38. Presumably, as a trustee of the Rockefeller Foundation, George Woods knew a great deal about the work of George Harrar even before the monograph was published.

31. According to Brown (p. 134),

The traditional wheat varieties, characterized by tall, thin straw, often fell over . . . when farmers applied more than 40 pounds of nitrogen fertilizer per acre, causing severe crop losses. In contrast, crop yields of the short, stiff-straw dwarf varieties [which came originally from a gene incorporated in Japanese wheat] continued to increase with applications of up to 120 pounds of nitrogen per acre. Given the necessary fertilizer and water and appropriate management, farmers could easily double yields.

32. Theodore W. Schultz, *Transforming Traditional Agriculture* (New Haven: Yale University Press, 1964), p. 132. If land is defined as the original and inde-structible powers of the soil, then land with fertilizers and land with irrigation is land to which capital has been added.
33. Ibid., p. 137.
34. Ibid., pp. 205–206.
35. The Bank's annual report for 1966/67, p. 11, stated: "[A] main develop-ment . . . [has been] the increased number of projects financed or under investi-gation by the Bank which involve . . . farm credit, livestock production, land set-tlement, seed improvement, grain storage, and training and extension work."
36. Article IV, Section 3 (b). For a more detailed analysis of local currency fi-nancing, see Edward S. Mason and Robert E. Asher, *The World Bank Since Bretton Woods* (Washington, D.C.: Brookings Institution, 1973), pp. 275–294.
37. May 1, 1964, cited in Mason and Asher, pp. 227–278. Woods's memoran-dum was probably derived from an earlier memorandum (April 24, 1964) entitled "The Financing of Expenditure in Local Currency," written, in all probability, by Hugh Collier or Raymond Cope. Page 278 reads:

During the period beginning with fiscal year 1961–62 and ending with fiscal 1967–68, the Bank disbursed $3,271.1 million in loan commit-ments made during this period. Of these disbursements, 71.6 percent rep-resented foreign expenditures, 27.3 percent were local expenditures, and 1.2 percent were undetermined.
During the same period IDA disbursed $1,342.5 million of the cred-its signed in these years. Of this total, 82.8 percent represented foreign expenditures and 13.9 percent local expenditures; while 3.3 percent was undetermined.

But see "A Conversation with Gerald Alter," pp. 21–22: "One of the fields in which I got into a bit of a controversy with George Woods was . . . in the analy-sis of the investment programs of the Latin American countries: the availability of complementary domestic finance. . . . One of the things we used to do was to ex-amine the foreign-exchange contents of investment programs, and, in the Latin American area, the tradition was pretty much not to finance the local-currency expenditures of individual projects. In some of the poor countries, the Bank had few compunctions about local-currency financing. . . .
"After becoming department head, I came up with proposals for local-cur-rency financing which I thought were justified, but George Woods became in-creasingly impatient with my attempts in this area."
38. Reconstruction loans to European nations [and to Japan and Australia] were program loans, because the precise projects to be financed were not specified. As Mason and Asher (op. cit., p. 290) have pointed out, however, "to evaluate a multi-year lending program, even if it consists entirely of projects, inevitably involves the Bank in the same kind of analysis of country performance as does a program loan."
There may be a presumption that loans for specific projects (in contrast to program loans) are more likely to induce a rapid increase in real gross national

product the more underdeveloped the country, but this is far from a usable rule of thumb. To be sure, an industrial country is more likely to be creditworthy in the first place, more likely to have the knowledge needed to plan its own projects. But Bank loans are fungible: they may be used in fact to finance the least productive project in an array of possible projects. Projects may be chosen because of the high import content rather than, necessarily, because of the high resulting productivity. In any event, as Albert Hirschman has described, many projects turn out differently than had been anticipated. See Albert A. Hirschman, "The Principle of the Hiding Hand," in *Development Projects Observed* (Washington, D.C.: Brookings Institution, 1967).

39. Annual report 1966/67, p. 11.

40. See Mason and Asher, pp. 345–359. The idea originated with a proposal to expand the lending authority of the Export-Import Bank, but, in January 1949, President Truman announced his Point Four program of technical assistance, and Richard Demuth prepared a memorandum for World Bank president John J. McCloy that recommended such an organization be established as a subsidiary of the World Bank. Nelson Rockefeller, chairman of President Truman's advisory board on international development, concurred and recommended that the United States take the lead in creating an International Finance Corporation as an affiliate of the World Bank. The United Nations kept the idea alive, though some in the United States argued that it would be wrong to use funds of the United States government to acquire shares of ownership in private enterprises overseas. In the end, spurred in part by a rival proposal sponsored by the Special United Nations Fund for Economic Development (SUNFED), the United States government agreed to accept an IFC with an initial capital of $100 million *provided no financing of equity was involved.* Loans were contemplated, but a limit of $2 million was initially decreed by the president, Robert Garner, as the maximum possible investment in any individual project.

41. According to Mason and Asher, p. 356: "Rosen was the only individual in the Bank Group whom Woods believed capable of putting together deals of this kind."

42. See Chapter 2.

43. See Chapter 2, note 29. Diamond wrote his first book, *Development Banks,* on the staff of the Economic Development Institute (EDI). After three years with the EDI, Diamond returned to be a division chief in the Europe, Africa, and Australasia area department. In 1960, he became assistant director of the Western Hemisphere area department.

In a transcribed interview (World Bank/IFC archives, Oral History Program, July 17, 1986, p. 77), Diamond said: "In the Philippines a peculiar situation arose. George Woods promoted the company. He organized the steering committee and guided its deliberations. The World Bank loan and the IFC investment were made in December 1962, approved by the Board . . . on December 20. So the IFC and the Bank got into the act financially just as Woods became president. And then every year there was a hell of a hassle at the shareholders' meeting.

"No Filipino shareholder held a significant amount of shares so he could dominate, if not control, the composition of the board of directors. . . .The first chairman of the board was Francisco Ortigas, who had been personally chosen by Woods as first chairman of the steering committee and then as chairman of the board. We always sent him a proxy saying for purposes of quorum you vote and for purposes of the election we rely on you to vote our shares. IFC had complete trust in him. He usually told us in advance what the situation was and who it was that he thought we ought to support, and we said we supported that slate. This went on for two or three years, but finally George said, 'I'm fed up with this. We never will get a stable situation there unless one of the Filipino shareholders holds a considerably larger stake.' He identified who this might be and sold IFC's shares to him. The shareholder then nominated the chairman of the board after Ortigas left. He was chairman until four or five years ago. That was the reason for the very early sellout.

"In my time of dealing with development banks overall, which means up until 1972, it never happened again. And I'd be reasonably sure it hasn't happened since. But it was an interesting case. I think George was right. I might add that the Filipino Bank did settle down afterwards. The battling on the board and among the shareholders ceased. The man who became the second and long-time Chairman was a very sensible and very able person. That was George's solution, a solution to an unexpected problem. It worked."

Though a representative of the IFC usually voted the equity shares it had purchased, the IFC never purchased more than 25 percent of the shares. The IFC held its shares in trust, so to speak, for people in the private sector to whom one day it hoped to sell the shares.

44. See "The Reminiscences of Dr. Martin Rosen," *George D. Woods Oral History Project* (New York: Oral History Research Office, Columbia University, 1985). See also Friedman, IV, p. 41; and Robert W. Oliver, "A Conversation with Ladislaus von Hoffmann," *Conversations About George Woods and the World Bank*, Washington, D.C., February 11, 1988, p. 14. Ladislaus von Hoffmann joined the IFC in July 1960 after working for a German chemical company. He spent three years in the Middle East building up the company's export business after graduating in 1949 in Freiburg, Germany, with a master's degree in business and economics. At IFC von Hoffmann became an investment officer, working closely with the Kuwaiti Investment Company. In the early 1960s, he became deputy director of the Asia and Africa department of the IFC. When William Gaud, who succeeded Martin Rosen in October 1969, retired in 1974, von Hoffmann succeeded Gaud. In our conversation about IFC investments, he told me, "One of the problems we had to struggle with was that the mandate of IFC included a provision that we should not compete with private capital. So one of the check points in any transaction was, 'Is this something where we are really substituting for private capital or is it something which wouldn't be financed otherwise?' Fairly Byzantine discussions took place on this subject from time to time."

45. Stanley Raymond Cope was director of the Europe area department and deputy chairman of the loan committee in 1964. He received a Ph.D. in economics from the London School of Economics and joined the merchant banking firm of Guinness, Mahon and Company. During World War II, he was secretary of the airborne forces. He was in the finance division of the control commission for Germany, 1945–1946, before returning briefly to Guinness, Mahon and then was with the Esso Transportation Company. He joined the World Bank in 1947, serving in the loan (i.e., the operations) department for five years before becoming assistant director and then director of operations in Europe.

46. The interest equalization tax applied to residents of the United States who purchased certain foreign securities. It was passed by Congress in late 1963 because it was supposed that there was an excessive outflow of private U.S. capital, which produced a basic balance-of-payments deficit. See Walter S. Salant, et al., *United States Balance of Payments in 1968* (Washington, D.C.: Brookings Institution, 1963).

47. Mason and Asher, p. 407. According to the 1965–1966 annual report of the World Bank and IDA, the Bank's net income during the year was $143.7 million, the special reserve was $289.7 million, and the supplementary reserve was $663.8 million. The Bank's net income for fiscal 1964 was $97 million and for 1965 $137 million, though this included $35 million that would have been allocated to the special reserve in previous years.

48. Black was not personally opposed to a transfer of the Bank's profits to IDA. Black told Woods, "If you do that, you won't find me snapping at you even though I laid it on the line that I would not let money go from the Bank to IDA."—Robert W. Oliver, "A Conversation with Aron Broches," *Conversations About George Woods and the World Bank*, Washington, D.C., November 7, 1985, p. 2. (Broches, a leading Dutch lawyer who was present at the Bretton Woods Conference, started to work for the Bank in 1946. He succeeded Davidson Sommers as general counsel in 1959.)

49. *IDA in Retrospect* (New York: published for the World Bank by Oxford University Press, 1982), p. 20.

50. Much of the following discussion of aid coordination is derived from Mason and Asher, pp. 514–537. The Aid-India Consortium consisted of most of the European nations, Japan, Canada, and the United States. For an interesting discussion of the work of William Diamond after he became director of the South Asia programs department and chairman of the Aid-India Consortium after October 1, 1972, see Diamond, pp. 42ff.

51. See Chapter 5.

52. Bank-sponsored consultative groups were established in the 1960s for Colombia, the Congo, East Africa, Ethiopia, Ghana, Korea, Malaysia, Morocco, Nigeria, the Philippines, Sri Lanka, and Thailand.

53. Harold N. Graves, Jr., "The Bank as International Mediator: Three Episodes," in Mason and Asher, p. 612.

54. Construction of the Mangla dam on the Jhelum River, authorized in 1960 and dedicated in 1967, preceded the Tarbela dam.

55. Dr. Peter Lieftinck was professor of economics at Erasmus University until 1940 when he was interned in German concentration camps, initially at Buchenwald and later in Poland. He nearly starved to death. Upon his release in 1945, he became finance minister in the first postwar cabinet of the Netherlands. In addition to being a professor of economics before the war, he had learned a great deal about the Bretton Woods Conference (which in 1944 had negotiated the IMF and the World Bank). By chance, while a prisoner of war, he had seen an article, dropped by a guard, about the Bretton Woods Conference. He had written to the Red Cross for more information and, in due course, had received in return a considerable packet of information about the conference.

For seven years as finance minister, during which he led the Netherlands from austerity to recovery, he was also a governor of the World Bank. He attended the inaugural meeting of the Bank at Savannah, Georgia, and he negotiated the $200 million World Bank reconstruction loan to the Netherlands. He became a good friend of Eugene Black and mentioned to Black at one point that, when he had finished his work in Holland, he would like to continue his career on the staff of the World Bank.

In June 1952, Lieftinck chose not to rejoin the cabinet. Shortly thereafter he received a telephone call from Black asking him to be his representative in Turkey, with which Black was having problems. Lieftinck was willing. He said, "Well, if you think I could do that. . . ." He worked as special representative to the president of the Bank in Turkey. Later, he led the general economic survey mission to

Syria, after which he performed the same function in Jordan, and then in Lebanon, whereupon, in 1955, as noted he became the executive director for the Netherlands, Yugoslavia, Israel, and Cyprus.

Lieftinck began his study of the Tarbela dam in late 1963 and finished it in 1967. It was in two parts: the first, completed in early 1965, dealt with the proposal for building the dam itself; the second outlined a program for using Pakistan's water and power. Lieftinck died in 1989.

56. See Robert W. Oliver, "A Conversation with Dr. Peter Lieftinck," *Conversations About George Woods and the World Bank*, Washington, D.C., November 19, 1985, p. 7.

57. See Graves, in Mason and Asher, pp. 339–341, 595–643.

58. Broches, p. 5. Aron Broches was the principal draftsman and negotiator of the treaty. Once the Centre came into being, Broches was elected its first secretary-general.

59. Broches, p. 10.

60. Diamond, p. 50.

CHAPTER 7

THE
FRUSTRATIONS
OF
GEORGE
WOODS

A worried George Woods, December 13, 1966

Presidant John F. Kennedy named the 1960s the Development Decade, and so for a while it seemed to be.[1] The Inter-American Development Bank was created in 1961. The Asian Development Bank was added in 1966. The African Development Bank, which served more than thirty newly independent countries, followed. The Organization for Economic Cooperation and Development (OECD), which succeeded the Organization for European Economic Cooperation (OEEC) at the Chateau de la Muette in Paris, became a forum where developed countries, including the United States, Canada, and Japan, could discuss mutual economic problems, including the assistance they might provide to less-developed countries. The United Nations Conference on Trade and Development (UNCTAD) was started by the Third World nations as a sort of counterpart to OECD, largely to discuss the commodity problem but also to lobby for more assistance from the developed countries. And the International Development Association (IDA) was created as a grant-type arm of the World Bank Group. But, while more organizations were involved, "the amount of finance moving from the developed to the underdeveloped world," as George Woods noted in an article in *Foreign Affairs* in January 1966, "is not rising, and the present trend is for the growth of the low-income countries slowly to lose momentum." Indeed, Woods predicted, "If present trends are allowed to continue, there will be no adequate improvement in living standards in vast areas of the globe for the balance of the century."[2]

> The aim of the Development Decade [Woods noted] is for the underdeveloped countries, as a group, to reach a yearly rate of economic growth of 5 percent. In the period 1950–54, the rate of increase in their gross national product did approximate that figure. But in 1955–60, it dropped to 4.5 percent; and in 1960–64 it was 4 percent. When allowance is made for population growth, per-capita income in about half the 80 underdeveloped countries which are members of the World Bank is rising by only 1 percent a year or less. . . . The average per-capita income in this lagging group is no more than $120 a year.[3]

Woods's words have been prophetic thus far for most of South Asia, most of Africa south of the Sahara Desert, and much of Latin America

and the Caribbean. In East Asia, on the other hand, real per-capita income from 1965 to 1988 (measured in 1980 prices) almost doubled (to
$650), though it started from a lower base.[4]

Woods's pessimism was due in part to the fact that the Bank was denied access to the U.S. security markets in 1966. Indeed, money remained
tight in the United States and Europe throughout Woods's term of office.
According to William Diamond, at one point "Woods said that, when he
accepted the presidency of the Bank, had he realized that he would be
spending so much of his time and energy persuading governments to put
up money, he never would have accepted the position."[5] This was the
downside of Woods's term in office; this was the basic frustration Woods
endured; heightened, perhaps, by Woods's perception that he must promote development in our time and compounded, perhaps, by Woods's determined, at times irritable, character and personality.

In his *Foreign Affairs* article, Woods also pointed out that

> when all amortization, interest and dividend payments are taken into ac-
> count, the backflow of some $6 billion from the developing countries off-
> sets about half the gross capital inflow which those countries receive.
> These payments are continuing to rise at an accelerating rate, and in a
> little more than 15 years, on present form, would offset the inflow com-
> pletely. In short, to go on doing what the capital-exporting countries are
> now doing will, in the not too long run, amount to doing nothing at all.

In this Woods was also prophetic. "The solution of the debt problem
is within the power and the means of the developed countries. They can
ease their own terms, and they can disperse finance through other chan-
nels. One of the latter is the Bank's affiliate, IDA, the other major institution for transferring capital to the low-income countries on conces-
sional terms."[6]

In January 1966, George Woods was beginning the fourth year of his
five-year term as president of the Bank. He would be sixty-five years old
on July 27, 1966. He had suffered a heart attack and a near-fatal
aneurysm. He was tired. Some thought that he deliberately sought to
make important decisions only in the mornings. By mid-1966, he was beginning to wonder who might succeed him as president. He was of two
minds about a second five-year term. On the one hand, he was not a quit-
ter: he was anxious to steer the Bank into calmer waters, to finish the job
he had set for himself in his first annual (1963) address to the board of
governors, to guarantee the financing he felt was needed for the entire
World Bank Group, IDA in particular. On the other hand, he had been
rebuffed in India, which he had most sought to help. He was having increasing trouble with his executive directors, the U.S. Treasury Department was reluctant to endorse increased sales of World Bank bonds in

U.S. security markets, and the U.S. Congress was hostile to increased IDA assistance, particularly if the IDA assistance did not result in offsetting U.S. exports.

Woods must have yearned occasionally for the surcease and tranquility of the home in Portugal that Louise had found for him; for the stimulation of his investment-banking friends; and the happiness of the Fifth Avenue, New York, apartment to which Louie and Woodsie retreated on weekends whenever they could. George Woods was a New York banker, not a Washington bureaucrat. Woods had grown up in the business world surrounded by people like John Macomber, Harry Addinsell, James Coggeshall, and Arthur Dean. He loved to see friends at the "21" Club, but he remained distant socially from his World Bank colleagues. "You would have to see the same people you work with," Woods once remarked. "Who wants to do that?" Louise Woods added that Woods didn't socialize with staff of the Bank in part because he knew that it would be difficult to fire anyone he knew socially.[7]

By the end of June 1966, the staff of the World Bank and IDA numbered 1,326, comprising nationals from sixty-eight countries.[8] Geoffrey Wilson, a vice-president, had resigned in 1965 to become deputy secretary in the United Kingdom's Ministry of Overseas Development. He was succeeded soon thereafter as vice-president by Mohamed Shoaib, a former finance minister of Pakistan and executive director of the World Bank.

Between June 30, 1963, and June 30, 1966, the African members of the World Bank increased from eleven to thirty-two.[9] As mentioned in Chapter 3, most of the African countries south of the Sahara had been wards of various European nations when the World Bank began. Following the reorganization of 1952, the Bank was divided into three area departments, one of which was for Europe, Africa, and Australasia. But by the beginning of Woods's presidency, after most of the African nations had gained their independence, Africa merited an area department of its own. Eugene Black had appointed Leonard Rist, former director of the economics department and head of the staff economic committee, as his special representative for Africa, but the new Africa department was begun in 1962 under Pierre L. Moussa.[10] Moussa returned to France in 1964 to become president of the Fédération Française des Sociétés d'Assurances. Abdel Galeel El Emary, the former finance minister of Egypt, succeeded Moussa.

In fiscal 1962/63, the most important African Bank loans were to Ghana ($47 million) to finance the Volta dam project and to Nigeria ($13.5 million) to finance port facilities in Lagos. At the 1967 annual meeting, in Rio de Janeiro, George Woods met with a group of African governors of the World Bank Group and told them with some enthusiasm:

The African countries have often felt that the Bank group was not doing
enough for them. There was probably some validity to this some 3 to 5
years ago, but it is far less true today. In 1966–67 we provided $86 mil-
lion in Bank loans, and $91 million in IDA credits. IFC investments in
Africa totalled $7 million. The share of Africa in the Bank group's oper-
ations has been growing steadily from 5.7 percent of the total in 1960–61
to 10.4 percent in 1963–64 and 14.7 percent in 1966–67. The Bank
group's effort on behalf of African countries is, perhaps, better measured
by the number of projects financed, which has increased from 3 in
1960–61 to 9 in 1963–64, and to 20 in 1966–67. At present we have
well over 100 projects in Africa under consideration. Our technical assistance has also expanded. In 1966–67 the Bank has made 3 grants for
feasibility studies and has agreed to be Executing Agency for 7 UNDP
studies. In fact, during the last year, 10 of our 18 new technical assistance activities were for projects in Africa. While I still do not consider
that the present situation is entirely satisfactory, it must be recognized
that substantive progress has been achieved.[11]

But the overall flow of official development assistance to Africa (bilateral
and multilateral) had remained static from 1961 to 1966 at about $6.6 bil-
lion annually.

In the early 1960s, John de Wilde, who had been acting director of the
staff economic committee, decided to investigate the problems of agriculture
in Africa south of the Sahara Desert.[12] In a pathbreaking two-volume study
carried out in Kenya, Mali, Uganda, Tanzania, Upper Volta, Chad, and the
Ivory Coast, de Wilde and his associates identified many reasons for the
paucity of agricultural output in much of Africa. Among these were the generally poor conditions of the soils; the irregular rainfall; erosion; the absence
of good harbors leading easily to the interior; the absence of formal education
among the farmers (other than the few Europeans who, after African independence, tended to abandon their plantations); the tribal or extended-fam-
ily relationship; disease; the scarcity of statistical information concerning
rainfall, climate, soils, and so forth; the general lack of mechanical equipment
or even animal-pulled ploughs; the widespread resort to burning the brush (to
create nitrogen in the soil) before planting; and the lack of income incentives
to innovate (in much of Africa in recent years, the lack of income incentives
for the farmers has been the consequence of bad government planning).

Though it has only about 10 percent of the world's population, Africa
is the second-largest continent in the world. In the 1960s, the proportion
of the population dependent on agriculture varied from a low of around 75
percent in Kenya to 90 percent or more in Liberia, Uganda, and Ethiopia.
In the case of Niger, Chad, and Upper Volta, subsistence farming was responsible for two-thirds of total employment.[13]

In his remarks to the African governors at the Rio conference in
1967, Woods also said:

Like yourselves, I am convinced that the land will remain for a long time the principal source of income and employment in Africa. You are aware of our efforts, including those of our resident missions in Eastern and Western Africa, to help governments identify and prepare agricultural schemes. The preparation of agricultural projects is often a long and arduous process and, in some cases, it takes a long time before tangible results are obtained. All the same, in 1966/67 we provided $40 million in loans and credits for agriculture, representing 21 percent of the Bank group's activities in Africa. As over fifty agricultural projects are now under consideration, I am confident that there will soon be an even greater expansion of our agricultural activities in Africa.

Woods referred to the growing importance of IDA. "You have seen that the share of IDA in total Bank Group financing in Africa has increased from 17 percent in 1963/64 to 49 percent in 1966/67, thus softening considerably the average terms of our lending. I . . . believe that the share of IDA in our lending operations in Africa should increase further. Indeed, Africa was one of my major concerns when I recommended a considerable increase in IDA's resources, and Africa would be among the main beneficiaries of the proposed increase."[14]

Michael Lejeune, who in 1970 became director of the East Africa area department,[15] said in an interview some years later: "This is an extremely difficult area in which to work, and I regret to say that many of the livestock projects that the Bank got into, not only in my time but subsequently, failed to achieve their objectives. . . .

"Africa . . . is a very difficult place to do business. In the rural areas one is up against all sorts of problems: customs, local governments, tribal matters, attitudes ingrained over the centuries which have not caught up with modern developments. The Bank, while pretty good at economics and so on, was, I must confess, pretty poor on sociological matters. . . . None of us really understood how African society worked. We did not speak the local languages. . . . These people communicated in their tribal languages, or possibly in Swahili or some other lingua franca which none of us knew at the time."[16]

Louise Woods devoted the whole of one lengthy interview to her travels in Africa with her husband. She told, for example, of a meeting between Jomo Kenyatta and Woods in Kenyatta's summer house in Mombasa. "Kenyatta had just said to Woodsie, 'You know, Mr. President, a countryman of mine was just murdered by his wife in Brooklyn, in your country.'

"Woodsie looked at him and said, 'Well, Mr. President, that will teach him a lesson.' With that, Kenyatta threw his head back and roared with laughter, and that made all of us relaxed."[17]

On an earlier occasion (Woods loved to tell this story himself), when Woods was in Ghana, President Nkruma invited Woods to Nkruma's home for a weekend to meet his family. Woods was having a good time when he turned to Nkruma and said, "Boy, you're really a White Man aren't you?" Nkruma seemed not to be disturbed; he perceived that he was being complimented.[18]

Julian Grenfell, who in 1966 had only recently joined the Bank, remembers having had breakfast with George Woods, George Wishart, and Abdel Galeel El Emary on the terrace of the Lake Victoria Hotel before Woods was to meet Milton Obote, then president of Uganda. Woods said to El Emary, "Tell me, Abdel, we haven't loaned any money to Uganda for a couple of years because we have disapproved of the economic policies Uganda has been pursuing. We seem to be agreed that we should start lending again if you're convinced that there are good things we can lend for. How important is it politically that we resume lending?"

El Emary replied, "It probably means the difference between Obote's staying in power and his going. If the World Bank does not announce that it is going to resume lending after your visit, this will be a real blow." "Do we need to keep Obote in power?" Woods asked. "Is there someone else who could do the job better?" "No," said El Emary, "there is only the army. If you lose Obote, you lose most of the good people who are with him at the moment and the army takes over." Woods said, "Then I guess we'd better make him a loan."

Julian Grenfell remembers wondering, "Is this the way the World Bank operates?" But he learned that this was very much Woods's style. Woods was much talked about as a man who only knew about investments, a sense of what needed to be done in certain countries to get their economies moving, but underneath it all, Grenfell concluded, Woods was a political man. He was a lot smarter than people gave him credit for. He could see that if we do this, we keep the president of an independent country in power. If we decline to do this, we're probably condemning him to a revolution.[19]

On another occasion, Woods met for the first time with the African finance ministers as a group during an annual meeting. They were very keen on their dignity and status. After the complaint session, it was Woods's turn to answer. Instead of referring to them as "Your Excellencies," he said, "I've listened to what you guys have to say. Now you listen to me." What he said to them made a lot of sense, but Woods was not at his most diplomatic.[20]

Munir Benjenk, deputy director for North Africa during much of the Woods presidency,[21] has told of a meeting between Woods and a delegation from Algeria headed by the finance minister. (Benjenk was translating from French to English, and vice versa). "'Our relationship with the World Bank is not productive,' the finance minister said. 'You are not doing anything for Algeria, and the reason you are not doing anything is

because we are a socialist country, and you're prejudiced.' Woods said,
'What makes you think that? Can you substantiate that? I don't believe
we have any prejudices. We apply the same rules for all peoples.' The minister said, 'Well, yes, you've done this,' and then for a few minutes we got
into a substantive conversation. Mr. Woods told him there are certain
things we cannot do, but the minister interjected, 'Of course you can't because you are prejudiced against socialist countries.' Woods looked at his
watch and said, 'Mr. Minister, you are repeating yourself,' at which point
I saw the ambassador go white. The finance minister had not understood:
he did not speak English. I thought for a second and decided I am not
going to translate it that way. Instead of saying, 'You are repeating yourself,' I said, 'Minister, this is very similar to what you said earlier.' Well,
the conference didn't last much longer. It broke up; it was a complete flop.
But I remember that the ambassador came to me and said, 'If you hadn't
translated it that way, we would have walked out of the room.' Of course,
the ambassador understood English perfectly well."[22]

There is another story involving Benjenk worth recounting at some
length because it sheds light on George Woods's very personal way of
doing business. Benjenk, after joining the Bank in 1963, some three
months after George Woods became president, worked for a year in the
development services department under Richard Demuth. Benjenk had
known Pierre Moussa in France, and in 1964 Moussa asked Benjenk to establish a new office in North Africa: Morocco, Algeria, and Tunisia. The
two vice-presidents, Knapp and Wilson, approved the proposal, but
George Woods had not been consulted. When someone put the proposal
before Woods, he exploded: "An office in North Africa? Absolute nonsense. Why should we have an office in North Africa? We hardly have any
business there. Let's start doing business first before we think of an office.
And who is Mr. Benjenk? Nobody has ever heard of Mr. Benjenk. No. No
office in North Africa."

Sometime later, Benjenk was summoned to Woods's office. Benjenk
had never seen Woods before. "Someone had the damn fool idea of sending you to North Africa," Woods began. "It doesn't make any sort of sense
at all. The only reason they can give for this is that you are a good man,
and you are not doing anything useful at the moment. I was curious and
asked for your file. You have done very well at OECD, and what you ought
to do in this place is to learn about the business of the Bank. . . . You must
become a banker. You've got to start lending money. . . . What you should
do is to take up a division in the operations department. You don't know
anything about that, but you will learn. We'll give you some assistance.
That's what you ought to do. . . . Is there any geographic area which is of interest to you?" "Well, yes, North Africa," Benjenk replied. "It would be of
great interest to me." Woods said, "Well, there is someone doing that job

now, but we can move him." "Thank you very much," Benjenk said and returned to tell his story to Moussa who said, "Very good, very interesting."

Moussa left the Bank soon thereafter, and Benjenk waited in vain for someone in the administration to inform him of his transfer to be head of the North Africa division of the Africa department. Demuth found a replacement for Benjenk, but two months went by. Benjenk went to see Michael Lejeune, director of administration, who said, "Well, Mr. Woods will let us know." It was suggested that Benjenk go to Europe to recruit for the young professionals' program.

When Benjenk returned in early January 1965, he met George Woods in the elevator. Woods said, "How do you like working on North Africa?" "I'm not working on North Africa." Benjenk replied. I am doing absolutely nothing." Woods said, "How come?" as he went white in the face. "Obviously," said Benjenk, "your instructions haven't percolated downward." "All right," said Woods, who looked as if he wanted to swear. Within an hour, things began to happen. Benjenk was called by Abdel Galeel El Emary, who had succeeded Pierre Moussa while Benjenk was away in Europe. "Yes, I know about this, but we were not quite sure. Of course you will come to the Africa department. By the end of the month you will be here." "So, in the end," Benjenk added, "I got the job—against the wishes of the establishment."

In another place in this interview, Benjenk said, "The World Bank, for a long time after that, was really a one-man show. No one argued publicly about the decisions of the president." From this experience, Benjenk concluded that if Woods "wanted to get things done, he had to push them through . . . this and similar events made me feel that a number of people close to him could not be trusted."23

Whether or not that was true, it is clear that Woods's style was somewhat different from Black's. Woods was more inclined to overrule his subordinates, to inject himself into decisionmaking after his staff had supposed the decision had been made. Most of the senior staff had been hired under Black and were accustomed to Black's way of doing business. Burke Knapp became the senior vice-president under Woods, but, on one occasion, even Knapp had an official reprimand put into his file by Woods. While Woods was unavailable overseas, Knapp, Lejeune, and various projects people decided that Morocco had violated a clause in a loan agreement and had so notified the government of Morocco. Woods reprimanded Knapp when he returned. Woods felt that only the president of the Bank could recommend a loan to the executive directors, and only the president could inform a government that it had violated a loan agreement.

Alexander (Sandy) Stevenson, former director of the South Asia department, has indicated that Woods got involved in Bank operations from time to time, though "it was not a very predictable thing. He sometimes appeared to act on a whim—in many ways admirable, because he had a lot of very sound instincts, but this made him difficult to work for. . . .

"We were trying at the time to increase IDA operations in Pakistan. The Pakistanis were particularly interested in getting IDA credits into what was then East Pakistan. We had lent for a small industry project in West Pakistan, and we were planning a similar operation in East Pakistan. Mr. Woods suddenly decided that we shouldn't be involved in small industry, so we had to abandon the project at a rather late stage. Mr. Woods didn't meet with us on that; it was Raymond Cope and Bill Diamond who called us in and told us. That was the day President Kennedy was shot, which is perhaps the reason I remember it. . . .

"[Woods] also decided at one stage . . . that we were expending too much effort on loans to . . . development banks [in small countries]. I had the unhappy job of going out to Singapore and telling the government there that Mr. Woods was not going to proceed with a loan we were in the course of working out. That, I think, was one of the most wrong decisions that could ever have been made, but Mr. Woods just didn't want to have anything to do with small development banks. I thought it was whimsical on his part, but once he had made up his mind, he had made up his mind."24

Benjenk felt that Woods's instincts were right ninety-five percent of the time. He was an instinctive man, a guts man. He would feel things that other people wouldn't feel. Therefore, he did not hesitate to overrule anybody, junior or senior, if he felt instinctively that something was wrong. He also thought the hierarchy of the Bank sometimes tended to be too arrogant and too supercilious in their treatment of the membership. He became more and more personal in his administration of the Bank. He started to think about people as being "good people" and "not good people"—as people he would trust and people he would not trust. And whenever he came to the conclusion that somebody wasn't on the same wavelength with him or with a country, he would move him, sometimes quite ruthlessly.25

Woods's method of making decisions on controversial points, according to Benjenk, was interesting. He would often call in two or three people who, he believed, had opposite views. He would listen to the opposing views and then make a decision. He sought Benjenk's and Demuth's opinions frequently. At the time in 1967 when he decided to create a new department for the Middle East and North Africa, he appointed Benjenk as deputy director. That same day an arrogant and unpleasant letter came in from the finance minister of a country, and Woods called in Benjenk and a colleague and asked how the letter should be answered. Benjenk's colleague said, "It is full of fire and brimstone and should be answered in a very strong way." Benjenk agreed. Woods asked Benjenk, "Do you want to keep your job?" "Yes," said Benjenk. "Then you have to remember one thing: we are not in the business of winning arguments with our member countries."[26]

Rainer Steckhan, who succeeded George Wishart as Woods's personal assistant in late 1965, said in an interview: "I think Woods was sometimes perceived as a loner in decision making, which I would say is not a fair statement. At the president's council meetings, . . . Woods gave everyone a chance to ask about his area. I think it did influence Woods's judgment and helped him make decisions. Woods could be very harsh with people, but I think it was his way of testing them. People were able to talk back to him, disagree with him. I've seen occasions when a senior official of the Bank disagreed with Woods, and Woods would say, 'You are totally wrong,' and the next day Woods would call him up and say, 'I think you are right.' It was his style."[27]

Julian Grenfell observed that "Woods didn't speak with a very happy turn of phrase. He could throw people off with his bluntness."[28]

Michael Lejeune observed one such display of Woods's volatility: "The president's council, on one occasion when I was meeting with them, were waiting in the anteroom outside [Woods's] office. Woods was on the telephone. . . . We had been waiting quite a while when someone from the group turned to Woods's secretary and said, 'Well, what do you think? Even though he is on the phone, should we go in or not?' She said, 'Yes, go in.' So we all went in and started to sit down at the conference table at the opposite end of his large office. . . . Woods slapped his hand over the telephone's mouthpiece and told us all to 'get out'—When he wanted us in he'd tell us. . . . When he had finished the telephone call, we went back in and he was as friendly as he could be. But it was not something one would have expected Black to do, and it's certainly not something McNamara would have done. It was just a different style, no doubt a style that people were totally accustomed to in the rough and tumble world of Wall Street, but some of the people in the Bank were surprised."[29]

Woods liked to deal immediately and quickly with problems that came up; he trusted his intuition. Coming out of the business world and not having an academic background, he was sometimes skeptical of what the academically oriented people in the Bank were up to. He was interested in making the Bank an important center of economic study about problems in the developing world, but he did not take to theoretical investigations naturally. He could be skeptical of people who did not come from the business atmosphere to which he was accustomed. They might be doing things that were tangential to the main work of the Bank. In Woods's mind they were wasting their time and the Bank's money. Sometimes he personalized his suspicion and came down hard on individuals. He might demote or even fire them.[30] Louise Woods would have said, "He didn't suffer fools gladly," but even the members of his senior staff and some of the executive directors were sometimes treated as if they should have worn dunce caps. In board meetings, it was not uncommon for Woods to begin questioning the staff himself, even though he had already gone over their recommendations with a fine-tooth comb. This was a technique he used, presumably to show the board that he was on top of the situation, but it may have been counterproductive: it implied a lack of confidence in his staff; it also implied that there were things the staff was concealing from the board and Woods challenged the board to find out what they were. This only led to more questioning. "Why are you going to do it that way?" It was almost as if Woods was courting controversy for its own sake.

Under the articles of agreement, the board of governors, with weighted voting, controls the Bank. The governors must agree to any amendment of the articles of agreement, but they normally meet only once a year. It is the executive directors, also with weighted voting, who are responsible for the day-to-day operations of the Bank. It is they who approve the loans the Bank makes. It is they who hire the president of the Bank.[31] The president of the Bank is an employee and the nonvoting chairman of the executive directors. The president has a five-year term that can be renewed at the discretion of the board. The president can re-sign in midterm. No president has ever been fired.

As recounted in Chapter 2, John J. McCloy accepted the presidency of the Bank only under certain conditions, among which was that he have the power to choose the U.S. executive director. He chose Eugene Black, and Black, in turn, felt that the prerogative to choose the U.S. executive director continued with him. Lejeune has indicated, "I don't in fact know whether [Black] was . . . consulted about the U.S. executive directors dur-ing his time, but it certainly is true that most of those who served in that capacity were congenial to Black. There was never, that I can remember, a serious problem of disagreement or confrontation with a U.S. executive director. On the contrary, it was Black's habit to work very easily with the U.S. executive director in all matters, and Black almost invariably had strong United States support for everything he did in the Bank."[32]

In the early days, the board met once a month. One of the items of discussion was whether or not the directors should be in residence in Washington. The articles of agreement specify that "The Executive Di-rectors shall function in continuous session at the principal office of the Bank and shall meet as often as the business of the Bank may require."[33] As time went by, all the directors were in continuous residence; the busi-ness of the Bank required the board to meet frequently. Toward the end of each fiscal year, there was a heavy amount of business in approving loans.

Over the years, there was also a change in the relationship between the board and the Bank's president. In the early years, senior staff members and members of the board were intimately acquainted with each other. There were regular monthly luncheon meetings of the senior staff and members of the board, and there was an annual party at the president's house for the executive directors, alternates, and the senior staff. As the Bank grew larger, this intimacy became less; as the business of the Bank grew heavier, the relationship between the board and the management changed.

These changes became more evident when George Woods became president. A difference in personalities between Black and Woods undoubtedly contributed to this, but that was only part of it. As had been foreseen when it was created, IDA tended to politicize the Bank. Relationships with Part I countries, those that contributed to IDA, as distinct from Part II countries, those that benefited from IDA, became sharper and matters were more hard-fought. The directors began to have technical assistants to help them in their work and to transmit matters to their leaders at home. The board itself became larger. Instead of being a group of sixteen or seventeen persons, with alternates who did not play a very large role, they became a group of twenty or more. Alternates and technical assistants or advisers played a larger role in relations with the staff.

Relations with the staff became different. When an executive director wished to discuss something with a department head in Black's and most of Woods's time, he would come down to the department head's office and talk about it. There came a time, however, when certain directors from developing countries stood on their dignity and insisted that department heads come to see them, even if it were a matter on which the director took the initiative. Then the directors began to insist that the department directors come to see them regularly to report on what was happening. At the same time, the general support by the U.S. government was changing. When Woods became president, he had no control over the appointment of the U.S. executive director, and the relationship between the president of the Bank and the U.S. administration became less close and congenial.

Black's way of ensuring that things would go smoothly in the board was to consult very widely ahead of time, individually or in small groups, those directors relevant to the passage of whatever it was that Black had in mind. Before matters ever got discussed in the board as a whole, Black knew very well where he stood with the directors and from what quarters he could expect support and from what quarters he could expect trouble.

According to Michael Lejeune, "All presidents do this. There was nothing new about it, but Black did it to a remarkable degree and with remarkable success. He had a way of charming the executive directors so that there was seldom any tension in the board about anything. Actually it was very relaxed. People could crack jokes and get away with it fairly regularly during Black's chairmanship.

"It wasn't quite the same with Woods. He was all business, and, while I don't doubt that he consulted executive directors, this still didn't prevent his running into trouble in his board from time to time. It's the evolution of relationships. I would have said that, in Woods's day, it became apparent that the board was testing its power vis-à-vis the president, and that it was seeking a greater role."[34]

However, Peter Lieftinck recalled, "Gene Black had a little more of an autocratic way of presiding than George Woods, who had a more democratic way. So it may be that under George Woods, there was more awareness by the members of the board of the needs of development financing than during the earlier years. That brought to a certain extent different people on the board. . . .

"I had the highest regard for Gene Black, but it was considered a little unusual to go against him, to quarrel with him. George Woods did not give the impression of a man who would take it amiss if you expressed a different opinion, so I do think that discussions may have been more lively under George Woods. I personally experienced both periods. . . . I always participated in the discussions and took a very great interest also in the method of project appraisal and project comparison and development planning and so forth. I always commented on the staff reports and on the project policies, but I don't remember more intense discussions or more differences of opinion appearing under George Woods than Gene Black."[35]

Of course, as discussed in Chapter 4, an additional reason for the increased work and tension of the executive directors involved the balance-of-payments problems of the United States.[36] The United States government—the Treasury Department and a majority in Congress in particular—were increasingly concerned about the dollar glut[37] and the inflation that began as a consequence of the Vietnam War, including the way in which that war was financed. President Kennedy had worried about the growing gap between the rich and the poor nations and had sought to do something about it, but President Johnson became preoccupied with domestic programs and the Vietnam War.

In his first address before the United Nations Economic and Social Council in April 1963, George Woods said:

> In the past year, the ability of a number of less developed countries to undertake new borrowing on conventional terms has continued to weaken: in fact, their external debt increased more than it had in the previous year, while their capacity to earn foreign exchange did not improve. In consequence, we face an urgent problem: If the pace of development in these countries is to be maintained *without overloading them with external obligations*, then ways must be found to assist them more and more with grants or with credits carrying lenient financial terms.[38]

Woods repeated his message to the Investment Bankers Association in December 1963:

> We ourselves, to be sure, have pointed repeatedly to the fact that in some countries, the burden of debt is rising toward a point where they will become doubtful risks. In these countries, for the time being at least, the Bank will be limited in its ability to operate. These clients will have to turn increasingly to sources able to offer capital on more lenient terms, including the Bank's own affiliate, the International Development Association.[39]

In 1963, Woods was optimistic.

> Within the years from 1948 to 1961, the gross national product of a representative sample of more than 60 developing countries rose by about 70 percent. This over-all rate of growth is higher than that achieved by the industrialized countries during the same years.[40]

In December 1963, Woods said:

> As you know, Bank loans and IDA credits are not tied; indeed, we normally insist that suppliers be permitted to compete on an international basis for orders that we finance. It is unfortunately true that although great progress has been made in the aid effort in many ways—in expanding its total volume, in easing amortization terms, in improving the choice of projects—there has been an increasing tendency to tie aid to the procurement of goods produced in the lending country. . . .
> From the point of view of the developing country, the most obvious consequence of tied aid is that it often makes it necessary to pay more for goods and services than would be the case if they were being bought in the open market.[41]

At the UNCTAD conference, on March 24, 1964, Woods drew attention to recent decisions to "enlist the cooperation of the Food and Agriculture Organization of the United Nations (FAO) in our plan to intensify our support of agricultural development on this broader scale."[42]

> In our efforts to do more to help create the facilities for the spread of education, we should have the cooperation of the United Nations Educational, Scientific and Cultural Organizations [UNESCO], with which we plan jointly to explore and support new projects. . . .[43] We have [also] undertaken more and more pre-investment studies of possible projects and sector programs, both as executing agency for the United Nations Special Fund and on our own.[44]

Woods announced that it was his intention "to recommend to the Bank's executive directors . . . that the Bank transfer to IDA a portion of the Bank's net earnings for the year, . . ." but he added that "even with such transfers from the Bank, the needs . . . which IDA was created to meet cannot be satisfied by governmental subscriptions at their present level. I earnestly urge, therefore, that the contributing governments participating in this conference reexamine the amount of their pledges to IDA in light of the pressing investments requirements of the developing countries as they may be revealed during the course of our deliberations here."[45]

From early 1964 until the end of his term as president, George Woods became increasingly concerned about, one might even say obsessed with, the problem of raising funds for the Bank and, in particular, for IDA. On May 20, 1964, the senior staff was informed that, for balance-of-payments reasons, the Bank had deliberately decided not to offer any bonds in the United States in 1964. Equally deliberately, it planned to offer $300 million or more in 1965. Meanwhile, the possibility of marketing more Bank bonds in Europe was being explored. In fact, the Bank sold only $200 million of World Bank bonds in the United States in fiscal 1964/65. Woods was pleased because he felt that the U.S. Treasury Department had accepted the proposition that dollars raised in the United States had led to greater U.S. exports, but in 1966 the Bank was refused permission by the Treasury Department to sell dollar bonds in the United States at all.

Aron Broches, the Bank's general counsel, has said, "We had one problem that disturbed Woods very much and that was that the United States was becoming difficult in giving the required consent to borrow. The World Bank is different from other borrowers. Even if a market is open to all comers, the World Bank nevertheless needs the consent of the government concerned. The Bank's articles of agreement so provide. Woods had very bad relations with [Secretary of the Treasury Henry] Fowler and it didn't take very long before Woods became concerned that the Bank might not be able to borrow the funds it needed to meet its obligations to its borrowers. He and I talked about the problem. Each country has the right to give or withhold its consent, but here was the United States, which at the time was happily voting in favor of a greater loan program, saying, 'You can't borrow in our markets,' even though the only way we could pay out on the loans we made was by borrowing in the United States market. This issue was never settled, but after a while it lost its practical importance."[46]

At the 1964 annual meeting of the World Bank Group in Tokyo, Woods felt able to predict "that IDA's resources will be replenished. The additional funds to be made available by 18 capital-exporting countries for commitment at least through June 30, 1966, will be more than $750 million."[47] Woods warned, however, that

> there is the all-important area closely related to the debt service problem—namely, the provision of adequate resources of foreign exchange for developmental investment and particularly investment on IDA-type

terms. This whole matter, as you know, was extensively discussed at the
Geneva Conference and in those discussions the Bank's representatives
participated actively. We have been asked to continue that participation
by undertaking a number of studies, all revolving around three basic issues: How best to achieve a major increase in the flow of public and private funds to the developing countries; how to assure that a greater portion of those funds is available on terms which do not unduly burden the
economies of the recipient countries; and finally, how most effectively to
apply those funds in a way that will permit development to go forward
smoothly despite fluctuations in export earnings.[48]

Interest rates were increasing in Europe and North America,[49] a sign of
rising inflation and a shortage of capital that made it necessary also to
raise the interest rates charged by the Bank to developing countries.
In an address to ECOSOC on March 26, 1965, Woods said:

> For the underdeveloped countries, the problems presented by a sharply
> rising burden of debt service continue to be fundamental. IDA was es-
> tablished five years ago as one means of easing this burden by making
> funds available over long periods and a minimal cost. Thanks to action
> completed during 1964 by the capital exporting countries, IDA's re-
> sources have been replenished by more than $750 million, bringing the
> aggregate of the Association's convertible funds to about $1.6 billion, in-
> cluding a grant of $50 million out of the Bank's net earnings for the fis-
> cal year which ended June 30, 1964. These resources will, it is estimated,
> be fully committed by the summer of 1966. We are therefore about to
> commence discussions looking to a Second Replenishment of IDA re-
> sources. I hope and expect that we can make annual grants to IDA out of
> Bank net earnings and that our members will give not only continuing
> but increasing financial support to the Association. The economically
> justified demand for capital on IDA terms continues to outstrip the funds
> available on these terms, and the demand is certain to grow rather than
> diminish.[50]

At the OECD meeting in Paris, in July 1965, Woods returned to the
theme of rising debt:

> Present total external public debt—long- and short-term—of the devel-
> oping countries, as a group, is estimated at about $33 billion, and amor-
> tization and interest payments on this debt may be as high as $3.5 billion
> a year. This debt amounts to about 15 percent of the combined GNP of
> the developing countries. Service charges on it have been rising by more
> than 10 percent per year, despite a few important rescheduling opera-
> tions, and they now amount to about 12 percent of the developing coun-
> tries' total export earnings.[51]

By the time of the 1965 World Bank Group's annual meeting in
Washington, virtually all of the available IDA funds had been committed.
In his address to that meeting, George Woods commented:

In the final analysis, the high-income countries in IDA's membership must decide what scale of operations they want IDA to undertake in the future.

In his concluding remarks, he was somewhat less reserved:

I have been encouraged by hearing from some of the Governors that their governments are well aware of the need for additional IDA resources in the near future and of their willingness to play their full part. I have also noted the widespread support for the policy of transferring a certain portion of the Bank's net income to IDA.[52]

Almost immediately after the annual meeting, however, Woods was telling his senior staff that the replenishment of IDA was the biggest problem for the immediate future.

In words that foreshadowed his successor's, Woods said at Columbia University on April 13, 1967:

This new [developing] world contains about two billion people—about two-thirds of humanity. Most of it is hungry most of the time, average calorie consumption is on the order of 2,000 a day—an intake which in Europe two decades ago, we regarded as being dangerously near the famine level. Between the income of an ordinary citizen in Western Europe and that of an ordinary African or Asian, the disparity is 10 or 15 to 1, with the contrast that implies between standards of shelter and education, work and equipment.[53]

On July 7, 1965, Livingston Merchant was appointed to succeed John Bullitt as executive director for the United States. Bernard Zagorin was his alternate. Merchant was taciturn and quarreled with Woods on occasion. M. W. O'Donnell, of Australia, who represented Australia, New Zealand, and South Africa, was succeeded in January 1967 by J. O. Stone, also of Australia, who was a thorn in Woods's side. Stone was excessively pedantic, nit-picking. He would raise questions at the board level that probably should have been asked of staff privately. Stone would ask, for example, if countries should be charged what it really costs to investigate IDA loans. He was referring tangentially to India. When Stone asked, Woods replied: "When we review the Bank . . . we are automatically reviewing IDA. One of the unusual things about the IDA situation is that if IDA stopped, if the governments decided not to support IDA any further, there wouldn't be any appreciable change in the expenses of the Bank."

Executive directors' board meetings were a great deal longer and more thoughtful than they had been. Everyone was brooding about IDA and the fact that, between them, India and Pakistan were getting about two-thirds of the IDA commitments. This did not sit well with Rene Larre, the French executive director, who was concerned with French West Africa.

It did not sit well with Mohamad Kochman, of Mauritania, who represented Senegal, Cameroon, Ivory Coast, Malagasy Republic, Rwanda,
Somalia, Togo, Central African Republic, Chad, Congo (Brazzaville), Dahomey (now Benin), Gabon, Mauritania, Niger, and Upper Volta. Nor did
it appeal to Manuel San Miguel, of Argentina (or Luis Escobar, of Chile),
who cast the votes of Argentina, Chile, Uruguay, Bolivia, and Paraguay;
nor with Jorge Mejie-Palacio, of Colombia, who cast the votes for Brazil,
Philippines, Colombia, Ecuador, and the Dominican Republic. It probably
did not appeal to Dr. Luis Machado, the dean of the board, who was from
Cuba, though he did not any longer represent Cuba: he represented Mexico, Venezuela, Peru, Haiti, Costa Rica, El Salvador, Guatemala, Panama,
Honduras, and Nicaragua.

Woods would point out that there were more poor people in India
and Pakistan than in the whole of Africa and Latin America, but the
competition for IDA funds created jealousies. Woods tried joking with the
directors. On one occasion he remarked airily, "If there aren't any questions, are there any comments? If there aren't any questions or comments,
a motion is in order." The directors laughed. On another occasion, when
Woods had pushed a motion through the board, a member rose, furious,
and exclaimed, "Mr. Woods, this is irreglamentary" to which Woods
quickly replied, to accompanying laughter, "Doctor, we'll soon have to
have simultaneous translations."[54] But Woods was having more difficulty
with his board.[55]

He was also having difficulty with some elements of the press. In a
scathing article, Kurt Block, associate editor of *Barron's*, argued that

> George Woods of the World Bank tends to mislead. Thus, he complains
> to his governors that "a banker without money is like a doctor without
> pills." He added: "With the widespread shortage of capital, the World
> Bank and IDA are facing a serious financial problem."
>
> Whether the governors know it or not, the problem arises from Mr.
> Woods's deliberate three-year effort to run down the Bank's liquidity.
> . . . Had he maintained adequate reserves, he could now afford "even in
> a world of the highest interest rates in 40 years" to skip a year or two of
> borrowing. If his pillbox is empty, the doctor has nobody to blame but
> himself.

Block implied that the World Bank and the Aid-India Consortium
had been wasting the economic assistance they had been lending or giving to India and Pakistan because "both countries are arming for the next
'confrontation' and nourishing hostile sentiments against each other. . . .
[Furthermore] despite huge multibillion-dollar outlays, income per capita
of [India's] helpless subjects has not risen by one iota."[56]

George Woods's star was not high in the sky above Capitol Hill.
Woods did work the Hill, the Treasury Department, and the White House,

it was said, but not effectively. Several members of Congress had lost their seats in recent elections because they had supported foreign aid. As George Woods himself said in an informal talk to the Council on Foreign Relations in 1964: "In the United States, the foreign aid bill has a rougher passage through Congress in every succeeding year. Disappointment with the results of foreign aid is widespread."[57] Critics claimed that there was no real consultation between the Treasury Department and Congress about IDA. If congressmen asked the Treasury for documents about the Bank, they were turned down. The Treasury people thought the World Bank people were overpaid; they traveled first class, even in the United States.[58] At no time had IDA offered any real evidence of benefits to taxpayers from expenditures. It was asserted that the congressional staff could not go, except in an informal way, to talk to people in the Bank. Everyone remembered Eugene Black as a warm person who entertained congressmen, but George Woods entertained little.

George Woods must have been aware of congressional attitudes. He sought to counter these by hiring as a consultant and lobbyist Senator A. Willis Robertson, a Democrat from Virginia, whose term of office expired on December 31, 1966,[59] and he announced that, as of January 1, 1967, most Bank employees would no longer be able to travel first class in the United States, the only exceptions being executive directors and Bank officers of department-head rank or above. That would bring the Bank's practice into line with the United States government and most large corporations, would save $50,000 a year, and remove a possible target of criticism at a time when efforts were being made to obtain additional funds from Congress. A new department of program evaluation and control was also established in February 1967, under the direction of John Williams, who had been deputy director of the Africa department.[60]

It was something of an accident of history that George Woods was given the task of raising money to replenish IDA. The Treasury Department had carried the ball (along with Senator Monroney) in sponsoring the original IDA bill. It was also responsible for the first IDA replenishment, which, in George Woods's eyes, was disappointingly small and unnecessarily delayed. The Treasury Department became committed to reducing the outflow of U.S. capital and to resisting inflation, which would discourage U.S. exports while encouraging imports. President Kennedy and his secretary of the treasury, Douglas Dillon, were also committed to maintaining the integrity (preventing the devaluation) of the dollar.

When Henry Fowler became secretary of the treasury in April 1965,[61] he specifically asked Woods to negotiate the second IDA replenishment if Woods wanted to expand IDA replenishments during a period of U.S. balance-of-payments deficits. Woods, in turn, asked Irving Friedman to estimate how much more the Bank should seek for IDA. Friedman proposed $1 billion a year in 1965 dollars, so Woods became determined to seek $1

billion a year, and Woods was obliged to go cap in hand, as Irving Friedman put it, because he did want to increase IDA replenishments.[62]

Fowler said many years later that "until Mr. Woods retired from the
Bank, . . . we had very close working relationships. . . . A good deal of the
financial planning and execution of the program of the World Bank for
lending depended upon the ability of the Bank to borrow in the United
States . . . bond market and in turn upon the consent of the U.S. government acting through the U.S. governor. That was my role. . . . And it also
involved acting as an agent of the World Bank before the U.S. Congress
in getting the necessary approvals . . . of the IDA funds."[63]

On September 8, 1965, Woods warned his senior staff that, in his
forthcoming speech to the annual meeting of the board of governors, he
would encourage the eighteen Part I countries to think about the need for
IDA-type financing; and after he had delivered that speech, he commented that the replenishment of the IDA was the biggest problem for
the future.

On June 15, 1966, Burke Knapp reported that a recent review of IDA
resources indicated that IDA commitments by the end of 1966 would ex-
haust the $300 million carryover of uncommitted funds and the $75 million transfer to IDA of the Bank's 1965/66 net profits. The review had
been prompted by the Bank with a desire to contribute its full share of the
nonproject assistance required by India's consortium program. This alone
would involve IDA credits of $115 million.

On July 13, 1966, Woods announced that he would soon present his
request for the second replenishment of IDA to the executive directors
representing Part I countries. On December 28, Woods said that money-
raising was the most important problem immediately confronting the Bank
and IDA. Discussions with the U.S. Treasury Department encouraged him
to believe that there would be a Bank bond issue in the United States before the end of June 1967, and the outlook for IDA replenishment had also
improved, but it would take some time to reach an understanding with the
United States and other Part I countries. It was inevitable that there would
be some interruptions of IDA's capacity to enter into firm commitments to
extend additional credits. The well had temporarily run dry.[64]

In a letter of March 31, 1967, Secretary of the Treasury Henry Fowler
indicated to Woods that the U.S. government was prepared to recommend to Congress that the United States participate in an aggregate IDA
replenishment of $2.4 billion, in which the United States would provide
40 percent (rather than 42 percent) of the total: $600 million would be
payable in fiscal year 1968/69, $800 million in 1969/70, and $1 billion in
1970/71. But the proposal contained the proviso to which other nations,
the French in particular, objected. As stated in the 1967/68 annual report
of the World Bank and IDA, the proposal was that

IDA would call upon the U.S. contribution to meet disbursements on new credits only for the amount needed to finance procurement in the United States. Thus, during that period, payments under the second replenishment would have no adverse effect on the U.S. balance-of-payments. Amounts deferred, however, would be subject to call, thus permitting the entire amount of the replenishment to be committed. As a necessary corollary to this deferment arrangement for the United States, a number of other participating countries agree to permit a compensating acceleration of IDA's drawings upon their contributions in order to meet its disbursement requirements.[65]

In the senior staff meeting of April 26, 1967, John Williams announced that the Bank would begin to charge IDA a straight management fee instead of attributing IDA costs to the Bank. On May 3, George Woods announced that a meeting would be held in Paris on May 8 and 9 to discuss the IDA replenishment. On May 17, Woods reported to the senior staff that the U.S. replenishment proposal had encountered widespread criticism in Paris, not only because of the high level of the proposed replenishment, but also because of the relative shares of the Part I countries and the balance-of-payments conditions placed upon acceptance by the U.S. Treasury Department. On July 14, Woods threatened not to recommend a transfer to IDA from the Bank's 1966/67 net income.

By the time of the 1967 annual meeting of the board of governors in Rio de Janeiro, the IDA replenishment issue had still not been resolved. George Woods said, in part, in September 1967:[66]

> For the second consecutive year, I must report to you that finding finance for the operations of the Bank and IDA is a dominant continuing problem. In the case of the Bank, the consequence of a high rate of disbursement plainly must be large borrowings. Since our last meeting we have arranged to borrow $700 million, of which $380 million was new money and $320 million was for refunding.
>
> Over the past year, IDA has been able to make commitments and carry on its operations, due in large part to extraordinary support given to the Association from several sources. The Swedish government, for the sixth consecutive year, made a welcome special contribution to IDA. The Swiss government (a nonmember) has started legislative machinery for authorizing a loan to IDA on the same highly concessionary terms IDA accords to its borrowers. . . . And the Bank, with the approval of the Governors at last year's Annual Meeting, made a transfer to IDA from its net earnings of fiscal year 1965/66.

Woods referred in passing to the "fact of rapid population growth—now proceeding fast enough to double the population of the less-developed countries in a single generation. Here in Brazil, it is expected to double in 20 years," but, he added, "the world is not going to be saved simply by chemical fertilizers and 'the pill.' The changes needed by the less-developed countries touch intimately all of society. They will come about as part of a larger transformation of social and economic organiza-tion—as part of the larger process we call economic development. In that process, education must play a pervasive part."

Woods discussed trade with the governors of the Bank:

> The total exports of the less-developed countries have not been growing sufficiently fast. For some countries, the lag in export growth has been caused, in part, by mistaken policies—among them, over-valued ex-change rates and too much priority to import substitution, no matter how uneconomic. . . .
>
> Suppose that the exports of the less-developed countries, instead of declining as a proportion of world trade had been able last year to main-tain the same modest position that they had occupied five years earlier. On that supposition, the less-developed countries would have had a 1 percent larger share of world exports—and that 1 percent would have earned them well over a billion dollars more of foreign exchange than their exports actually did earn in 1966.

Woods warned that "the available amount of international develop-ment finance is falling farther and farther behind the economic capacity of high-income nations to provide it, and farther and farther behind the capacity of developing countries to use it productively."

In Woods's concluding remarks on September 29, he amplified:

> It was but a few years ago that the principal limitation on the World Bank Group's activities was a shortage of well-prepared and economically sound projects in countries where the general economic position war-ranted financial assistance. We had faith that through patient effort and with technical assistance from the Bank and other sources, the ability of many of our less-developed countries to prepare and carry out useful projects could be improved. But this was faith. The process had never been tried on a large scale before. We could not be sure it would work.
>
> Today things have changed greatly. We have been able to identify more projects which are, or soon will be, ready for financing than we now have the resources to finance. These are located in many more countries than ever before. This is an encouraging fundamental change. It reflects, not a decrease in our resource availability, but a substantial in-crease in the ability of our member countries to prepare and carry out productive investment.

Woods then repeated the proposal Secretary of the Treasury Henry Fowler had made in the letter of March 31, 1967.

> Several other contributing countries have accepted the amounts pro-posed by the United States, but the amount of the replenishment and the kind of balance-of-payments protective devices which should be

incorporated in the replenishment agreement are still under negotiation.
. . . The Governor for the Netherlands has suggested . . . that the time
has come to convene a special high-level meeting . . . as soon as possible for the purpose of reaching a firm agreement regarding the replenishment of IDA resources. This is a constructive suggestion which should
receive full consideration by all concerned. I expect to act on it; and I
trust that . . . we shall be able within the next month or two to resolve
the outstanding issues regarding amounts and conditions and to reach
conclusions that will enable IDA to operate.

As it turned out, however, it would be almost two years, well into the
McNamara presidency on July 23, 1969, before the United States ratified
the second IDA replenishment, thus making that replenishment legally
possible. Eleven countries had made advance contributions before that
date, but the replenishment totaled only $1,200 million for three years,
$400 million per year. The United States was permitted to delay payment
of its pro-rata share until July 1, 1971, when the full third replenishment
of IDA would be in order, but the U.S. share of the total was only 38 percent. It had been 42 percent in 1960 as well as in 1964 when the first IDA
replenishment was negotiated.[67]

Under the headline, "Happy Fund, Troubled Bank," an article appeared in the Sunday, September 24 edition of the *New York Times*, the
day before the Rio conference was to convene, with a picture of a dejected
George Woods sitting, his hands folded in resignation. The story began:
"An optimistic International Monetary Fund and a troubled World Bank
begin their annual meetings here Monday." After discussing the "Happy
Fund," the article continued,

The World Bank, on the other hand, is faced with an undercurrent of
distress on three counts: The development of many of the poor countries
remains unsatisfactory, despite the help they have received. India is the
major case. The Bank itself—and particularly its "soft loan" affiliate, the
International Development Association—is having a harder time raising
money. The IDA is completely out of funds and awaits agreement among
the rich countries for more.

There has been some unpublicized friction between the president of
the Bank, George D. Woods, and the board of executive directors, representing the member countries.

The directors, it is understood, have agreed to extend Mr. Woods'
term for up to another year beyond its expiration at the end of 1967. Mr.
Woods had no desire for another full five-year term, but the question of
a short-term extension, it has been learned, brought to a head the dis-
satisfaction of some members of the board.

The matter has been smoothed over, but now a serious search has
begun for Mr. Woods' successor. Meanwhile, the real problem of drum-
ming up more money for IDA remains. The rich countries, 18 of them,
are the ones who are asked to contribute, and they have been unable to

agree in negotiations stretching back to before last year's annual meetings of the Bank in Washington.

The Bank, and Mr. Woods, want as much money as possible, wholly
untied to the individual balance-of-payments problems of the donor
countries. The United States is willing to contribute much more than in
the past, providing that the other rich countries do so and also providing
that contributions to IDA do not create a major new drain on the balance of payments.[68]

One can only conjecture about who talked to Edwin L. Dale, Jr., the
reporter for the *New York Times*, of the "friction" between George Woods
and the executive directors. William Bennett has suggested that Livingston Merchant, the U.S. executive director, was the source,[69] though
many people on the staff as well as other executive directors knew about
Woods's confrontational manner.

Irving Friedman has said, "If there was hostility between Woods and
some of his board members, it wasn't expressed to me, . . . I didn't go and
ask an executive director if he was upset or not by what George Woods
had said. I did, however, speak to executive directors quite frequently, because I had this habit from Monetary Fund days. I would not interpret the
New York Times [article] as a leak from a board member. I'd say it came
from the staff. I got much more of a sense of arrogance from some of the
staff members."

"I remember at the governors' conference in Brazil walking into his
office—it was the closest I ever saw George Woods to crying. He looked
completely busted up with his head down, looking at [the Dale] article.
His comment to me was, 'Irving, why do people do this sort of thing?'"[70]

From that time on, Woods was determined to find a presidential successor as soon as possible. He had done his best for the World Bank in difficult circumstances, but some of what Benjenk referred to as "the establishment" were hostile to Woods. Irving Friedman said, "Woods was not a
man that his staff feared. There was more caution in making hostile remarks [about Woods] when I first came [in August 1964]. By '67, some
staff were openly critical. I was hearing such remarks, but I heard them in
confidence; I never repeated them to Woods."[71]

Following his dejection at Rio, Woods quickly regained his equilibrium and soon thereafter delivered the greatest speech of his career in the
World Bank.

Notes

1. See George D. Woods, "The Development Decade in the Balance," *Foreign
Affairs*, Vol. 44, No. 2, January 1966, p. 206. See also George D. Woods, "The
Price of Expansion," *Forum*, February 1966 pp. 16–19.

2. Woods, "The Development Decade in the Balance," p. 207.

3. Ibid.

4. See *World Development Report* (New York: published for the World Bank by Oxford University Press, 1989), p. 7. See also the IMF staff's *World Economic Outlook*, May 1991 (Washington, D.C.: International Monetary Fund, 1991), p. 13.

5. Transcript of interview with William Diamond, July 17 and 22, 1986, by Robert W. Oliver, Oral History Program, Bank/IFC archives, p. 50. See also "Mr Woods's Reply" to the executive directors at Woods's last meeting, March 18, 1968:

> It goes without saying, I have no regret about having taken this post toward the end of 1962. If I knew about it as much then as I know about it now, I'm not sure I would have taken it [laughter]. It turned out to be a much more exacting, a much more complicated, a much more demanding post than I thought it was going to be, but with it all, I'm very happy that I was given the opportunity to join the organization here and I'm very happy with the years and associations both that I've had in these buildings and in this post.

6. Woods, "The Development Decade in the Balance," pp. 212ff.

7. Robert W. Oliver, "A Conversation with Louise Woods," *Conversations About George Woods and the World Bank*, New York, November 8, 1985, p. 42.

8. See the 1965–1966 annual report of the World Bank and IDA, p. 24. In recent years, the staff of the World Bank and IDA has numbered over six thousand.

9. See the 1962–1963 annual report of the World Bank, pp. 53–54, and the 1965–1966 report for the Bank and IDA, Appendix 4. The African members of the Bank in 1963 were Ghana, Ivory Coast, Niger, Nigeria, Senegal, Sierra Leone, Somalia, Sudan, Tanganyika, Togo, and Upper Volta.

10. Pierre Moussa was brought from the French Ministry of Overseas Territories to be director of the Africa department. Moussa was a graduate of the prestigious Ecole Normale Superiore, an inspecteur des finances, and had the French equivalent of a Ph.D. He had published two books: *Les Nations Proletaires* and *L'Economie de la Zone Franc*, both published by Les Presse Universitaires de France. John Williams of the United Kingdom was the deputy director of the Africa department, and Andrew M. Kamarck, the economic adviser. Moussa wrote the preface of Kamarck's book, *The Economics of African Development*.

Moussa left the Bank near the end of 1964 largely because he felt he had too little independence and because George Woods created the president's council without appointing Moussa as a member. Kamarck wrote (personal correspondence, March 5, 1992): "Not appointing [Moussa] was a big mistake on the part of Woods. From my experience in the Bank, I would rate Moussa at the very top as an administrator, policymaker, leader. He would have made an excellent president of the Bank."

11. George Woods, "Draft of Remarks to the Governors from Africa," September 22, 1967, pp. 1–2.

12. John C. de Wilde, et al., *Experiences With Agricultural Development in Tropical Africa*, 2 vols. (Baltimore: published for the International Bank for Reconstruction and Development by Johns Hopkins Press, 1967). See also Andrew M. Kamarck, *The Economics of African Development*, rev. ed. (New York: Praeger Publishers, 1971).

13. Kamarck, p. 34. It may be noted, however, that the terms of trade may shift against developing countries. As George Woods pointed out in an address to the United Nations Conference on Trade and Development, Geneva, March 25, 1964, p. 4,

> Some 30 countries, accounting for nearly half the trade of the developing world, are dependent on a single commodity for more than half their export earnings; and many other countries are dependent on only two or three. . . . To use but one striking example, the Latin American countries increased the volume of their exports of primary commodities by 25 percent during the period from 1956 through 1962, but they actually earned less foreign exchange in the last year of the period than in the first.

14. George Woods, "Draft of Remarks to the Governors from Africa," p. 2.
15. Sudan, Ethiopia, the Congo, Kenya, Uganda, Tanzania, Malawi, Zambia, and Zimbabwe.
16. Robert W. Oliver, "A Conversation with Michael Lejeune, II," *Conversations About George Woods and the World Bank*, Washington D.C., November 19, 1985, p. 11. Lejeune, after starting in 1946 in personnel, became a loan officer and a division chief. In 1952 he became deputy director of the Europe, Africa, and Australasia area department and then of the Far East department. In 1964, George Woods asked him to be director of administration; then, in 1967, he became head of a new department dealing with the Middle East and North Africa, to which Europe was later added. In 1970, he became director of the East Africa department and then became executive secretary of the Consultative Group on International Agricultural Research (CGIAR), which the World Bank was largely responsible for creating. He retired from CGIAR in 1983.
As director of administration, Lejeune saw another side of George Woods, who had assumed responsibility for designing the menus in the Bank's dining rooms. Woods paid a great deal of attention to the design and construction of the building, overriding the decisions of architects and administrators on such matters as how much space should be allotted to a cafeteria and how much to an executive dining room. Of Woods the constant meddler, Louise Woods said, "He ran the Bank like a corner drug store."—John T. Mason, "Interview with Mrs. George David Woods" (Interview 3, January 14, 1983), Oral History Project, Columbia University, p. 105.
17. Ibid., p. 123.
18. See Robert W. Oliver, "A Conversation with Irving Friedman, V," *Conversations About George Woods and the World Bank*, Washington, D.C., July 23, 1985, p. 17. George Wishart remembers the story differently. Nkruma was lamenting to Edgar Kaiser, who was traveling with Woods, that it was difficult to take action in certain matters. "Well," said Edgar, "you are free, white and twenty-one, are you not?" They all laughed.—George Wishart, personal correspondence, May 25, 1992.
19. See Robert W. Oliver, "A Conversation with Julian Grenfell," *Conversations About George Woods and the World Bank*, Washington, D.C., July 15, 1986, pp. 1–2.
20. Robert W. Oliver, "A Conversation with Munir Benjenk," *Conversations About George Woods and the World Bank*, Washington, D.C., November 18, 1985, pp. 24–25.
21. Munir Benjenk, born in Turkey, lived there until he was nineteen, being educated at English and U.S. schools in Istanbul. After graduating from the

London School of Economics, working for the BBC, and serving in the Turkish army in the Far East during the Korean War, he joined the OEEC in Paris. In Sardinia, as director of a technical assistance project, he met a World Bank team and in 1963 was induced to join the Bank.

22. Ibid., pp. 22–23.
23. Ibid., pp. 5–11.
24. Robert W. Oliver, "A Conversation with Alexander Stevenson," *Conversations About George Woods and the World Bank*, Washington, D.C., November 18, 1985, pp. 23–25.
25. Benjenk, pp. 19–20.
26. Ibid., pp. 17–18.
27. Robert W. Oliver, "A Conversation with Rainer Steckhan," *Conversations About George Woods and the World Bank*, Washington, D.C., November 13, 1985, pp. 8–9. Steckhan, after working for the Ford Foundation in Germany, joined the Bank in the young professionals program in 1964. Before becoming Woods's assistant he worked in the projects department, the Europe area department, and the legal department. A lawyer by training, he worked for Woods until March 31, 1968, and then for Robert McNamara until the end of June 1969 when he became deputy director of the East Africa area department. He later became director of the Central Africa area department, acting director of the West Africa area department, did a stint at the Harvard Business School, and then became director of the European office. In 1983, he became director for the western half of Central and South America.

Steckhan told me (Steckhan, p. 2): "I think the idea of the young professionals program . . . was further to diversify the staff—that is, to get more nationals from a greater variety of countries. I believe this was one of George Woods's greatest achievements."

28. Grenfell, p. 1. See also Robert W. Oliver, "A Conversation with William Bennett, *Conversations About George Woods and the World Bank*, Washington, D.C., January 20, 1988, pp. 15–16; and Robert W. Oliver, "A Conversation with Aron Broches," *Conversations About George Woods and the World Bank*, Washington, D.C., November 7, 1985, p. 20.

29. Lejeune, II, p. 29.

30. See, for example, the reference to Nathanial McKitterick in Chapter 3. Lejeune reported (II, p. 28): "On one occasion, he called me as Director of Administration in charge both of personal and household matters to make sure that this man was demoted and put in a particularly small office. He could do that kind of thing once in a while. . . . While he was usually very friendly with the staff, the staff were . . . a little [afraid] of him because these stories got around. He could be abrupt. He could be unduly abrasive."

31. Thus far they have always looked to the president of the United States, who represents the largest single member country with the greatest voting power, for his nomination of a president of the Bank. But this is only a tradition. Also by tradition, the managing director of the International Monetary Fund is a European. Harry Dexter White, who, along with Lord Keynes, was primarily responsible for drafting the Bretton Woods Agreements, had been in line to be the first managing director of the Fund, in which case the president of the Bank would probably have been a European. But when President Harry Truman refused to appoint White (because of charges that White had leaked information to the USSR), the managing director of the Fund became a European, partly to prevent White from continuing as a candidate for the job of managing director.

32. Lejeune, I, p. 22.

33. Article V, Section 4, (e).

34. Ibid., p. 29. By the early 1970s, the annual reports of the Bank began to be issued over the signatures of the executive directors rather than the president of the Bank. After McNamara became president, he got around the directors by letting them have their annual reports while he developed the economic section of the annual report into his own, separate, *World Development Report*.

35. Robert W. Oliver, "A Conversation with Dr. Peter Lieftinck," *Conversations About George Woods and the World Bank*, Washington, D.C., November 19, 1985, pp. 15–16.

36. See especially Chapter 4 on balance-of-payment problems.

37. See Robert W. Oliver, "Bretton Woods: A Retrospective Essay," the California Seminar on International Security and Foreign Policy, 105 (June 1985), p. 55: "Gradually . . . the dollar ceased to be scarce. Indeed, in the early 1960s, as American investors sent dollars into exchange markets to buy the local currencies needed to finance American investments abroad, the world began to experience a sort of dollar glut. More and more currencies became freely convertible, at least to pay for imports, and stable, equilibrium exchange rates mattered a great deal. In such a world, the International Monetary Fund also mattered a great deal."

38. "The Activities of World Bank and Its Affiliates," New York, April 5, 1963, pp. 12–13. Italics added.

39. "Address to the Investment Bankers Association," Hollywood, Florida, December 5, 1963, pp. 8–9.

40. Ibid., p. 13.

41. "Address . . . to the Economic and Social Council of the United Nations," New York, December 18, 1963, p. 13.

42. Address delivered in Geneva, March 25, 1964, p. 12.

43. Ibid., p. 13.

44. Ibid., p. 19.

45. Ibid., p. 17.

46. Aron Broches, p. 24. The problem continued through the McNamara presidency, but McNamara "solved" the problem largely by borrowing heavily in Germany, Kuwait, Japan, and Switzerland. See William Clark, "McNamara at the World Bank," *Foreign Affairs*, Vol. 60, No. 1, Fall 1981, p. 169. This increased purchase of World Bank bonds outside the United States contributed to the general outflow of capital from Europe and Japan that was associated with a decrease in the "favorable" balance of trade of the United States.

47. Address to the boards of governors of the Bank, International Finance Corporation, and International Development Association at Tokyo on September 7, 1964, p. 2. The first IDA replenishment in current dollars turned out to be $745 million for the years 1965 to 1968.

48. Ibid., p. 10. The same year (1964), Dragoslav Avramovic and others published for the Bank a study, "Economic Growth and External Debt," showing that in the period 1955 to 1962 the public and publicly guaranteed debt of a representative sample of developing countries more than doubled and that amortization and interest payments on this debt more than trebled.

49. See 1965–1966 annual report, World Bank and IDA, p. 30.

50. Address to the Economic and Social Council of the United Nations, New York, March 26, 1965, pp. 14–15.

51. Statement to the ministerial meeting, development assistance committee, July 22, 1965, p. 7.

52. Address to the boards of governors and concluding remarks, September 27 and October 1, 1965, pp. 10 and 15. IDA had been instituted in 1960 at an initial capital of $1 billion that was to be used over five years. It was divided into two parts. The eighteen high-income, or Part I, countries having the largest subscriptions (required contributions) were to pay $751 million (100 percent of their subscriptions). The remaining, or Part II, countries were obliged only to pay in 10 percent of their subscriptions: $24 million. Ireland, Israel, and Jordan paid all of the remaining 90 percent of their subscriptions in convertible currencies; Ireland, Mexico, Panama, Spain, and Yugoslavia paid a portion in dollars. The remainder of the Part II countries exercised their prerogative to withhold the 90 percent portion of their subscriptions. In 1962, when it became apparent that the bulk of the IDA funds would be committed long before June 30, 1964, the governors of the Bank requested the executive directors to review the future needs of IDA, and the directors recommended that IDA be replenished periodically by contributions from the Part I member countries, based essentially on the formula for the contributions in 1960. The first replenishment began on June 30, 1965. The Part I nations were Australia, Austria, Belgium, Canada, Denmark, Finland, France, Germany, Italy, Japan, Kuwait, Luxembourg, the Netherlands, Norway, South Africa, Sweden, the United Kingdom, and the United States.

53. "Finance for Developing Countries: A Time for Decision," Gabriel Silver Memorial Lecture, School of International Affairs, Columbia University, April 23, 1967, p. 4.

54. Steckhan, p. 15.

55. A hint about the difficulties Woods was having toward the end of his presidency may be gleaned from the following passage from William Clark's autobiography, *From Three Worlds* (London: Sidgewick and Jackson, 1986), pp. 240–241. Clark describes Robert McNamara's first meeting on April 9, 1968, with the executive directors and their alternates. McNamara was flanked by four or five of his most senior officers: "The meeting went extremely badly. One by one, the executive directors attacked a staff paper on the effects of devaluation on the Bank's assets. After ninety minutes, McNamara crisply halted the discussion, withdrew the paper and promised further discussion on the matter at a later date. There ensued a discussion led by the United States Executive Director, Livingston Merchant, in which he soundly criticized certain contract award practices. Finally, under Any Other Business, some questions were raised about the 'Grand Assize,' to which the President replied cautiously that the matter was still in the preliminary discussion stage. . . .

"In the afternoon, McNamara informed the President's Council that he had found the morning's board meeting a pretty horrifying experience. In three hours, nothing had been achieved, and there had been no single mention of development. He had come to the Bank to deal with development issues . . . not to participate in a debating society. In the future, no proposal should be taken to the board unless it was already firmly established that it had the support of the majority of the voting power. At this point there was much moaning amongst the old hands about the poor state of relations between the Bank staff and the board which the new president had inherited from his predecessor."

56. Kurt Block, "Toward Economic Growth," *Barron's*, October 3, 1966, p. 5. But see pp. 12–13.

57. Talk given by Woods in New York, May 27, 1964, reading copy, p. 13.

58. Lieftinck (p. 14) recalled: "In those years, Pierre Paul Schweitzer, who was managing director of the Fund, felt strongly that something should be done

GEORGE WOODS AND THE WORLD BANK

to mix the various nationalities and races among the staff in the Fund and that some joint recreational facility might be helpful. Such things more often existed in Europe than here. So he sponsored strongly the Bretton Woods Recreational Center. . . .

"Schweitzer contacted George Woods and said that this should be done by the Bank and the Fund together. . . . But George Woods turned him down. He said that if Congress finds out that Bank money has been used for an investment in a recreation center, 'I will be in trouble with the Congress and the Administration, and that will hurt my capacity to raise money for IDA.'"

59. Senator Robertson, a member of the House for fourteen years and of the Senate for twenty years, had been chairman of the Senate Banking Committee.

60. This was done in part because Woods sought to control overly large, temporary missions abroad.

61. Henry Fowler, a lawyer, served as under secretary of the treasury when John F. Kennedy was president and Douglas Dillon was secretary. He later went to Goldman Sachs Investment Banking Corp. in New York.

62. See Chapter 4.

63. "The Reminiscences of Henry J. Fowler," *George Woods Oral History Project*, Oral History Research Office, Columbia University, 1984, p. 6.

According to William Bennett, when George Woods was president of the Bank, "I can assure you, that George's feelings about Henry Fowler were unprintable. I listened to him several times on the subject."—Bennett, p. 17. But Irving Friedman has said: "Fowler [was] genuinely devoted to getting IDA replenished. . . . We wouldn't be talking the magnitudes today [1974] were it not for 'Joe' Fowler."—Friedman, I, p. 76.

After George Woods retired from the World Bank, the Woodses and the Fowlers became good friends. Henry Fowler became chairman of the board of the Institute for International Education, and the Fowlers lived for a time at 825 Fifth Avenue, New York, where the Woodses also lived.

64. See "U.S. Controversy over Funds for IDA," *Washington Post*, December 29, 1966, p. 3. See also Chapter 4.

65. Annual report, p. 26. George Woods invited Richard Demuth and Irving Friedman to discuss balance-of-payments safeguards with U.S. Treasury officials. Two main types of safeguard were proposed during 1966. One of these, as suggested by Demuth, was a form of tied aid. This was rejected by George Woods as indicated in Chapter 4. The other, as suggested by Irving Friedman, was a plan to defer for a period of years the negative effects on the U.S. balance of payments. The wording of the Friedman approach is more nearly as stated in the annual report for 1967–1968, but the European negotiations did not result in the allocation of $1 billion a year for IDA. In addition to the U.S. proposal for balance-of-payments safeguards, other issues included the control by donor countries over IDA's management and lending policies, the aggregate amount of additional resources to be made available to IDA, the share of resources to be contributed by each of the participating countries, and the geographical distribution of IDA credits.

66. Address, September 25 and 29, 1967, pp. 2, 4, 6, 8, 9, 14, and 16.

67. By 1981, it would fall to 27 percent.

68. Edwin L. Dale, Jr., "Happy Fund, Troubled Bank," *New York Times*, September 24, 1967. p. F1.

69. Bennett, pp. 14–15.

70. Friedman, IV, p. 36.

71. Ibid. Woods seemed to take out his frustration on Harold Graves, who had served Black and Woods as director of information and primary speech writer. Woods apparently felt that, as director of information, Graves could have prevented the *New York Times* article. William Bennett later concluded, "Harold couldn't possibly have stopped that story. It was too good." Bennett added, rather ruefully, "Harold was an excellent PR man. He was probably the best speech writer the Bank ever had."—Bennett, p. 15.

But Woods had been considering replacing Graves for some time. At one point Graves had sought to leave the Bank to assume the presidency of the "Franklin Book Program." Graves acknowledged that he "wasn't very happy with Woods's regime; I was critical of things he was doing."—Robert W. Oliver, "A Conversation With Harold Graves, I," *Conversations About George Woods and the World Bank*, Washington, D.C., July 17, 1985, p. 19. In Graves's own words: "I think [Woods] felt that this information department should have made a bigger contribution toward helping him deal with [the IDA] problem.

"The Bank, for the first time really, at least for the first time in a long time, was faced with the necessity for dealing with the Congress of the United States, and Woods was meeting all sorts of people up on the Hill who had never heard of the Bank or didn't understand what the Bank was about. He thought that by this time, surely, the Bank should have been a household word on Capitol Hill. It wasn't, and so I think this was a source of concern for him, and a source of discontent. Without knowing, I think this was the major problem."

CHAPTER 8

THE GRAND ASSIZE, McNAMARA, AND WOODS'S FAREWELL

George Woods receiving an honarary Doctor of Law degree
from Columbia University

G eorge Woods was by no means alone in his insistence that the nations with low per capita income needed IDA-type assistance if their governments were to avoid too rapidly rising international indebtedness. Public opinion in much of Europe, particularly in the Netherlands and the Scandinavian countries, was supportive. The Canadians, the Italians, and the Australians also backed Woods's initiatives. There was considerable doubt among some economists in the United Kingdom that rapid growth could be sustained in the Third World, but the Overseas Development Institute (ODI), of which William Clark was the director, wanted to try.[1] In his memoirs, Clark wrote:

> By 1967, with the [Development] Decade definitely out of steam, I turned my mind to what could be done to get the boilers fired up again. Somehow a new sense of urgency had to be injected into the international development effort. As Barbara Ward was eloquently insisting, the population growth rate in the Third World was a ticking time-bomb. If the Development Decade had been launched on the optimistic forecasting of how much could be achieved, the time had now come to broadcast very bluntly to the world at large how much stood to be lost, by developed and developing nations alike, if the effort was not revived.[2]

Clark decided to bring together a small group of people "of unquestioned expertise and commitment to the development effort, in the hopes that a brainstorming session might lead us to a plan of action."[3] What was needed, Clark believed, was an authoritative, well-researched statement by a panel of distinguished experts of the reasons why the decade was faltering.

Clark invited a few friends to meet over the weekend of April 8–9, 1967, at Sir Edward Boyle's capacious house in Sussex, southern England.[4] Among them were René Maheu, head of UNESCO; Axsel Freiherr von dem Bussche, a friend concerned with the equivalent in Germany of the Peace Corps; Andrzey Krassowsky, an ODI staff member interested in rural development; Barbara Ward (Lady Jackson);[5] and George Woods, who had attended an ODI annual meeting in 1965 and had become acquainted with Clark at that time. It was supposed that Lord (Oliver) Franks,[6] who had been instrumental as the British ambassador to the United States in establishing the OEEC during the Marshall Plan, could be induced to head the panel of distinguished experts when the time came. The suggestion that emerged from the weekend deliberations was that they should seek to regain the enthusiasm of the Marshall Plan days, and Clark was deputized to work on the problem.

About six weeks later, with Clark in Washington for meetings of the Society for International Development, Woods asked Clark for help. Woods said, "I'm going to make a speech in Stockholm to the bankers. I'll write the banker's part, but I wonder if you would write the part suggesting a Franks Commission."[7] For his part, Clark asked if the World Bank might finance the work of the proposed commission. This agreed, Woods added, according to Julian Grenfell, who after Clark's death wrote the last two chapters of Clark's memoirs, "You have to get someone who can really put together a great speech."[8] Back in England, Clark sought out Barbara Ward and induced her to collaborate in the effort. "Woods was very happy with that, and so was Barbara Ward."[9]

On September 11, Harold Graves, director of the information department, cabled Barbara Ward officially advising her that the Swedish Bankers' Association had invited Woods to speak to them on October 27. "This would be a very distinguished audience, and Mr. Woods believes this would be an excellent point from which to launch some of your ideas concerning possibilities of the Nineteen-Seventies as set forth in the draft you sent him last June."[10]

On September 15, Ward wrote to Woods:

> The more I look at the behavior of the British and German Governments or the capers of Congress—between the extremes of Ellender and Fulbright, the more convinced I am that our whole post war international economic policy will simply drain away unless some fresh movement of public opinion, bringing new pressures to bear on parliamentarians, can be effectively launched. The Christian bodies are beginning to organize.[11]

Woods entitled his talk to the Swedish Bankers' Association, "Development—The Need for New Directions."

> I am particularly happy [Woods began] to be here today at this meeting of the Swedish Bankers' Association and to be able to tell you how much we at the World Bank appreciate the splendid support and encouragement we receive from the Swedish community. In addition, I believe that, in this uncertain and not altogether promising moment in world economic development, Sweden's exemplary support for the International Development Association has an importance and significance beyond the actual capital sums it has made available. For I believe that the

plight of the developing peoples—the two-thirds of humanity who are striving to cross the threshold of modernization—is the central drama of our times.

Woods briefly described the mechanism of IDA lending, pointing out that, apart from outright grants, it was the most concessionary finance available and assuring the bankers that the same rigor was applied to IDA lending as to lending by the World Bank itself. He added, however, that IDA's funds were nearly exhausted. "Our worldwide crisis today may seem less acute [than in 1947 after the first framing of the Marshall Plan], but, I assure you, it is vaster and deeper and even more complex. . . . Left alone, it can only grow worse. And at the back of that possible deterioration lies the risk of stark crisis—in food, in work, in hope—for over half the human race."

Woods reiterated that the flow of official aid, net of amortization, had not increased much above the $6 billion a year reached in 1961. There had been some increase in the flow of private capital, though most of this was going to developing countries possessing marketable mineral resources. He attributed the failure of the development decade in part to the perception that waste, inefficiency, and even dishonesty deflected resources from development:

> The picture of pervasive waste and failure is simply not borne out by the facts. It is precisely because this relatively rapid growth [of the developing countries] has been going on now for up to two decades that [their] absorptive capacity . . . is steadily increasing. . . . We at the Bank ask that IDA's resources be increased to a billion dollars a year. . . . And these investigations convince us not only that the flow of assistance on concessionary terms must be greatly increased, but also that the developing countries will be able technically, managerially and administratively to absorb that flow.

Woods drew a distinction between the major developed powers who experienced their greatest expansion during the nineteenth century or before and the less-developed nations at the present time. Earlier "their trends of population growth, urbanization and mechanization helped and reinforced each other." For present-day developers, he said, "the spurt of population is taking place ahead of the means of feeding and absorbing it—at a time when farming is still insufficiently modernized to provide increasing food for the whole population and at a time when the trend in industry is to need fewer but more highly skilled workers." Woods continued:

> In some measure, the developing countries today, like the nations of Europe in 1948, are caught in a series of interlocking contradictions and bottlenecks which cannot be broken by purely conventional means. The

need is for exceptional action on a sufficient scale. The need is to launch
a contrary movement in which growth feeds saving, saving generates
more growth, and both together help two-thirds of humanity over the
next two critical decades—critical because, although population increase
will only begin to slacken over the next 20 years, the groundwork can
nonetheless be laid for successful modernization and greater stability
later on.

The alternative—of stagnation, frustration and disappointed hopes
—will leave the great majority of our fellow men hungry, restless and reduced to a sort of delinquent despair. I, for one, do not believe that our
small planet can survive half-sated and half-starved. I believe the case
for exceptional responses and exceptional measures to be unmeasurable.

We are ready at the World Bank, together with interested governments, to help to select and finance . . . a group of experts. I am ready
to put at their disposal all the information and statistical material the
Bank has accumulated and, if requested, to second staff to their service.
Such a *Grand Assize*—judging the world's record and prospects of growth
—should in any case precede any attempt to round off our faltering
Decade of Development with a genuine reformation of policy.

Woods added, almost as a footnote, "Today we have the resources, the
experience and the knowledge to narrow the separation between the rich
and the poor. But we are held back by lack of direction and lack of will.
We may have stolen the Promethean fire, but at present we do little more
than complain that it is burning our fingers."[12]

On November 4, the *Economist* sought to rally support:

In 1967, economic assistance from rich countries to poor ones is set upon
a grim, ebb tide. As a percentage of national income, it has fallen in all
but two or three aid-giving countries. . . .

What has gone wrong? The facts themselves are not unfavourable.
Poorer nations, in spite of confusions and turmoil, have managed on the
average to approach the development decade's aim of a 5 percent annual
growth rate. The rich nations have not run out of resources for the effort.
On the contrary, they have added some $350,000 million to their com-
bined incomes since 1961. The failure lies elsewhere: in a weakening of
the political commitment to the whole idea of aid, and an erosion of
popular support. . . .

It is not an academic question, but a problem of human survival, to
ask how this drift can be arrested. And in such a predicament it is clear
that any possibility, however frail, of reversing the trend has to be
explored. . . .

This is, in essence, the proposal which Mr. George Woods, President of the World Bank, put forward in Stockholm last week. Recalling
the decisive part played in the Marshall Plan by the Franks report, he
called for "a grand assize" to examine and report on the whole field of
economic assistance. No doubt the problems are tougher, the perspective
longer, the facts more complicated. But the stakes are greater too.[13]

The Stockholm speech was a great speech, written, for the most part, by a grand lady.[14] Woods must have felt fulfilled: he had finally said exactly what he wanted to say about the development decade, the rising public debt of the poor nations, and the need for grants or concessionary loans from the rich nations. He had fulfilled whatever obligation he may have felt to John F. Kennedy and Eugene Black.

Julian Grenfell has said: "I think there was a transformation of Woods in the second half of his term of office. He came to an understanding that the presidency of the World Bank and the institution of the World Bank could do a lot more than he had imagined when he first came in. . . . He began to realize that his voice counted in the growing and expanding community of people who were really interested in creating an international network of development officials and people in politics. He found himself willy nilly as president of the Bank in all of that. In the last two years . . . he moved out of being an autocrat head of the World Bank to being an international statesman."[15]

Grenfell also remarked: "I think the Stockholm speech was saying, 'Look I am leaving the Bank. This is my last public pronouncement. For God's sake listen. This is what is going to happen.'

"The enthusiasm for 'the Grand Assize' which, at that time, they thought Oliver Franks was going to head, was very much rooted in his . . . writing-on-the-wall syndrome. He thought that things could easily get out of hand. He understood very clearly what people like Edward Boyle, Barbara Ward, René Maheu, and William Clark were saying to him which was that this development decade has run out of steam. The money that is going in is simply not doing the job. It's raising GNP, standard of living, but it's not having much effect on poverty. I think [Woods] understood that quite clearly."[16]

Meanwhile, rumors were circulating when George Woods delivered his Grand Assize speech that Robert McNamara, U.S. secretary of defense, would succeed Woods as president of the Bank.[17] Woods had had lunch with McNamara at the Pentagon from time to time,[18] but he was first attracted to McNamara as a possible candidate for president of the Bank on May 18, 1966, when McNamara spoke to a meeting of the American Society of Newspaper Editors in Montreal:

The World Bank divides nations on the basis of per-capita income into four categories: rich, middle-income, poor and very poor. . . . Since 1958, only one of these [rich] nations has suffered a major internal upheaval on its own territory. But observe what happens at the other end of the economic scale. Among the 38 very poor nations, . . . no less than 32 have suffered significant conflicts. . . .

Even in our own abundant societies we have reason enough to worry over the tensions that coil and tighten among underprivileged young people who finally flail out in delinquency and crime. . . .

The conclusion of all this is inescapable. Given the certain connection between economic stagnation and the incidence of violence, the years that lie ahead for the nations in the southern half of the globe look ominous. . . .

Development means economic, social and political progress. It means reasonable standard of living, and reasonable in this context requires continual redefinition; what is reasonable in an earlier stage of development will become unreasonable at a later stage. As development progresses, security progresses, and when the people of a nation have organized their own human and natural resources to provide themselves with what they need and expect out of life, and have learned to compromise peacefully among competing demands in the larger national interest, then their resistance to disorder and violence will enormously increase. . . .

The role of the United States must be to help provide security to these modernizing nations, provided they need and request our help and are clearly willing and able to help themselves.[19]

George Woods approved of what Robert McNamara had said. Given his own struggle with the secretary of the treasury, Henry Fowler, moreover, Woods may have supposed that the World Bank Group would benefit from having as its president a man who was close to the White House. Whatever the truth of that, once Woods's mind was made up, with single-minded resolution he continued to seek McNamara as his first choice to succeed himself.

At a press conference on November 30, 1967, Woods explained:

I undertook as a moral commitment . . . to serve in this post for five years, starting with January 1, 1963. . . . I never intended to stay here in the World Bank indefinitely. My own personal appraisal was that I was a little bit old for the job at the time when the U. S. Governor, Doug Dillon, approached me on it. I've kept my apartment in New York; I've lived in a hotel here, and I've always expected to serve out my term and be relieved.

But I became aware of the fact that there wasn't any particular activity on anybody's part to find a successor. . . . I concluded that the only way I was going to be relieved was if I should go about finding my successor myself. This was also the advice I had from a couple of old and valued friends. . . .[20]

I came to the conclusion that it might be well to look away from the investment banking and banking fraternity. It was well known, I am sure, to a great many of you gentlemen that the World Bank . . . is not really a Bank. . . . We are, in fact, a development finance company engaged in the business or profession of financing development in the less-developed parts of the world. . . . [This] involves a great deal more than making loans. It involves advice and technical assistance of all sorts. . . .

After deliberation I came to the conclusion that one man—I thought of two or three—but the one man who would be outstandingly qualified was Mr. McNamara, although I confess I was a little doubtful about his availability. . . .

Bob McNamara had lunch with me here in the Bank on the 18th of April of this year [1967]. . . . Subsequently, I talked to him from time to time. . . . We didn't call each other on the telephone and talk about this with any regularity, [but] he understood that he was my candidate for this post. He gradually got to understand why he was. I kept sending him copies of reports and speeches and descriptions of our activities at regular intervals, he and his wife were guests of my wife and me with others at dinner, and I never failed to take the opportunity of reminding him that I thought he was the man for the post.[21]

Woods reached an agreement with his executive directors in August 1967 that his contract as president could be extended for up to a year beyond December 31, 1967. He specified that the period would be shortened if an acceptable successor was found. McNamara was Woods's clear choice, but Woods was trying to tie up the total package before news of his preference became known.

While Woods was vacationing in Portugal, he received a telegram from Luis Machado, dean of the executive directors: SENDING YOU TODAY THROUGH THE COURTESY OF THE AMERICAN EMBASSY A PERSONAL MESSAGE ON BEHALF OF ALL EXECUTIVE DIRECTORS. The message, dated August 18, 1967, said, in part:

The Executive Directors have been discussing informally the question of the presidency of the Bank beyond the expiration of your contract. They have been informed that you have indicated your desire to relinquish the presidency as soon as a suitable successor is able to assume office. The Executive Directors have unanimously expressed their regret at this fact, but have agreed that in the circumstances they should embark urgently upon a search for a successor. It seems possible, however, that no successor may become available to take office by the end of the year and, that being so, the Executive Directors have in mind the need to provide for some interim period. In considering that possibility they have been made aware not only of your own generous offer to stay on for some period of time, if necessary, but also your desire to be relieved of your responsibilities as soon as a suitable candidate can take office.[22]

George Woods, in his pursuit of Robert McNamara, had to obtain the agreement of Livingston Merchant, the executive director for the United States, and Henry Fowler, the U.S. secretary of the treasury and governor for the United States. Sometime during September, the executive directors reached an understanding that, by October 31, Livingston Merchant would propose one or more candidates for the post of president of the Bank Group. On October 14, there was a meeting in the office of the secretary of the treasury at which specific names were proposed by Fowler, Merchant, and Woods. Fowler wrote, "Douglas Dillon, David Rockefeller, David Bell, Tom Mosher." Merchant wrote the same names. Only George Woods wrote, in addition to David Rockefeller, the name: "Bob McNamara."[23]

On November 8, Woods called McNamara, who was too busy for an extended conversation on the telephone. Woods asked if he might ride with McNamara from the Pentagon to the White House. In the car, Woods said, "This World Bank thing is coming to a head. I don't know what the names are going to be. As long as I have a vote, your name is going to be one of them. I thought you ought to know, Bob, that there was [an] intention to have the names submitted by October 31. The U.S. didn't make that date, but it seems to me it's liable to happen anytime."[24]

On November 16, in the office of the secretary of the treasury, Henry Fowler, Woods was told that President Johnson had chosen McNamara as his candidate to succeed Woods. In a prepared statement on November 30, McNamara said: "About the middle of October, I was informed by the President that nominations to succeed Mr. Woods would soon have to be made, and he asked if I was still interested in serving as head of the Bank. I answered in the affirmative. . . . The President told me . . . that he would do whatever he could to help me. . . . [But] no date has been set for my departure from my present post and the assumption of my new duties."[25] On Sunday, November 19, or Monday, November 20, Woods called McNamara to tell him that his name was going to be presented that Tuesday to the executive directors of the Bank by Livingston Merchant.

News of McNamara's approaching nomination was leaked to the London *Financial Times* on November 27; and there were leaks the day before in India and in Florida (by a Spanish-language newspaper). All these leaks were embarrassing to Woods because the executive directors had not yet confirmed the nomination of McNamara by Livingston Merchant. Indeed, the directors were not due to meet in executive session until December 5.

On November 28, the *New York Times* carried the headline: "MCNAMARA IS NAMED BY U.S. TO HEAD THE WORLD BANK: JOHNSON MOVE A SURPRISE." Subheadlines stated: "Shift Due in 1968" and "Capital Sees No Hint of Any Change in Policy on War." The text contained the following excerpts:

> Word of the shift, expected to take place next year, caused stunned surprise in Washington. . . .
> Senator Mike Mansfield of Montana, the Senate majority leader, said tonight that he had not heard of Secretary McNamara's nomination until informed by the press. "I think it's a serious loss for the country," he said. "I think he is by far the best man in the Cabinet and the best

Secretary of Defense we have ever had. I know of no one who can replace him and keep civilian control of the Defense Department as he
did.". . .

The date of McNamara's taking office, if he is approved, is not certain. But it was reliably reported that the date would be next spring or
earlier—in any case before the Presidential election.[26]

The following day, a headline in the New York Times read: "Shift of
McNamara Raises Speculation of Rift on War"—"Friends Say He Backs
Bombing Restraint and Opposes Missile Defense—White House Silent on
Reasons for Move."[27] "The portrait of Mr. McNamara," the New York
Times reported, "is that of an intensely complicated man who conveys one
impression of his beliefs and emotional attitudes to friends who share
these convictions and feelings and who conveys a significantly different
impression to friends who do not. The first group portrayed McNamara as
a man who is increasingly troubled by the course of the Vietnam War. He
would like to suspend the bombing campaign against North Vietnam because he considers the air war a dubious exercise that is hardening North
Vietnamese resistance and prolonging the war. The second group, who are
not troubled by the war, doubt that McNamara is distraught. He's a tough
man, but after seven years he's tired. In Europe, McNamara was viewed as
a Dove who was forced out of office by the Hawks in the military."[28]

The New York Times said editorially on November 29:

As a management expert Mr. McNamara may feel tempted to transform
the World Bank as thoroughly as he transformed the Pentagon. Mistakes
have been made in development finance, which is still in its infancy, and
there is ample room for innovations designed to improve efficiency and
accelerate economic growth. But development goes far beyond a mastery
of techniques and the introduction of systems analysis. More than anything else, it requires new dedication and an increase in help from the
rich countries that are now so dubious about aid and so parsimonious in
their assistance.

The problem has been emphasized by George D. Woods, retiring
president of the World Bank, whose reign has coincided with the emer-
gence of a large number of new independent nations at a time when the
resources for their development have been drying up. Mr. Woods has pi-
oneered in providing loans for education and agriculture, which had previously been neglected, and in stressing the need for more multilateral assistance. His awareness of the growing gap has led him to suggest a "grand
assize," an inquest similar to the one that preceded the Marshall Plan, in
order to bring about a fresh sense of urgency in spurring development.

Mr. McNamara can make maximum use of his enormous capacity
for management and leadership by seeing to it that such an inquest is
carried out. The task of development is too large and too complicated to
be handled by any one nation. What is needed is a long-term program
that is supported by all of the industrialized states. With his grasp of the

magnitude of the problem and his abilities to cope with it, Mr. McNamara appears the man for the next Decade of Development.[29]

On November 30, President Johnson issued a press release that stated:

Some time ago, Mr. McNamara reported to me that Mr. Woods had talked to him about succeeding Mr. Woods as President of the [World] Bank. Mr. McNamara said he was interested in the World Bank post as an opportunity for continued service. He assured me of his willingness to remain as Secretary of Defense so long as the President considered it to be necessary, but he believed the service would benefit from the appointment of a fresh person.[30]

Years later, in a telephone conversation with me, McNamara indicated that "during the latter portion of my period in Defense, serving as [President Johnson's] secretary, we had a big difference of opinion regarding the Vietnamese War, and we just came to a parting of the ways. Partially to facilitate my departure, but also because of the deep affection I think he had for me, at one point he said, 'Bob, you can have anything you want. What is it you want? I heard you talk about the World Bank. Is that what you want? If that is what you want, that is what you will have.'"[31]

On December 5, George Woods was finally able to write a letter of congratulation to McNamara, adding: "I will at all times stand ready to assist you in any way possible."[32] On December 13, Woods introduced McNamara to the senior staff of the Bank and mentioned that McNamara had always been his first choice to be his successor. On February 21, 1968, he was able to add that McNamara would assume the presidency on April 1.

News of McNamara's impending appointment came against a backdrop of other news. President Johnson conferred with the secretary of the treasury, Henry Fowler, and congressional leaders on the long-stalled tax-increase proposal.[33] The House Ways and Means Committee was demanding sharp cuts in the president's budget proposals before it would consider a 10 percent income-tax surcharge to fight inflation, then running at an annual rate of nearly 4 percent, and to finance the rising costs of the war in Vietnam.

The United States had enjoyed seven years of prosperity. Real output had increased by more than 40 percent. Per capita income after taxes had increased by 29 percent, measured in constant purchasing power. But the pernicious wage-price spiral, which was to bedevil the U.S. economy for nearly twenty-five years, had begun. The unemployment rate in December 1967 had fallen to only 3.7 percent.[34] The booming economy following the tax cuts of 1964 and 1965 had induced revenue increases sufficiently great to produce balanced budgets in those years, but, with virtually no cyclical unemployment in 1966 and 1967 and with the already high levels

of defense spending piled on top of normal private demand, the economy was overheating rapidly. The president had recommended a 10 percent surcharge on corporate and individual income taxes to extend
through June 20, 1969. With rising interest rates, which would ultimately reduce investment spending, however, his request was not quickly
acted upon.

The dollar was falling under increasing pressure from the French
franc, the German mark, and the recently devalued British pound. The
basic balance-of-payments deficit of the United States was rising. West
Germany's central bank announced on November 27 that it would sell
dollars for German marks to reduce the "dollar overhang." It would buy
the dollars back, if necessary, at an interest rate of 1.75 percent for up to
three months.[35]

In Canada, the president of France, Charles de Gaulle, challenged the
French-speaking people of Quebec to break away from English-speaking
Canada. The Canadian prime minister, Lester Pearson, replied, "I do not
propose to deal in any detail with General de Gaulle's statement of yesterday, a statement obviously very carefully prepared and made in the
press. General de Gaulle's statement will without doubt arouse discord in
Canada. I am sure the people of this country will be restrained in their response to it, as I am in mine today, so as not to serve the purpose of those
who would disunite and divide our country."[36] Lester Pearson lost the next
Canadian election, but he was to return to prominence when he became
the principal author of the Pearson commission report—the outcome of
George Woods's Grand Assize proposal.

At one point in George Woods's November 30 press conference,
Woods was asked by Edwin Dale, of the *New York Times* (the man who
wrote the "Happy Fund, Troubled Bank" article): "Will you finish the IDA
replenishment before you leave?" Woods replied:

> Mr. Dale, there's just no way to answer this. I don't know what to put in
> as the benchmark as to when I'm going to leave office, and whether
> IDA's completed or not depends on how far in advance of the date I fi-
> nally do leave office. . . . After we have a meeting of minds with the re-
> sponsible Ministers of Finance, then, in these countries—18 of them—
> there is legislative action. All I can say is that IDA replenishment is in
> the forefront of the questions that I have today, and we're moving for-
> ward with the governments in the resolution of that IDA question. I sin-
> cerely hope that in the measurable future—by that I mean by the end of
> December—there will be . . . a meeting of minds between the President
> of IDA and the responsible Finance Ministers. I still think this can be
> done. We're having different kinds of meetings, in different places in the
> world on different aspects of it. There will be a meeting here in Wash-
> ington as a matter of fact—next week—on one aspect of it. There [will
> be] a meeting in London later on in December. We're getting along.

Shortly after his address to the Swedish bankers, Woods abandoned hope of obtaining $1 billion annually for the second replenishment of IDA. He agreed to settle for $400 million a year and left it largely to Burke Knapp and Irving Friedman to work out the details.[37] Woods told his senior staff that he was disappointed that world conditions did not make a higher level of replenishment feasible. He did not, however, regret putting forward his original proposal. It had focused attention on the issue of multilateral concessionary aid. The United States had accepted the billion dollar a year figure in principle, and no one had objected that aid on that scale could not be effectively used. In late January 1968, Woods announced that the proposals for the IDA replenishment put forward in the memorandum he had sent to the Part I countries on January 16 had been accepted by Italy and Sweden. He added that it could be safely assumed that the U.S. Treasury Department would initiate steps to obtain congressional approval. Germany, France, and Japan all accepted later that week, but the $400 million per year did not become operational until July 23, 1969, when the U.S. Congress passed the enabling legislation.

News of McNamara's nomination was concealed from most of the staff of the World Bank until November 28 when the *New York Times* broke the story. Aron Broches guessed that the "handwriting was on the wall" when he read in the society pages of the *Washington Post* that Mohamed Shoaib, a former minister of finance for Pakistan and now a vice-president of the World Bank, and his wife had given a dinner for the McNamaras and the Woodses.[38] But it came as a shock to Irving Friedman, who was told in the corridor by Burke Knapp that McNamara was going to be the next president. Friedman had heard speculation that Douglas Dillon or David Rockefeller might be chosen, but the secretary of defense had not crossed his mind. "I remember feeling disappointed, not because I had any strong feelings about McNamara, but because I still wanted George Woods to stay on," he said.[39]

When McNamara was in place as president of the Bank, Friedman suggested that McNamara might want to appoint his own economic adviser. "Oh no, Irving," McNamara replied, "I've heard a great deal about you. I want you to stay. But you have to promise me. . . . You know I have a weakness for numbers. Please protect me from my weakness for numbers."[40]

In preparation for the McNamara presidency, Friedman, Kamarck, and Emanuel Levy, the statistician, sought to improve the statistics in the economic briefs of developing countries.[41] As early as December 1966, Kamarck had assembled statistics for various countries in a loose-leaf binder that he referred to as Country Economic Briefs. In July 1967, C. F. Owen, secretary of the economic committee, had circulated a memorandum from Kamarck to the economic advisors of the area departments explaining why the committee needed a wide variety of data, though this led to grumbling among the area department economists about the extent of the data Kamarck wanted. On January 10, 1968, Kamarck himself sent a memorandum to the economic advisors in which he pointed out that, whenever the economic committee considered a country and new recommendations were prepared, the data should be updated. In addition, in March and September of each year the area department economists were to review all their countries to make sure no data were misleadingly out of date. Kamarck also sought qualitative evaluations. Statements about performance and creditworthiness might be a single word such as *Eligible*, but statements concerning poverty should include data about income per capita. A general evaluation should be a description of the current economic situation and a summary statement of the economic committee's most recent conclusions and recommendations. A large part of the value of the data, Kamarck argued, lay in their being internationally comparable. Thus, the comparative data division, under Levy, had general responsibility for this work, but the division needed to work with the area departments. It was desirable, said Kamarck, to have as complete a set of briefs as possible ready for McNamara when he took over.[42]

On November 27, 1967, Woods called William Clark in England to say, "Tomorrow there is going to be an announcement that Robert McNamara will succeed me as president of the World Bank. I would like you to consider whether or not you could take the place of the director of information when Bob McNamara comes to the Bank." Clark said that he would certainly think about it, and Woods said, "When you've thought, come across and see us." According to Robert Asher, who interviewed Clark in 1983, Clark left for Washington three days later—not, Clark said, "because I was desperately anxious to hold the post—I didn't know enough to say yes or no—but because I thought it was a sort of challenge that one shouldn't hesitate to try out."[43] According to Clark's memoirs, published in 1986 after Clark's death, Clark did not go to Washington until mid-January 1968, after having sent Woods a letter indicating that he regarded the position of director of information at the World Bank as an extension of what he had been doing for nearly seven years at the Overseas Development Institute. He added, however, "I am not the international civil service–type carrying out a brief handed down. I want to be involved in some aspect of policymaking, and I regard my function as an emissary of leaders of opinion worldwide."[44]

In any event, when Clark arrived in Washington he was taken by George Woods and Richard Demuth to see McNamara in the Pentagon. He had an agreeable meeting with the secretary of defense. McNamara had talked with David Ormsby-Gore (Lord Harlech), the British ambassador to Washington during the Kennedy presidency, about Clark, and McNamara said that he was looking forward to working with Clark.

McNamara stipulated that he would be in place at the Bank on April 1 and invited Clark to do the same. Clark joked that, if McNamara had no qualms about their both beginning their careers on April Fool's Day, he would suppress his own. They grinned and shook hands. Clark instantly felt that McNamara was a man he could work for and with. As George Woods later told Clark, "I think your body chemistry works."[45] On February 21, Woods presented Clark to the senior staff of the Bank and indicated that Clark, on April 1, would become the new director of information.

Meanwhile, Woods had arranged to add Sir Denis Rickett to the staff as a vice-president, in large part to maintain liaison with the governors and executive directors of the Part I countries responsible for replenishing IDA. Rickett would retire as the British Treasury's second secretary in time to join McNamara's president's council during the first week of April. Woods, who was anxious to avoid another confrontation with Part I countries, induced Sir Denis to join the McNamara team, and with that Woods felt that he could hand over the reins to his successor. The third replenishment, largely negotiated by Rickett by June 1970, was supposed to be $900 million a year. Once again there would be difficulty with Congress, but Woods had done a proper job of preparing the way for McNamara.

Woods was a lame duck president for four months. He traveled to New Delhi, India, to address the UNCTAD conference in February. His ambition was to emphasize the need for more IDA assistance, but—as recounted more fully in Chapter 5—many Indians took exception to some of his statements. Three days after Morarji Desai, the Indian deputy prime minister and finance minister, had written to Woods thanking him for amending his words, Woods repeated much of what he had said to UNCTAD. At the World Conference of the Society for International Development on March 7, he said:

> The development business is in trouble. Some of the high resolve with which the business was begun 20 years ago has gone. A sense of disillusionment is not confined to the industrial countries: in the less developed countries too, there is disappointment and an impatience for results. . . .
>
> The first message is this: That [for] every developing country sincerely committed to accelerating its economic progress, the development job is doable. And it is doable largely with the knowledge and skills already at our command, provided only that adequate and appropriate finance is available. . . .
>
> The second message is this: Whatever the importance of the other justifications, there is one justification that overrides all others—and that is the moral imperative to do what can be done to alleviate poverty, illness and despair wherever they may be found.[46]

This was George Woods's swan song. He had chosen a successor who was on his wavelength. The presidency of the World Bank Group was to be a continuous process. All that remained was the official transfer of power.

On April 1, the day after President Johnson's announcement that he would neither seek nor accept the Democratic party's nomination for a second term, Robert McNamara and William Clark arrived at their new desks.[47] That afternoon, Woods called on McNamara to talk about the Grand Assize. As it turned out, Franks was unable to take on the leadership of the commission and McNamara settled on Lester Pearson, Canada's former prime minister, who accepted McNamara's invitation in August 1968.[48] Pearson (with some help from McNamara and Clark) quickly chose as his fellow commissioners Edward Boyle of Britain, Roberto Campos of Brazil, Douglas Dillon of the United States, Wilfred Guth of Germany, W. Arthur Lewis of Jamaica, Robert Marjolin of France, and Sabura Okita of Japan. He had the final report of the commission in the hands of the governors of the Bank at their annual meeting in 1969.

Most of the report recommended more of the same, with one notable exception. Jamaica's Lewis, professor of political economy at Princeton University, suggested that IDA should be separated from the Bank: IDA should have a separate board, perhaps even a separate staff, for it was necessary to separate proposals for action among the poorest countries from proposals for action among the more wealthy countries. IDA should have a poverty-oriented program, argued Lewis, who subsequently received the Nobel Prize in economic science. Lewis was espousing a suggestion that had come from the UNCTAD conference earlier in 1968. To this suggestion, McNamara responded, "If there is going to have to be a move toward dealing with the poorest, the change should come on the part of the Bank, not on the part of IDA." McNamara said, in effect, "Don't detach IDA from the Bank; rather, let IDA lead the Bank into right paths."[49]

The U.S. public was unimpressed by the Pearson commission report. In 1969, their thoughts were more on extricating themselves from the Vietnam quagmire and the voices of George Woods and Robert McNamara were drowned out. *The Pentagon Papers*[50] was many times more interesting than *Partners in Development*, the report of the Pearson commission.[51] Barbara Ward sought to rally support. Robert McNamara began to speak about the bottom 40 percent and then about Absolute Poverty.[52] Clark spoke to two hundred members of the staff on the results of the Pearson commission but received a "very cool response from the older members,"[53] many of whom were U.S. citizens. The response of the younger staff was more favorable.

The influence on McNamara himself was considerable. He used *Partners in Development* as a sort of guidebook and he often carried it with him on his travels. And he turned increasingly to a constituency abroad in his

successful search to increase the funding not only of the Bank but of IDA.
By the time of the fourth IDA replenishment, which began in 1972,
Robert McNamara had almost achieved the billion dollars a year George
Woods had sought, though the contribution of the United States had
fallen to 38 percent—from 42 percent. By 1981, it had fallen to 27 percent. By June 1968 the capital subscriptions of the World Bank had risen
to almost $23 billion, over $20 billion of which was subject to call to meet
the obligations of the Bank. It was an international guarantee fund that
served as backing for the bonds the Bank sold. By June 1970, capital subscriptions had risen by an additional $3 billion, thus permitting the Bank
to increase further its outstanding bonded indebtedness—though increasingly in non-U.S. markets.[54]

McNamara sold a record $1.2 billion in World Bank bonds in 1969,
compared with $700 million in 1968 and an average of $275 million a
year during the Woods years. In early September 1969, the World Bank
sold a $175 million issue of two-year bonds to fifty-six central banks at an
average interest rate of 8 percent, an all-time high interest rate. According to *Business Week*, McNamara's critics by then included John J. McCloy
and Eugene Black.[55] In late 1968, Robert W. Cavanaugh, treasurer of the
World Bank since its founding, resigned in protest over McNamara's ambitious plans.[56] Martin Rosen resigned in 1969 to enter private business.
McNamara was using the Bank, as well as IDA, in his attempt to deal with
poverty in the world.[57]

On Wednesday, March 27, 1968, noting that the meeting of the senior
staff was his last as president of the World Bank, Woods said that it was the
best qualified staff in the world of development finance that McNamara
would be taking over. He was grateful for their patience and cooperation.
Knapp replied that Woods was leaving an indelible stamp on the Bank.
With his restless energy, he had been a great fermenting agent, dissolving
any complacency that might have existed in the Bank or the developing
world and setting up chain reactions in both that would continue.

On Thursday, March 28, the day after Woods's meeting with his senior staff, he met informally with his executive directors, but Dr. Luis
Machado presided. "For five and a quarter years," Machado began,
"George [Woods] has been our chairman. I think that he has presided over
more board meetings than any other president in the Bank. In the early
days we met twice a month, then it became one every week, but lately
we've been meeting not only twice a week but mornings and afternoons.
I think if he'd stay longer, we'd probably be meeting at nights also, which
would give us a good excuse to be away from home. George, we're going to
miss you as chairman of this board. Even the flags around this room will
miss you. We'll miss you for two reasons: look at all the time and energy
we have spent for five and a quarter years to teach and train and educate

a chairman, and, by the time he knows how to preside at a meeting, he's quitting [laughter]. Besides that, it is going to be very difficult for us to get accustomed to being without you."

Dr. Otto Donner, the director for Germany, presented Woods with a traditional gavel made from a cherry tree in the Bretton Woods. His remarks referred to the energy and pertinacity Woods had exhibited. "It is true we had dabbled [in the education field], but we really had not entered [it] properly yet. You did so. You spoke of the necessity of doing more for agriculture and the sense of enhancing productivity . . . long before the world began to speak of the neglect with regard to agriculture. . . . I remember with particular pleasure also the way you approached the IDA problem and . . . of arranging the transfer of Bank earnings to IDA. You widened the horizon . . . for the IFC. All of your achievements . . . lie under the direction of widening the horizons for the [World] Bank Group."

"May I have a word?" meekly requested George Woods. "No," Machado responded quickly with a grin. "You're just like any other director. Wait your turn." He then asked Dr. Peter Lieftinck to make another presentation.

Lieftinck gave Woods a scrapbook containing clippings and photographs of the Woods years. Again Woods sought the floor, but Machado turned instead to Mohamed Kochman of Mauritania, who represented many of the countries of North Central Africa. Kochman read a resolution praising Woods for "bringing to the organizations the happy combination of unrivaled knowledge and experience of financial affairs [and] a deep concern for the peoples of [the] developing countries and an understanding of their problems."

Georges Prescoff of France was recognized as the latest newcomer to the board. "I have found . . . that you have kept the . . . virtue of a young man. You are difficult to satisfy. You are an exacting man. You have a strong feeling of impatience, which we hope we all had when we were in our twenties. . . . If I may, I have no present to give to you. I will just, perhaps for the first time, say a French sentence in this board: '*Ce n'est qu'un au revoir.*'"

Machado teased Woods: "Well, George, now you felt for a few minutes how directors felt when they were anxious to talk."

Woods responded, "Thank you Luis. Thank you gentlemen. Yes, I have, for the first time around this table, had the sensation of frustration I'm sure several of you have had." Woods referred to people who said they were going to speak only a few minutes and then talked for twenty. To laughter, Woods added, "I must confess that I never enjoyed Otto Donner's remarks as much as I enjoyed them today." Woods also joked about Louise Woods: "This girl I'm married to really loves publicity . . . for her husband. . . . She has less than no interest in general news of the world. On her behalf, I particularly say thank you for these books. I especially appreciate your patience, which once or twice I consciously was trying. I wanted to reach an end before it was too late, . . . and always you were most cooperative. As a group, I'll never forget you."[58]

The final event of the farewell to George Woods was a banquet held in the John Quincy Adams Room of the State Department on Friday evening, March 29. Woods had driven down from New York that afternoon with Richard Demuth.[59] Except for Denis Hudon of Canada, all the executive directors and the president's council were there with their wives. Dr. Machado repeated some of the themes of the previous day.

"George Woods, you are the victim of the American [retirement] system. You are retiring as president of the World Bank at the peak . . . of your career. At the time when you could be most useful to our organization, at the time where under the constant stewardship of your board of directors, you have learned to run the Bank. . . .

"The world is too busy to write a history about everyone who is born, and it would only recognize in its pages those men and women who were born with unusual qualities and attributes to bring them out from the mob and let them stand for something worthwhile and constructive. And if you go through the pages of history you will find that history will always recognize those who were gifted at birth by nature with two great qualities: imagination and courage. And George Woods has both of them. . . . As president of the World Bank, he immediately was faced with the hunger, the misery, the sickness, the poverty of an overpopulated world. And immediately this . . . man from Wall Street became the dreamer of the World Bank. His fantastic imagination told him exactly what had to be done."

Machado talked about Woods's emphasis on "new methods to develop [the] agricultural industry" and spreading "education to the masses." Machado spoke about Woods's "visions of what had to be done to raise the enormous money required to take this job to a successful completion. He had the imagination, but in addition, President George Woods had the courage . . . to fight for his dreams. . . . He had the courage to go around and tell the developed countries of the world that they were not giving enough money [and] that the money they had to give had to be on the most liberal terms required to make the development of the underworld possible."

Machado then presented Woods with a copy of *Bank Notes*, the staff journal whose sixteen-page edition summarized Woods's records in office and included the signatures of the almost 1,500 members of the staff. Machado also presented Woods with a picture of an old Spanish town— the "silent witness that through the years has listened to every one of your conversations on the telephone, every one of your interviews, that has accompanied you in your moments of depression and your moments of enthusiasm."

In responding, Woods said that he was proud of the job that had been done on recruitment, particularly of the 109 "young professionals" who had come to the Bank, only fourteen of whom had left. He was also proud of the recruitment job he had done on Bob McNamara. "I think he's going to blow new life and new enthusiasm, new energy into our newer programs, particularly education and agriculture." Woods joked about not being much in favor of exercise. "I may be getting to the point where I am old enough to take up golf." He also drew a distinction between bilateral foreign aid and development finance, which not only provides "the money for the projects to increase productivity in the poorer countries of the world," but also "includes . . . providing the advice, the knowledge, the experienced advice about the economic planning of those countries and equally importantly the advice of the experienced people that know about projects of the type we finance—those in our projects department." Finally, Woods admonished the staff, "Don't be discouraged by the fact that instead of a billion dollars a year for the next three years we have four hundred million dollars in IDA. . . . We'll live through it. . . . And in our own way, we keep doing the best we can for our friends, rich and poor."

As is befitting a lady, Louise Woods had the last word. She remarked, "This is terrible to come last. Everybody's tired and wants to go home. But I would like to say to all of you that your generosity and your kindness and consideration to me in the five years we've been here have just been glorious to live with and glorious to be a part of it. I have never, I guess in my whole life, lived in an atmosphere of affection that I feel you have for me, nor have I ever given so much of my affection to any group of people as I have to all of you."

Louise Woods mentioned in particular Marjorie Billings, who had "in a period of five years invited for me over 1,500 ladies for tea in our home. She was the inspiration [for] the idea we had in 1963 for the participation of wives in the annual meetings." She singled out for commendation Mrs. George (Molly) Wishart, Mrs. Geoffrey (Judy) Wilson, Mrs. Martin (Judy) Rosen, Mrs. Harold (Judy) Graves, and Mrs. Orvis (Elizabeth) Schmidt. She thanked the gentlemen—George Wishart and Rainer Steckhan in particular—who had accompanied the Woodses on their travels, and closed with the words that these had been "the happiest five years of my whole life, and I'm very grateful to all of you."[60]

* * * * *

For a month, George Woods occupied an office on the eleventh floor, just below McNamara's office. Woods expected McNamara to seek his advice from time to time, but McNamara never called. Woods spent most of his time talking to his stockbroker in New York or working with Julian Grenfell on the preparation of the speech Woods would deliver before the World Affairs Council in Pittsburgh.

Woods rejoined the board of directors of the First Boston Corporation on May 15, 1968. He also served First Boston as a paid consultant. On April 25, 1968, he rejoined the board of the New York Times Company, which he had served from 1959 until he became president of the World Bank. He also joined Mrs. Arthur Hays (Iphigene Ochs) Sulzberger and her son, Arthur Ochs (Punch) Sulzberger, as one of three trustees who would carry out the terms of Adolph S. Ochs's will. (Adolph Ochs was the grandfather of Arthur Ochs Sulzberger, the current publisher of the *New York Times*.) Early in 1968, he became chairman of the board of the Henry J. Kaiser Foundation, a position he retained until 1971. He received an honorary degree from Notre Dame University (of which he was also a trustee), to add to ones from Allegheny College (1963) and Columbia University (1966).

George Wishart, who traveled with the Woodses and was George Woods's personal assistant for over four years, has spoken of Woods's "great love of America." Wishart said, "Above all, he prided himself on being a New Yorker. When I used to drive with Woods into New York City from the airports, as we crossed the Triborough bridge and came into view of Manhattan, Woods would say to me: 'George, isn't it *WODER-FUL* [sic]; that's my town.'"[61]

Woods was very close to the Kaiser family, Edgar Kaiser in particular, but he was a New Yorker through and through. His other close friends were the Rockefeller brothers, John D. III, Nelson, and David in particular;[62] André Meyer; the Sulzbergers of the *New York Times* and their writers Tom Wicker and Russell Baker. One of Woods's favorite sayings was that "the people who matter, know."

Before Woods became president of the World Bank, he and Louise were in the audience as Leonard Bernstein conducted Aaron Copland's Orchestral Connotations, which had been commissioned by the New York Philharmonic Orchestra in celebration of its opening season in Lincoln Center. The concert took place on Sunday, September 23, 1962, and included works by Beethoven, Mahler, and Vaughan Williams. The chairman of the board, John D. Rockefeller III, wrote in the opening week program, "Lincoln Center exists because leaders in the arts, education, business, labor, the professions, philanthropy, and government believe that the arts are a true measure of a civilization." George D. Woods was one of the twenty-one directors of the Lincoln Center for the Performing Arts and was also chairman of the board of the Vivian Beaumont Repertory Theater of Lincoln Center.

Woods was appointed chairman of the New York State Urban Development Corps by New York Governor Nelson Rockefeller on June 26, 1968. He served as a member of the board until 1974.[63]

On December 12, 1968, Woods became chairman of the board of the International Executive Service Corps, succeeding David Rockefeller, president of the Chase Manhattan Bank and a principal founder of the corps. The corps—the Businessmen's Peace Corps—had been founded in 1964 to provide experienced U.S. executives to businesses in developing countries. Wood was chairman for six years.

In May 1969, Governor Nelson Rockefeller announced that Woods would be a member of the U.S. presidential mission to Latin America. Woods was one of thirty-six members of the mission whose report was submitted to President Nixon in August.[64] Woods later wrote to Rockefeller, "While, as you know, I had some question as to the advisability and even feasibility of the Mission, now am delighted to have been a part of it and proud to be identified with the recommendations you have made to the President."[65]

George Woods's personal files are filled with correspondence to and from the Rockefellers. On August 18, 1971, for example, Nelson Rockefeller wrote to Louie and George, "I can't tell you how much we loved our visit with you [at your home in Portugal]. There are no two more wonderful people—and we were simply crazy about your house and the beautiful things in it, as well as the garden and the swimming pool. And, too, I just can't begin to thank you for the parties your arranged, and, of course, I was thrilled with the shopping. . . . We look forward to seeing you after Labor Day."[66]

Woods served in the 1970s as president of the Foreign Bondholders Protective Council, which succeeded in arranging some payment to the U.S. holders of the long-defaulted bonds of such East European governments as Romania and Poland.[67] George and Louise Woods were still actively supporting good causes early in 1982. Martin E. Segal, chairman of Lincoln Center for the Performing Arts, Inc., wrote to the Woodses, "With your support as a Founder, we are planning to form a Chairman's Council of Lincoln Center. You are among the first to come to mind as part of this core group." The Woodses immediately sent $2,000.

But more and more, George and Louise looked forward to spending the summer months in Portugal. In the spring of 1982, Woods was told that he had an inoperable brain tumor. His appetite diminished until he could no longer eat. One day in mid-August he discovered that he could no longer climb down the ladder to the swimming pool He died six days later—August 20, 1982—at age eighty-one. There was no funeral or memorial service. His ashes were scattered in the East River. Louise followed George in death—from cancer—on August 23, 1986. Her ashes, too, were scattered in the East River.

Irving Friedman, who provided the author with six lengthy interviews, said in one of them: "You couldn't impress Woods with your position, or your money, or the way you looked, or the clothing you wore, or the car and the chauffeur you had driving around. It just didn't impress him at all.

"He enjoyed people for what they were rather than as part of a social group. He didn't refer much to social groups. He didn't . . . refer to the fact that 'I had dinner with the former French ambassador' . . . or something like that. He was a very one-on-one kind of a person. Because of this one-on-one relationship, he was rarely on stage. You rarely saw him in a public, generalized capacity. He was always a very intimate person. . . .

"He seemed to take great delight in the mobility of American society. He never talked about his own mobility. When you talked to him, you wondered if he was talking about himself. He didn't talk about himself. He was always talking about [his experience] in semiphilosophical terms. He was a great admirer of the American system."[68]

Back in 1966, when Woods was in his prime, David Lilienthal, former head of the Tennessee Valley Authority, called on Woods in his tiny office in the United Nations building to talk about increasing productivity on the farm. As Lilienthal recalled it, Woods welcomed Lilienthal into his office by saying, "They didn't tell me you were waiting." Woods wore a "warm grin and a welcoming glint of the eye that marked him off from any banker I have ever known—and most other men who have had their way for decades.

"Few are the men who have great power over the lives of others and can remain unaffected by that fact. Harry Truman was the greatest example I have known. But George Woods, though different in almost every other way, runs him a close second."[69]

In March 1977, Lilienthal wrote in the copy of his *Journals* that he presented to Woods:

FOR GEORGE WOODS
A GREAT PUBLIC CITIZEN
AND A WISE MAN OF BUSINESS

Notes

1. A first in history at Oxford, Clark during World War II was press attache at the British embassy in Washington, returning to London as the European editor of the *Encylopaedia Britannica* and part-time editor of the *New Statesman*. He became diplomatic correspondent for the *Observer* and press advisor to Sir Anthony Eden during the Suez crisis. In 1965, he became the first director of ODI. Broadly

speaking, the Overseas Development Institute was funded one-third by the Ford Foundation; one-third by British business; and one-third by the British government. Clark became the vice-president for external affairs in the World Bank, which he served from 1968 to 1980. Author of six books, Clark died in 1985.

2. William Clark, *From Three Worlds* (London: Sidgewick and Jackson, 1986), p. 231.

3. Ibid.

4. Boyle had been treasury minister and minister of education. This account relies heavily on Clark's memoirs and Patricia Blair's and Robert Asher's separate interviews of Clark on October 4 and 5, 1983, Bank archives.

5. Barbara Ward had just been appointed by Pope Paul VI to the pontifical commission for justice and peace. She was the author of a number of significant books about international economic issues, including *The West at Bay, India and the West, The Rich Nations and the Poor Nations,* and *Only One Earth.* In the 1950s, she was a principal writer for the *Economist.* In 1973, she became president of the International Institute for Environment and Development, retiring in 1980, to be succeeded by William Clark. In the last six months of her life, she received from Prince Philip the Royal Society of the Arts' Gold Medal for her work on conservation. Too ill to attend, she sent a message: "Give them my thanks for this honour, particularly because it is what I care about most, the conservation of the world in which all mankind may have a decent life and have it more abundantly." Barbara Ward died on May 31, 1981.

George Woods and Robert McNamara were members of the Barbara Ward memorial fund committee.

6. By 1967, Lord Franks was provost of Worcester College, Oxford.

7. Blair's interview of Clark, October 4, 1983, p. 3.

8. Robert W. Oliver, "A Conversation with Julian Grenfell," *Conversations About George Woods and the World Bank,* Washington, D.C., July 15, 1986 (Addendum, February 10, 1988), p. 31.

9. Ibid.

10. Transcript of outgoing wire. At about this time, Woods told Graves, "Harold, I'm not happy with your department. I don't know what's wrong with it, but there is something wrong with it; and I've asked Michael Lejeune if he will look into this and see if we can work this out."—Robert W. Oliver, "A Conversation with Harold Graves, I," *Conversations About George Woods and the World Bank,* Washington, D.C., July 17, 1985, p. 19. See also note at end of Chapter 8. Things were not worked out to Woods's satisfaction, however. Perhaps Woods had already decided to offer William Clark Graves's job. Clark was more sympathetic to Woods's point of view. On October 16, Graves was officially transferred to the development services department as an assistant to Richard Demuth. Lars Lind, a Swede and assistant to Graves, became acting director of the information department.

11. Personal correspondence.

12. Address given in Stockholm, October 27, 1967. Italics added.

13. *Economist,* November 4, 1967, pp. 490–491.

14. William Clark and Harold Graves had a hand in writing the speech, which went through at least four drafts. According to Julian Grenfell, however, Barbara Ward "did the entire draft. It was very much her own speech."—Grenfell, p. 31.

Clark wrote in his memoirs: "Cunningly, to lure Oliver Franks, [she] included a passage recalling that before Europe could enter wholeheartedly into the experiment of the Marshall Plan, an official body of experts under Franks' leadership had been drawn up from the participating nations to study the whole range of programs and policies required to achieve European recovery. 'What was needed now,' she wrote, 'was a "Grand Assize" which should precede any attempt to round off the faltering [Development] Decade with a genuine reformulation of policy.'"— Clark, *From Three Worlds*, p. 232.

15. Grenfell, p. 6. Grenfell also said, "Woods was not a particularly likeable person to the board. They regarded him as autocratic, grouchy and determined to have his way. . . . He lacked social grace. He was not good at small talk really. In his declining years, [however,] he became a man of great charm. When he retired and I was living in New York as the [Bank's] representative to the UN, I used to have lunch with him quite often. He was a man full of wisdom and charm. We talked about theater and music."—Grenfell, p. 5.

16. If Grenfell is correct in his assessment, Woods's emphasis on the poor was one of the important bridges that Woods built between the Black and the McNamara years. Black was largely concerned with the growth of preindustrial societies; McNamara was largely concerned with reducing absolute poverty. These are, of course, not mutually exclusive alternatives.

17. Clark, p. 233.

18. Martin Rosen recalled: "George used to go over to the Pentagon once a week or every two weeks and have lunch with [Cyrus] Vance, who was undersecretary [of defense] at the time. [He was] a Wall Street lawyer who had been close to George prior to . . . their coming to Washington, and McNamara frequently joined them for these lunches."—"The Reminiscences of Martin Rosen," George D. Woods Oral History Project, Oral History Research Office, Columbia University, May 15, 1984, p. 17.

19. Robert S. McNamara, "The Essence of Security," *Reflections in Office* (New York: Harper and Row, 1968), pp. 141–162. Before joining the Kennedy administration, McNamara had a distinguished career with Ford Motor Co. Born on June 9, 1916, in San Francisco, he received a master's degree at the Harvard Graduate School of Business Administration. McNamara then joined a California accounting firm. In 1940 he returned to Harvard to become an assistant professor and was also a consultant to the War Department in the establishment of a statistical control system for the air force.

He volunteered for active military duty in World War II but was turned down because of nearsightedness. On leave from Harvard, he went to England as a civilian consultant for the War Department. Subsequently commissioned in the air force, he was awarded the Legion of Merit. After the war, the Ford company was having managerial and financial problems and McNamara and nine other statistical control experts were hired as a team. They immediately started asking all kinds of questions and became known as the Quiz Kids. The nickname was changed to the Whiz Kids when they instituted reforms and operational savings throughout Ford's worldwide plants.

McNamara became president of the Ford company in November 1960, one day after John F. Kennedy was elected president of the United States. Kennedy offered him a cabinet post and in January 1961 McNamara was sworn in as secretary of defense.

20. The "old and valued friends" were John J. McCloy and Eugene Black. See James Reston, "McNamara Departure: A Puzzle Still," *New York Times*, November 30, 1967, p. 16.

21. Transcript of press conference, pp. 3–5. William Bennett had suggested that Woods knew by the beginning of 1967 that he was not going to be reelected president for a second full term. "That was pretty well known around the Bank. . . . I think it hurt him terribly. I think he felt that he was doing a good job in a

very difficult time."—Interview by Robert Oliver, Washington, D.C., July 1986, p. 2. Julian Grenfell, on the other hand, believed that Woods was not disappointed. "He didn't want to serve on as president. I think, with some justification, he felt he had positioned the Bank for the new era."—Grenfell, p. 13.

22. Woods's personal papers. Woods had agreed to stay on for an interim period of up to one year to accommodate President Johnson's request that his secretary of defense complete the military budget for fiscal year 1969 before he left.

23. On March 23, 1967, Woods had suggested J. Richardson Dilworth (Rockefeller Brothers), Orville Freeman (secretary of agriculture), Kermit Gordon (Brookings Institute), and McNamara. Others who were mentioned included, in alphabetical order with their dates of birth: David Bell, U.S., 1919; Guido Carli, Italian, 1914; Lord Cromer, British, 1918; Douglas Dillon, U.S., 1909; Thomas Gates, U.S., 1906; Felipe Herrera, Chilean, 1922; William McChesney Martin, Jr., U.S., 1906; Louis Rasminsky, Canadian, 1908; and David Rockefeller, U.S., 1915. The birthdates were probably in response to an undated memorandum in Bank files entitled "Desired Qualifications for President of the World Bank," among which was that he should preferably not be older than fifty-five, thus allowing for two five-year terms of office.

24. Press conference held by Woods on November 30, 1967.

25. *New York Times*, November 30, 1967, p. 16.

26. *New York Times*, November 28, 1967, 1ff.

27. *New York Times*, November 29, 1967, pp. 1ff.

28. Asked if he regarded McNamara as a good secretary of defense, Senator Everett Dirkson said, "Yes I do. He had conviction. He had an excellent brain, and he didn't have to rely on aides in committee hearings."—"McNamara shift queried in Senate," *New York Times*, November 29, 1967, p. 17.

29. *New York Times*, November 29, 1967, p. 46.

30. *New York Times*, November 30, 1967, p. 16.

31. Robert W. Oliver, "A Telephone Conversation With Robert McNamara," January 30, 1986, p. 4.

32. Woods's personal papers.

33. *New York Times*, p. 47.

34. *Economic Report of the President*, February 1968 (Washington: Government Printing Office, 1968), pp. 6 and 9.

35. *New York Times*, November 28, 1967, p. 67.

36. *New York Times*, November 29, 1967, p. 21.

37. See Edward S. Mason and Robert E. Asher, *The World Bank Since Bretton Woods* (Washington, D.C.: Brookings Institution, 1973), pp. 408–411.

38. Robert W. Oliver, "A Conversation with Aron Broches," *Conversations About George Woods and the World Bank*, Washington, D.C., November 8, 1985, pp. 22–23.

39. Robert W. Oliver, "A Conversation with Irving Friedman, V," *Conversations About George Woods and the World Bank*, Washington, D.C., July 23, 1985, p. 34. "Woods was very quick to tell me how pleased he was that McNamara was appointed. . . . If George Woods spoke well of him, chances are that I would too. McNamara was a disappointment because I enjoyed my relations with George Woods. As far as I was concerned, the most pleasant appointment for me would have been a continuation of the same person."—Ibid., p. 36.

40. Ibid., p. 35.

41. See Chapter 4.

42. There are tables in the George Woods collection at Columbia University (unnecessarily under tight security still) giving information about a great range of

statistics for 1967 for all the countries that were members of the Bank. They include information about gross national product, savings, investment, consumption, and so forth. An attempt was also made to categorize LDCs as being Bank or IDA worthy. For a recent judgment about statistical information, see Nicholas Stern, "The Economics of Development: A Survey," *The Economic Journal*, Vol. 99, No. 397, September 1989, pp. 597–685.

On December 19, 1968, Friedman sent a memorandum to the chief economists of the area departments in which he noted that there had been general agreement every time the matter was discussed that it would be useful to have a statement of the economic work needed in any given country. Friedman proposed that the chief area economists, with the advice of the working party for each country, should outline the future work needed. By then, five-year economic projections had been prepared for thirty-nine countries, a major purpose of the tables being to provide a comprehensive view of each country's five-year development prospects. During 1968, the problems of collecting comparable data were ironed out sufficiently so that tables were being presented to McNamara as a new device for assessing creditworthiness as well as eligibility for Bank or IDA financing.

43. Robert Asher, "Interview of William Clark," October 5, 1983, p. 2.

44. William Clark, *From Three Worlds* (London: Sidgewick and Jackson, 1986) pp. 234–235. Clark's memoirs (pp. 233–234) are slightly at variance with Asher's account. This is probably because the last two chapters ("The World Bank 1968–1980" and "Going Home") of the memoirs, though written with great care by Julian Grenfell, were completed, from Clark's notes, after his death in 1985.

45. Asher, p. 2. See also Clark, *From Three Worlds*, p. 235. Clark noted (p. 237): "On the staff of the department was someone who had worked for me in London at the beginning of the sixties. I had given Julian Grenfell his first job after coming down from Kings, Cambridge. . . . When I arrived I found him in charge of the department's African interests. . . . I eventually sent Julian to Paris to head our information and public affairs operations in Europe, and then, during the second half of my stay at the Bank, he was our ambassador to the United Nations in New York."

In 1974, under Robert McNamara, William Clark became vice-president for external relations. Among other duties, he traveled with McNamara just as Harold Graves had traveled with Eugene Black. See William Clark, "McNamara at the World Bank," *Foreign Affairs*, Vol. 60, No. 1, Fall 1981, pp. 167–184.

In *From Three Worlds* (p. 234), Clark observed that George Woods "might not be the world's greatest diplomat, but his energy, imagination and political courage were clearly being devoted to turning the Bank, to the real benefit of its developing member countries, into something it had not been hitherto. I was later to form the firm opinion that Bob McNamara's subsequent huge expansion of the Bank would have been a much tougher and riskier undertaking but for the ground work laid by his predecessor during the relatively short presidency. Bob was of the same view."

Clark also recalled (p. 237) that the information department he had inherited had "a professional staff of twenty-one people plus support staff [which] had been under the interim care of its deputy director, Lars Lind, since the departure of its previous director, Harold N. Graves, Jr., to a different department of the Bank. I already knew that Lind, a Swede, had had his difficulties with George Woods, but it took me no time at all to conclude that Woods had misjudged his man. I found Lars professionally extremely able, very dedicated and most likeable. . . . He was later to succeed me briefly as Director of the Information Department when I was promoted to Vice-President, External Relations in 1974. . . . One could not have asked for a wiser and more helpful deputy for a newcomer such as myself, and he proved a most valuable colleague and good friend through the seven years we were together."

46. Keynote address to the tenth anniversary conference, Washington, D.C.

47. According to Aron Broches, Woods "had . . . hoped to arrange a deal with McNamara that McNamara would resign [as secretary of defense] at the end of Johnson's term [January 1969], which would give Woods another year. That did not work out. President Johnson is supposed to have said that if McNamara wanted to leave, he should do so as soon as possible."—Robert W. Oliver, "A Conversation with Aron Broches," *Conversations About George Woods and the World Bank*, Washington, D.C., November 7, 1985, p. 20.

McNamara himself has indicated: "I think George wished to stay on at the Bank, not, maybe, for another full term, but at least for an additional period. I think the directors didn't wish for him to stay on."—"A Telephone Conversation with Robert McNamara," p. 4.

At another point in his interview, Broches said: "There was a lot of tension between [Woods] and the directors. It was so bad his last year that when McNamara came every director told him, 'Whatever you do, don't act like Woods. Don't have confrontations.' McNamara read three years of verbatim minutes, and for a while McNamara hardly opened his mouth."—Broches, p. 19.

48. Clark had suggested Pearson to Woods earlier, but Woods had said, "No, I think someone who has just lost office is not the ideal person."—Blair, p. 5.

49. Blair, p. 11.

50. Neil Sheehan, et al., *The Pentagon Papers* (New York: Bantam Books, 1971).

51. Report of the Commission on International Development, *Partners in Progress* (New York: Praeger Publishers, 1969). According to *Business Week*, ("World Banking McNamara-Style," September 27, 1969, p. 100): "The Pearson Commission report was to have been fresh and dramatic enough to fire a grand new debate on how to deal with world poverty. It is neither very dramatic nor very fresh. Its primary recommendations are for a doubling of the amount of aid funneled through such multinational organizations as the World Bank, and for developed countries to boost their infusions of official and private capital to the developing lands to 1% of their gross national product by 1975."

Julian Grenfell, on the other hand, has suggested that "the value of the Pearson report was that it drew attention to the fact that the Development Decade had run into a lot of trouble."—Grenfell, p. 32.

52. See Blair, pp. 12–16, and Robert W. Oliver, *International Economic Cooperation and the World Bank* (London: Macmillan, 1975), pp. 267–270.

53. Blair, p. 14.

54. In his 1983 interview with Robert Asher, William Clark observed, "I think that America has become very much more inward-looking, and very much less of a leader in world affairs, than when I first experienced it; and that makes me very sad. . . . I can only say that we were not, in my opinion, well served by American executive directors in the Bank. The executive directors, in my period, did very little to lead. They were nearly always obstructive, and always for the same reason: 'It's going to lead to trouble with Congress.'—Asher, p. 25.

55. "World Banking McNamara-Style," *Business Week*, September 27, 1969, p. 97.

56. See Deborah Shapley, *Promise and Power: The Life and Times of Robert McNamara* (Boston: Little, Brown and Co., 1993), p. 471. See also Andrew

Kamarck, "McNamara's Bank," *Foreign Affairs*, Vol. 60, No. 4, Spring 1982, p. 952: "In terms of the level of lending, the McNamara results appear impressive—$12.3 billion in total Bank and International Development Association lending in his last year [1981] compared with $1.3 billion in 1967 before he became president. However, if the inflation-distorted figures are deflated by the U.S. producer price index, the results are that in the McNamara years lending in real terms grew at a rate of under ten percent a year, while in the Black-Woods period, taken together, lending grew by just over ten percent a year."

57. See Hollis Chenery, et al., *Redistribution with Growth* (London: published for the World Bank and the Institute of Development Studies, University of Sussex, by Oxford University Press, 1974). But see also Shapley, *Promise and Power*, pp. 566–568.

58. George Woods's personal papers, "Memorable Hours."

59. Demuth commented in an interview many years later: "It really was extraordinary that George did contribute as much as he did in the first half [of his term], and then he lost confidence in himself for some reason or other. He lost the confidence of the board. He was fighting with them all the time. He was fighting with governments because he hadn't been able to carry out the IDA replenishment . . . even though the kind of agreement that was ultimately reached was obviously obtainable right from the beginning. In the end, I'm sorry to say, I don't think anybody except the executive director from Morocco (George and his wife had special relations with Tazi and his wife) was unhappy to see George go. The final banquet given for George was one of the saddest occasions I've ever been to because there was nobody there except Tazi and his wife who was sorry to see George go, and everyone knew that, including George."—Robert W. Oliver, "A Conversation with Richard H. Demuth," *Conversations About George Woods and the World Bank*, Washington, D.C., July 18, 1985, pp. 1–2. Among others, William Diamond, who was also present at the banquet, has taken exception to Demuth's remark. "It is not true that Mr. and Mrs. Tazi were alone in regretting Woods's departure. I regretted it, and I do not recall it as a sad event, as Dick does."—Personal correspondence, March 21, 1993.

60. George Woods's personal papers, "Farewell Dinner at the State Department, March 29, 1968."

On March 18, 1985, almost three years after George Woods died, Louise Woods sent a note to President A. W. Clausen, then president of the World Bank: "Dear Tom, I hope you will find time to read the enclosed transcript of remarks made on the occasion of the farewell dinner given to us by the Executive Director of the World Bank in March 1968, at the State Department."

Clausen replied, in part: "It's surprising how little the issues have changed over the years. And, of course, the statements provide a fitting and touching tribute to George's contributions to the World Bank and to yours as well."

61. George Wishart, personal communication, May 23, 1992.

62. On November 28, in the ballroom of the Plaza Hotel in New York City, Frank Pace, Jr., president of the National Institute of Social Sciences, presented the five Rockefeller brothers with gold medals for distinguished service to humanity. After his retirement from the World Bank, George Woods would become deputy chairman of the population group of which John D. Rockefeller III was chairman. John D., the oldest Rockefeller brother at age sixty-one, responded, "I am glad you require that the recipients of your awards be present in person. It gives me an opportunity to see my brothers." Noting that family planning and

population problems had been one of his chief concerns for many years, he quipped, "If my parents had been exposed to today's ideas of family planning, my brothers Win and David might not have made it."

63. On October 23, 1975, Woods testified that Edward J. Logue, the agency's chief executive officer, had been at odds with various bankers and that this had caused defaults by the urban development corps earlier in the year. See the *Wall Street Journal*, October 24, 1975.

64. *The Rockefeller Report on The Americas* (New York Times Edition; Chicago: Quadrangle Books, 1969), p. 5.

65. Personal correspondence of George Woods.

66. Personal correspondence of George Woods.

67. The Foreign Bondsholders Protective Council was formed in 1933 as a nonprofit organization to protect the interests of the holders of foreign securities which had flooded the U.S. capital markets before the Great Depression and were payable in dollars.

68. Friedman, V, Washington, D.C., July 23, 1985, pp. 39ff.

69. David Lilienthal, *The Journals of David Lilienthal* (New York: Harper and Row, 1976), p. 209.

INDEX

249

ABOUT THE BOOK
AND THE AUTHOR

Based on dozens of in-depth interviews, as well as the historical record, Robert Oliver has written a unique biography of George David Woods, who in 1963 became the fourth president of the World Bank.

George Woods transformed the World Bank from a relatively passive investment organization into an active leader of world development. He pushed for greatly increased lending in support of agriculture and education, worked closely with the United Nations, and revived and greatly strengthened economic analysis in the Bank itself. He also initiated measures to expand the equity investments of the International Finance Corporation and sought annual funding of one billion dollars for the International Development Association, the Bank's soft-loan affiliate. He retired in 1968 after inducing Robert McNamara to be his successor.

Oliver's lively biography offers not only a full picture of Woods and his pivotal contributions to the World Bank's development, but also reflects the changes that occurred in the 1960s within both the agency and the environment in which it functioned.

ROBERT W. OLIVER is emeritus professor of economics at the California Institute of Technology.